The Author as Hero

The Author as Hero

SELF AND TRADITION IN BULGAKOV,
PASTERNAK, AND NABOKOV

Justin Weir

NORTHWESTERN UNIVERSITY PRESS / EVANSTON, ILLINOIS

Northwestern University Press
www.nupress.northwestern.edu

Printed in the United States of America

10 9 8 7 6 5 4 3 2 1

ISBN 978-0-8101-2807-1

The Library of Congress has cataloged the original, hardcover edition as follows:

Weir, Justin.
    The author as hero : self and tradition in Bulgakov's Master and Margarita,
Pasternak's Dr. Zhivago, and Nabokov's The gift / Justin Weir.
        p. cm. — (Studies in Russian literature and theory)
    Includes bibliographical references and index.
    ISBN 0-8101-1881-5 (alk. paper)
    1. Russian fiction—20th century—History and criticism. 2. Self in literature.
3. Authorship in literature. 4. Mise en abyme (Narration) 5. Bulgakov, Mikhail
Afanas'evich, 1891–1940. Master i Margarita. 6. Pasternak, Boris Leonidovich,
1890–1960. Doktor Zhivago. 7. Nabokov, Vladimir Vladimirovich, 1899–1977.
Dar. I. Title. II. Series.
PG3098.4 .W452002
891.73'409384—dc21

                                                        2002001422

♾ The paper used in this publication meets the minimum requirements of the
American National Standard for Information Sciences—Permanence of Paper for
Printed Library Materials, ANSI Z39.48-1992.

Contents

Acknowledgments

It is a genuine pleasure for me to recognize the great debt I owe to colleagues, friends, and relatives who helped me complete this book. Andrew Wachtel, who encouraged me and gave me invaluable early advice and direction, deserves special mention. He and Gary Saul Morson have long served as model scholars for me and as sources of intellectual inspiration. I am grateful also to Carol Avins, Stephen Blackwell, Caryl Emerson, John Kopper, Timothy Langen, and William Mills Todd III for their criticism and suggestions. Paul J. Weir was an early, generous reader, and he helped make this a better book. Lena Lencek was an ideal colleague at Reed College, and I benefited from her enthusiasm and sound judgment. Many others at Northwestern University, Reed College, and Harvard University provided guidance and goodwill at all the right moments. Susan Harris and Susan Betz at Northwestern University Press were understanding and helpful throughout the publication process. The support of Joy Masterson Weir was remarkable in every way, and I dedicate this book to her.

Introduction

> The clearest, most memorable and important
> feature of art is how it arises, and the world's
> best works, in telling of the most diverse things,
> are in fact narrations of their own birth.
> —Boris Pasternak

I begin with this oft-quoted passage from Pasternak's *Safe Conduct* because I am interested in how art is conscious of its origins. The frequent citation of this passage in literary scholarship reveals, moreover, how accustomed we have become to the discourse of "meta." Metafictional narrative devices have long been a focus of scholarly criticism, and the past several decades have witnessed a boom of tricks in art, literature, film, and other media that pull back the curtains and disclose the inner workings of storytelling in all its forms.[1] The examples are legion. Even the nightly news employs cuts to the booth, allowing viewers to eavesdrop on voice-over directions from the producer. Journals of contemporary fiction advertise "Please no more stories about writers!" in order to stave off the hordes of authors who seem to have taken too literally the familiar maxim, "Write from your experience." At some point, too much meta-information grinds art into sausage—and we no longer want to know how it is made.

This study is devoted to the use of a particular metafictional device, the *mise en abyme,* in Mikhail Bulgakov's *The Master and Margarita,* Boris Pasternak's *Doctor Zhivago,* and Vladimir Nabokov's *The Gift.* A *mise en abyme* is a representation of the entire novel within a single image or passage in the novel. By describing how the *mise en abyme,* itself often a work of art, is created, the novel seems to narrate its own birth. And this narrative description of the birth of art allows us to begin to describe each novel's preconception of what authorship itself meant to each novelist.[2] More is at stake than mere reflexivity. Novels that narrate how they were written play on our expectations of how novels in general are written. They also foreground the activity and necessity of our interpretation of them. *The Master and Margarita, Doctor Zhivago,* and *The Gift* use the reflexivity of the *mise en abyme* to reconfigure the relationship of selfhood to literary tradition in modern authorship.

In order to appreciate how Bulgakov, Pasternak, and Nabokov conceived authorship anew, we need first to consider their changing attitudes toward selfhood and literary tradition. When the nineteenth century ended, Russian novels did not stop "being about" psychology; rather, a heightened modernist self-awareness (already detectable in aspects of Tolstoy, Dostoevsky, and others) precluded the continued depiction of people in ways that concealed how literary form inherently influences characterization. That relationship between literary form and the form of selfhood implied by literary character emerged in critical debates about the "new" Russian novel of the 1920s. Once authors or critics begin to talk about how the individual and society are to be depicted in "new" versus "old" forms of literature, they already testify, if only implicitly, to particular conceptions of literary evolution.[3] Literary evolution, reflexivity, selfhood, and authorship—these are my main thematic concerns, and the *mise en abyme* puts them in special relation to one another. While there is probably little value in documenting all the various auto-referential devices in *The Master and Margarita, Doctor Zhivago,* and *The Gift* that could justifiably be called *mises en abyme,* their use is crucial when it touches upon those broader themes.

THE NEW NOVEL

> Prose should soon occupy the place that not long ago belonged exclusively to poetry.
> —Yuri Tynianov, 1922

The 1920s witnessed a renewal of artistic prose in Russian literature after two and a half decades during which poetry predominated. The success of this return to narrative fiction is usually attributed to Boris Pilnyak and Evgeny Zamyatin, as well as to other "Serapion Brothers," such as Konstantin Fedin, Lev Lunts, and Vsevolod Ivanov. These authors wrote mostly shorter prose works, and it was not until mid-decade that the genre of the novel, thought to have been worn out by Tolstoy and Dostoevsky and rendered impossible by Andrei Bely's *Petersburg,* was brought again to center stage by various literary critics and authors. Curiously, the reason for this renewed interest derived not from any critically acclaimed novels but from the *lack* of a "new" novel.

Contemporary critics, picking up on the terminology of critics of the twenties, sometimes refer to this period in Russian literature as both a revival or rebirth of the novel and a time of novelistic crisis.[4] Literary genres rarely disappear from the literary-historical register, however. During the years in which poetry predominated, many novels were in fact written by Bely, Merezhkovsky, Sologub, and others. Moreover, there is good reason to be skeptical of outcries of a literary "crisis." The passage of time, the taste of the reading public, and (one hopes) the good sense of critics, together mark traditions and constitute canons. Such processes would seem to require the perspective of historical distance and thus make the term "crisis" meaningless.

But, then again, not all literary crises are the same. Russian literature and criticism were closely interrelated: theorists like Victor Shklovsky and Yuri Tynianov were themselves novelists by the mid-twenties, and, in general, authors of fiction often joined critics in bemoaning the state of the contemporary novel. Thus the discourse of the crisis may open a window on more speculative aspects of literary history or evolution; for it is possible to ask about the structure of the literary consciousness of a period, especially when it is marked by its own heightened awareness of the dilemmas of literary change. The means by which people think about literary evolution evolve in identifiable ways that simultaneously exhaust old discursive potentials and create new ones.

Literary evolution is at the crux of the crisis/rebirth of the novel in the twenties. This proposition is self-evident because some sort of conception of literary evolution is presupposed by the very notion of a crisis or a *rebirth*. Yet literary evolution also informs the debates on the novel in a more general fashion. The twenty-five years of modernism that preceded the crisis/rebirth of the novel can be characterized by a heightened consciousness of the role of tradition. The futurist command to throw Pushkin from the "steamship of modernity" reveals the strong grip of the canon no less than the symbolists' attempts to find their forebears in Tyutchev or Baratynsky. Even the Serapion Brothers, whose calls for autonomy in art ostensibly shun Russian traditions, when they do make programmatic statements (as, for example, in Lev Lunts's essay "To the West!"), seek to enrich the tradition rather than dispose of it. Finally, one should not forget state-sponsored attempts to co-opt the Russian novelistic tradition, and especially Tolstoy, into the new Soviet literature.[5] Maxim Gorky's sprawling, proto-socialist realist novel *Mother*, for example, is stylistically regressive, though politically progressive.

Most important, the association of crisis and rebirth is deeply ingrained in the Russian appreciation of literary history, for the two have gone together at least since the time of Vissarion Belinsky. In his "Literary Reveries," Belinsky complained of the lack of continuity between pre- and post-1830 Russian literature, the "unnatural break" of crisis and regeneration that indicated, to Belinsky, the country's lack of a literature of its own: "Such abnormal leaps are, in my opinion, the best proof that we have no literature and, consequently, no history of literature; for not one of its phenomena was the outcome of another, not one of its events originated from another."[6] Belinsky does not say there is no new worthy literature; he says there is no organic continuation of a *Russian* literature in what is new. The terms of his obsession with literary tradition never entirely leave the Russian critical idiom, not even after the 1917 Revolution; and Belinsky's privileging of literature as the sine qua non of Russian cultural identity remained potent through most of the twentieth century.

In a 1924 essay Boris Eikhenbaum displays the same self-consciousness about literary tradition witnessed in Belinsky, only he narrows the generic spectrum of his comments to the novel:

> But which is the path for the novella, for the novel? Just now it turns out that Russian writers have not become translators and editors of translations in vain, and Russian readers have not begun to read only "international" literature in vain. *What is happening is nothing other than what happened in Russian literature of the [18]30s.*[7]

What is remarkable about this statement is not Eikhenbaum's revelation that Russian literature is searching for a "path" for the novel, but that this searching for a path is itself part of a Russian tradition. Literary history apparently repeats itself, but now the progenitors of tradition are conscious of being self-conscious.

The heightened self-awareness of literary tradition in Eikhenbaum and Belinsky is important to any discussion of Russian literary evolution. Literary evolution, like all concepts that are based on the possibility and nature of development over time, requires the elucidation of a mechanism of change. The mechanism Eikhenbaum points to is translation. By translating foreign novels, Russian authors acquire new literary models that have the potential to be significant for the Russian tradition in ways that they may or may not have been for the original tradition. Translation becomes, in effect, a transitional mode, or perhaps just the sign of a transition, between successive stages in the literary tradition—but it is not the only possible mechanism of change. Simply the *identification* of some sort of mechanism of change is imperative in debates about literary evolution. Belinsky, by contrast, viewed continual borrowing as a disadvantage, an additional sign that Russia had no tradition.

Georg Lukács's famous 1915 description of the novel as a sign of man's "transcendental homelessness" and as that which "seeks, by giving form, to uncover and construct the concealed *totality* of life" shares in a "synthesizing" or totalizing impetus of the Russian debates on the novel in the twenties.[8] The novel is somehow supposed to capture within itself the entire (contradictory) world. Yuri Tynianov, in his 1924 essay "The Literary Present," calls a return to the novel "essential and necessary" because its "large form" is capable of recapturing the "sense of genre" missing in contemporary literature.[9] Later in the same essay Tynianov distinguishes two important novelistic functions, the mimetic and the synthetic: "In order that literature capture everyday reality, it should not reflect it, for that literature is too much of an unreliable and crooked mirror, it should collide in some way with everyday reality."[10] The metaphor of the mirror provides one method of capturing reality, but it is neither the only nor necessarily the best way to do so. An artistic "collision" with everyday reality suggests a means of synthesizing its disparate aspects, rather than merely reflecting them.

The novel is the placeholder of so many different literary theories in the first decades of the twentieth century that its generic flexibility is stretched nearly to the breaking point. In the final pages of Lukács's *The Theory of the Novel*, the possibility of a new novel in Dostoevsky serves as a potential future utopia of lost epic society. Victor Shklovsky's influential theory of "defamiliarization" (остранение) is based principally on his analysis of prose, especially in Tolstoy's novels. Mikhail Bakhtin counters any Tolstoyan tendencies not with poetry but with the elevation of Dostoevsky's novels to the status of a new art form; and Bakhtin's idea of "dialogue" is explicitly defined as the work of prose, not of "monologic" poetry. And within just a handful of years of these other theories, socialist realism began drawing heavily on the novelistic models of Gorky's *Mother* and Gladkov's *Cement*. That the novel genre can even accommodate the nearly untenable theory of socialist realism, what Regine Robin calls "an impossible aesthetic," tells us that the rediscovery of the novel in the 1920s was significant not in and of itself but in how capacious the novel's synthetic properties were thought to be.[11]

Tynianov and Lukács, like Eikhenbaum and others, seem to agree in principle that the novel genre captures, totalizes, or synthesizes reality.[12] Yet in their descriptions of the mechanism of literary evolution they differ greatly. Tynianov develops in the late twenties an intricate model of evolution in which literature is treated as a dynamic system. Lukács, after his adoption of Marxism, relies on a deterministic base-superstructure model, though his treatment of literary evolution remains more psychologically perceptive than many Soviet Marxist approaches.[13] To judge by his work on Tolstoy, Eikhenbaum's sense of literary evolution shifts from an early, more mechanistic and formalistic concept of change to a later, more fluid and biographical concept of literary change.

DO POETS HAVE INTEGRAL SELVES?

By virtue of an odd coincidence, within the space of a year, two of the twentieth century's most famous poets eulogized the novel. In his 1923 essay, "Ulysses, Order, and Myth," T. S. Eliot declared that Joyce's use of Homer was on the order of a "scientific discovery," making *Ulysses* something other than a novel: "[T]he novel," he writes, "is a form which will no longer serve . . . instead of being a form, [the novel] was simply the expression of an age which had not sufficiently lost all form to feel the need of something stricter."[14] One wonders whether Eliot simply preferred "stricter" genres.

Only a year earlier, Osip Mandelstam also predicted "the end of the novel" in a provocative essay, explaining that "when we entered the epoch of powerful social movements and organized mass actions, both the stock value of the individual in history and the power and influence of the novel declined."[15] Mandelstam's understanding of the synthesizing function of the novel is spelled out in terms of a temporal coherency.

In Mandelstam's view, what the novel has done best as a particular form of literature is to depict people as actors on the world historical stage. The hero of the novel is both an individual with his own highly structured personality traits and a typical agent of historical progress, of social interaction at a given historical moment.[16] By this definition, Bazarov, to take as a (simplified) example the hero of Turgenev's *Fathers and Sons,* would be not just a single man, but also a typical Russian nihilist of the 1860s and therefore a representative of an important political movement in Russian history. In this sense the novel is the literary form most capable of merging two sorts of (already complex) chronologies: one, biography, depicts the order of events in an individual human life; the other, history, depicts the order of events that affect a society or country. This merging of chronologies exemplifies a temporal coherence that is essential to Mandelstam's idea of the novel.

The cataclysmic events of the twentieth century, Mandelstam assures us, have destroyed our concept of individual biography. It makes no sense to speak of individuals and historical events together, as if telling the story of the one could also tell the story of the other; for the individual is no longer able to act in a meaningful way. This loss of individual biography thus eliminates the very basis upon which the novel is constructed: "A man devoid of biography cannot be the thematic pivot of the novel, while the novel is meaningless if it lacks interest in an individual, human fate, in a plot and all its auxiliary motifs."[17] Not two but now three orderings of time, or chronologies, Mandelstam suggests, constitute the temporal coherence of the traditional novel: biography, history (as in the history of a country), and the order of events within the novel. Whereas previously these three chronologies have coincided with, or complemented, one another—Bazarov, the Russian 1860s, *Fathers and Sons*—now they cannot.

In his analysis of the rupture of an apparently seamless temporal fabric, Mandelstam anticipates a notion that has received much critical attention in the past few decades. Michel Foucault and others have suggested that the chronologies that give shape to the way we tell human histories were found in the nineteenth century to be different from those that make up the human sciences—the histories of nature, language, and economy, for example. Natural history, historical linguistics, and political economy point toward internal laws of development in nature, language, and economy that, though deeply involved with—and impossible without—the actions of human beings, could not be used for telling human histories. Foucault phrases the dilemma in more provocative terms: "the human being no longer has any history: or rather, since he speaks, works, and lives, he finds himself interwoven in his own being with histories that are neither subordinate to him nor homogenous with him."[18] What Foucault seeks to explain—and I believe, Mandelstam himself senses—is that the breakdown of a uniform sense of time in turn fractures the representation of human beings: we must replace our discussion of a single unifying chronology with that of several, potentially irreconcilable, chronologies.

Mandelstam is clearly concerned with the synthesizing nature of the novel, so much so that the novel is unimaginable without it. He actually uses the term "synthetic" (синтетический) in this sense.[19] But this synthetism is strictly tied to the worldly coherence that serves as its immediate object: a simplified version of the mimetic function of literature (something Mandelstam by no means adheres to in his own artistic prose) is thrown together with the novel's synthetism. In other words, the integrity of the character's personality and indeed of the whole novel is rendered dependent on notions of an easily comprehended reality and an ordered history. Yet how can that be true? Novels are the generic umbrellas under which many different people and diverse experiences are gathered.

What is lost in this confusing dependence on mimesis is a tenable conception of the mechanism of literary change. The greater the determination of literary creation by historical fact, the more one-sided and impoverished the sense of genuine literary development becomes. One is struck by the conceptual distance evident here between Mandelstam and Belinsky, for whom the internal development of the literary tradition had an organic quality. Mandelstam never states directly that literature is determined exclusively by events in the real world. Nevertheless he allows himself such reductions as, "The flourishing of the novel in the nineteenth century was *directly dependent* on the Napoleonic epos."[20] Other, fuller theories of evolution, such as Tynianov's, counteract this one-sidedness by balancing extraliterary lines of development with intraliterary lines.

This conceptual shortcoming aside, Mandelstam transforms the synthesizing and totalizing function of literature into a novelistic imperative that is at once temporal and humanistic. By shifting his focus to the potential chronological unities within the novel, Mandelstam begins to define the integrity of novelistic form in terms of narrative itself. In semiotic terms, one may say that the novel is a meaningful whole (text) through the differential relationship of its signifiers—here, a chronological sequence—not through a given wholeness of the signified, that is, the world as an already given, conceptually meaningful whole.

Mandelstam "humanizes" novelistic form because he emphasizes that what is at stake in synthetism is the possibility of representing individual identity. One could ask: if biography can no longer serve as the basis of a novel, then can the novel, or any combination of literary devices, serve as the basis of the biographical image? Mandelstam leaves open the possibility that the individual, though no longer *given* biographically in the world and thus unable to serve as the structural basis of the novel, may be *created through* the novel, alongside the novel.[21]

Mandelstam was not the only one to reconsider the relationship between humanism and the novel. Zamyatin's dystopic novel *We*, for example, narrates the rediscovery of individual identity through autobiographic writing. And in Konstantin Fedin's 1914 novel *Cities and Years* one of the main characters remarks:

> But somehow I think that novels are written the way boxes are made. Every board must fit the other boards on all sides. That, at least, is how novels were written before the war. Now it's probably impossible even in a novel to bring more than two people together at a time. The glue is no good, it doesn't hold . . . Those boards which still hold must be separated, perhaps smashed, because they are artificially glued together and people can't be glued together into humanity with that kind of glue.[22]

Novels, because they typically confirm our expectations of real character development, frequently explore the topic of what it means to create an identifiably human life. Yet the novel was not the only genre that allowed an interrogation of the potentially (de-)humanizing effect of literature. Mayakovsky, for one, seems constantly to ask our rhetorical question (do poets have integral selves?), for he clearly could find no genre to integrate his personality fully. Even the passion play of his *Vladimir Mayakovsky: A Tragedy* fails to capture his personality; the final verse of the play actually ends on his name, Mayakovsky, as though to suggest that his real identity both marks the boundary of the literary text and exceeds its lyrically inscribed personality.

At the very least Mandelstam leaves one with the sense that the novel's own synthetism or integrity is necessary for the establishment of individual identity. Psychology, as created through a character's interaction with historical events, he implies, can no longer adequately render personality. That task is left to the text itself, which, through its organization, may in addition reveal the presence of an aesthetically creative "I" behind it. In Mandelstam's *The Egyptian Stamp*, both the inadequacy of his supposed "hero" (who is in many ways a conglomeration of literary clichés) and Mandelstam's reversion to the first-person narrator disclose this discursive center, where the author resides as the real hero of the story. The only *human* image rendered by Mandelstam's novella is of the individual who remains hidden (but is subsequently revealed) as the ideological or discursive center behind the text.[23]

With Mandelstam what was merely a literary historical moment, the rebirth of the novel in the 1920s, becomes a question crucial to the evolution of the novel genre. The novel takes as a formal imperative the synthesis of several potentially irreconcilable chronologies, a synthesis that was previously given in the assumed coherence between the individual, his historical time, and the story the novel tells. That chronologically coherent, formal substrate of the integral personality can no longer serve as the basis of organization for the novel, according to Mandelstam, but the complementary humanistic imperative associated with it remains and challenges contemporary novelists to constitute the individual in the text in some other way. The need to create characters differently changes the nature of the novel and forces us to reconsider literary change itself.

THE SYSTEM OF LITERARY EVOLUTION

> [Never] has a single generation had such an interest in transformation and changeability—in evolution . . . In Turgenev's time they didn't even think in such a way; *but why do we feel it so?* No doubt because we ourselves are changing and our minds are broadening.
>
> —Yuri Tynianov, 1928

Certainly Tynianov was more interested in evolution than the average Russian in the 1920s.[24] Nevertheless, the problems associated with literary evolution have always been pervasive in Russian literature and criticism. Even in Turgenev's time, a heightened consciousness of tradition was frequently evident—one need only note the occasionally striking similarity between the rhetoric of the "Nihilists" of the 1860s and the futurists of the second and third decades of the twentieth century. Tynianov is really speaking about, and trying to explain in a metaliterary way, the evolution of the way people think about evolution. "In Turgenev's time they didn't even think in such a way; *but why do we feel it so?*" Here and elsewhere, Tynianov points to the changing characteristics of a culture and shows how they are interrelated with (but do not determine) the changing products of that culture.

In his 1927 essay "On Literary Evolution," Tynianov set forth a concise but remarkable theory of literary evolution that, as one critic recently put it, "remains to a surprising degree unsurpassed today."[25] The novel genre is not the focus of Tynianov's theory, but one can see a resemblance between the way that Mandelstam conceives of the novel's synthetism and the way that Tynianov designs his comprehensive theory of literary evolution. Tynianov's theory is perhaps best suited, moreover, to the "new novel" of the 1920s and after, because it shares their overt interest in reflexivity.

To study literary evolution is, for Tynianov, to study the "mutability" of systems, which by their very nature are all encompassing: they account for every individual part within the whole. The first point that Tynianov makes, however, is that we cannot understand literary evolution if we consider the literary "order" (traditional sequence of "great" books) in isolation, because literature inevitably "collides with the neighboring cultural, behavioral, and social orders in the broad sense" (66).[26] Such an isolation of the literary order transforms the history of literature into "a history of generals."

Two additional dangers must be overcome in the study of literary evolution, according to Tynianov. We must, on the one hand, separate literary evolution from the examination of the genesis of individual works of literature, and, on the other hand, remove subjective value as our main criterion of judgment. The first inevitably devolves into psychologism and the identification of personal influences. The second leads to naive evaluations, which, in Tynianov's theory, are to be replaced by a consideration of literary phenomena in their intrinsic "evolutionary significance and character." Before accusing Tynianov of circular reasoning on this last point, we should say that he also considers literature as a system fundamentally interrelated with extraliterary systems. The way literature changes is in part determined by the way other contiguous social orders change. *Any* literary phenomenon can be placed within this changing system of systems, and an "evolutionary significance and character" is obtained for *all* literary phenomena.

But what does Tynianov mean by saying that literature and individual literary works are systems? In a "system," each element within the literary work is interrelated with every other element within that work and with the whole literary system. This interrelationship Tynianov calls the "constructional *function* of the given element" (68). This function is two-directional. First, the element is interrelated with like elements in other works and systems; this is its "auto-function." Second, the element is interrelated with unlike elements within the same work; this is its "syn-function" (68). Hence, no "immanent" study of a literary work is possible, as each element within the work is interrelated not only with other elements within the work (its syn-function) but also with elements of other works and systems (its auto-function). Thus Tynianov avoids the first danger: the consideration of the literary order in isolation.

It follows that the literary system is a "system of the functions of the literary order which are in *continual interrelationship* with other orders" (72). There is really no such thing as an evolving synchronic literary system, but if we could freeze time and look at the literary system as a synchronic system, we would find that a certain "dominant" group of elements comes to the foreground. "A work enters into literature and takes on its own literary function through this dominant" (72). Certain works are correlated with certain genres, for example, through their dominant characteristics. "We relate the novel to 'the novel' on the basis of its size and the nature of its plot development, while at one time it was distinguished by the presence of a love intrigue" (73). The dominant elements in the literary system differ over time, and this mutability necessarily points to their changing interrelationship with other nonliterary orders. The dominant in our novels, and in Tynianov's theory, might be reflexivity itself.

What exactly is the interrelationship of the literary order with neighboring orders? If the evolution of literature as a system involves its changing interrelationship with other orders, what is the *mechanism* of change? The neighboring orders may be called "social conventions," says Tynianov, and they "are correlated with literature first of all in its verbal aspect" (73). The interrelationship of the verbal function with social conventions is, in Tynianov's terminology, the *ustanovka* ("intention") of the literary work. The term *ustanovka* has multiple meanings for Tynianov and is central to his entire theory of literary evolution.[27] Jurij Striedter divides Tynianov's usage of *ustanovka* into three corresponding levels of intentional relation:

> For Tynianov, it is only through *ustanovka* that the work as a functional system also becomes a system with an intentional reference, and that the historical or evolutionary aspect becomes a cardinal point in his general theory. He distinguishes three levels of the intentional relation: (1) Every factor of a work of literary art has an intentional relation to the complete work of art as a system. (2) This system has an intentional relation to the system of literature and literary evolution. (3) Literature and literary evolution have, through language, which is both the medium of literary creation and the medium of social communication, an intentional relation to the entire human environment in its historical and social transformations.[28]

In short, *ustanovka* describes the relationship of the individual elements of a work to the whole work, the whole work to the system of literature, and the system of literature to the extraliterary environment.

It is important to notice the visual image that Tynianov's theory suggests, its ever-expanding layers of interrelatedness. Within each element of a work we see the whole work, in which we see the literary system, in which we may also see the extraliterary world of social conventions. There is no literary representation that, in principle, cannot be contained by such a theory and that cannot capture, in a special sense, the social world. The resulting multilayered image of an onion or a *matryoshka* doll, in which the part-whole interrelationships are reflected again and again, frequently appears in modern literature and is a kind of *mise en abyme*. Although Tynianov's theory of literary evolution is not marked by any particular genre preference, it perfectly describes the movement of a reflexive modernist novel.

It is impossible, of course, to determine what the exact relationship was between Tynianov's theory of literary evolution and self-conscious literature of the 1920s. The formalists were all drawn to examples of meta-literature: self-referentiality highlighted for them what was "literary" in literature. Tynianov stands out among critics because he was not only a participant in the literary debates of the time—he also devised a theory of literary evolution. The image of expanding concentric circles that capture and synthesize more of everyday reality as they collide with it proved as advantageous a model of novelistic construction as it was a model of literary evolution. Both in literature and in criticism, debates on the novel led to new ways of rendering the individual as an integral being within the world.

THE *MISE EN ABYME*

The term *mise en abyme* was originally coined by André Gide and refers to the heraldic image of a shield that contains in its center a miniature shield. The whole contains a reflection of itself, and the reflection incorporates the whole. Lately, the term has been used almost as a critical catchphrase to describe any variation of literary auto-reference. Usually *mise en abyme* refers to interpolated representations of the entire work, as for example in Gide's *The Counterfeiters* (*Les faux monnayeurs*), where Edouard's journal might be said to reflect the larger novel itself. One finds especially frequent reference to the *mise en abyme* in criticism of the *nouveau roman* and the new *nouveau roman*, two subgenres which were a primary focus of the term's great popularizer, Lucien Dällenbach.[29]

The definition that Dällenbach provides for the *mise en abyme*, to give a very condensed paraphrase, relies on the basic property of reflexivity in metanarrative, intra- or metadiegetic utterances in the text. A "metanarrative" is a segment of text "where an internal narrator takes over temporarily from the author or narrator."[30] "Diegesis" refers to the spatiotemporal universe of the narrative; a metadiegetic utterance could be a dream, and an (intra-)diegetic utterance might simply be a conversation or other conventional event in the narrative. *Mises en abyme* reflect, according to Dällenbach, the "utterance" of the narrative, the "enunciation" of the narrative, or the "whole code" of the narrative, terms he borrows from Roman Jakobson's communicative model of language. Defined simply, the utterance of the narrative is the text itself; the enunciation of the narrative refers to its production; and the whole code of the narrative refers to the text, its production, and its reception. Basic types of the *mise en abyme* may additionally be delineated according to the kind of duplication they engender: "a '*mise en abyme*' is any internal mirror that reflects the whole of the narrative by simple, repeated or 'specious' (or paradoxical) duplication."[31] In fine, the *mise en abyme* generates a reflexivity of the utterance, enunciation, or code of the narrative by way of simple, repeated, or specious duplication.

Reflections of the utterance of the narrative may be found throughout world literature. In *The Master and Margarita,* the Master's novel is a *mise en abyme* because it reflects by way of simple duplication the entire novel. The degree of analogy between the two works is open to debate but, practically speaking, whenever readers compare Yeshua to the Master or the fate of Bulgakov's novel to the fate of the Master's novel, they recognize the resemblance between the two. The textological history of *The Master and Margarita,* the fact that this "desk drawer" novel did not perish, tends to support the reading of the Master's novel as a *mise en abyme:* Woland's famous line, "manuscripts don't burn," seems to apply as much to Bulgakov's novel as to the Master's, though this is, of course, purely a coincidence of literary history and literary politics.

Vladimir Nabokov's *The Gift* provides an example of a reflection of the utterance by way of repeated or specious duplication, depending on how one views the novel's ending. If, on the one hand, at the end of *The Gift* the reader believes that the novel just completed is in fact the same as the novel Fyodor said he was going to write, then the duplicative aspect of the *mise en abyme* is repeated, perhaps infinitely; for *The Gift* is then a novel about the writing of *The Gift,* which is about the writing of *The Gift,* ad infinitum. On the other hand, if the reader believes that the novel Fyodor intended to write represents a shuffling of the facts (as Fyodor promised it would), then there is an obvious paradox: the novel the reader has just completed, *The Gift,* is a false account of how *The Gift* came to be written. If the novel is true, it is false; if it is false, it is true. Specious duplication of this sort recalls the infamous liar's paradox: "This statement is false."

Narratives making use of the *mise en abyme* do not always combine reflections of the utterance with reflections of the enunciation, but the two often complement one another. A telling sign for reflections of the enunciation is the protagonist's appearance as an author, poet, or artist. Narratives of the "work in progress" tend to contain this sort of *mise en abyme.* In *Doctor Zhivago,* Yuri describes his poetry as the preparation for a larger work of prose. His poetry thus becomes a reflection of a larger prose "work in progress," which may be related to the whole of *Doctor Zhivago.* By endowing Zhivago with many of his own characteristics, Pasternak bolsters our identification of a *mise en abyme* of this enunciative type. Nabokov makes frequent use of this type of *mise en abyme* in *The Gift.* Much of the novel, perhaps all of it, describes the working of Fyodor's imaginative processes as he writes poems, biographies, and, one presumes, an autobiographical novel.

The third object of reflexivity in the *mise en abyme,* that of the entire code, is especially intriguing, for, of the three, this type of reflection provides what I think is the best reason for turning one's interpretive attention to *mises en abyme*. The reflection of the code approximates the literary relationships among author, text, and reader, and outlines the aesthetic preconceptions of these relationships as they exist latently in the text. To put it more simply, here is where the text seems to say "read me this way." This *mise en abyme* is an intersection of interpretive authorities, where reader, author, and character test various readings in isolation from the remainder of the text but with significant implications for more global interpretations.

The reflection of the code in a *mise en abyme* is not necessarily isolated from reflections of utterance and enunciation. The three may in fact go together, as in Fyodor's *Life of Chernyshevsky* in *The Gift*. The reader is privy to that work as it is being written (enunciation), as it exists (utterance), and as an entire literary event (code), which includes its reception by a readership. In each of these three cases of *mise en abyme*, there is a differing degree of analogy to be drawn between Fyodor's *Life of Chernyshevsky* and Nabokov's *The Gift*. As I mentioned earlier, what complicates all the *mises en abyme* in *The Gift* are their duplicative aspects, which may or may not lead the reader into paradox.

A simpler and more typical example of the *mise en abyme* in its reflection of the code may be observed in Pasternak's *Doctor Zhivago*. Early in the novel Lara recalls as a metaphor of the loss of her virginity a painting in the private room of a restaurant where Komarovsky took her. She comments that when she first saw it she was not yet comparable to an expensive work of art. From the start, then, the painting represents Lara's objectification and loss of identity. This is clear enough. In addition, through this scene the notion of art as commodity enters into a dialogue with Zhivago's (and consequently Pasternak's) romantic aesthetics. The condensation of one of the novel's implicit aesthetic debates—the representation and reception of an object of art—constitutes this *mise en abyme* as a reflection of the entire code.

In this *mise en abyme,* and in others, one passage is taken to signify more than other passages in the novel; and while we all recognize that some novelistic scenes are more important than others, the need to put boundaries on the broad range of potential *mises en abyme* must be considered. Dällenbach adduces two general hermeneutic principles for interpretation of the *mise en abyme* that are worthy of repetition here:

> The first, a traditional one, takes us back to an earlier proposition, and holds that it is the whole of the text that gives meaning to each of its segments, and that one can therefore only give a reflexive value to a sequence if this is justified by the text as a whole. The second, which is complementary, involves not interpreting texts in a reflexive-allegorical way unless reflexivity appears as a theme in them, guaranteeing some sort of systematic view. Narratives whose reflexive character is only tacit, or localized, are recognizable by their emphasis on their referential, rather than their literal dimension.[32]

The example of Pasternak's Lara meets the first criterion because of the meta-aesthetic nature of the passage; dialogues on the use of art are relatively frequent in *Doctor Zhivago*. The passage meets the strictures of the second principle because Lara herself uses the painting as a tool of self-interpretation. When readers take her description of the painting beyond its referential dimension, they merely follow her lead.

Although readers are thus warranted to consider the reflective nature of this passage as a *mise en abyme,* the *mise en abyme* is not itself purely, mimetically reflective. Eikhenbaum, Lukács, Mandelstam, and Tynianov revealed the novel's capacity to synthesize, or present the world as a totality that integrates individual identity. Yet these critics were also especially concerned that the novel not over-rely on mimesis in its representation of contemporary reality. Two features of the *mise en abyme* relate directly to the mimetic and totalizing roles of the novel.

The mimetic dimension of the *mise en abyme* is unusual in that the device's reflection is by definition never simple but compound—a kind of mimesis of mimesis. Representation here is of the second order because the object of the *mise en abyme*'s reflection is not the world itself but the literary representation of the world. The mirror in the novel is, moreover, always "crooked," to use Tynianov's word, compressing or dilating meaning as though it were light passing through a lens. According to Dällenbach, "the fictional *mise en abyme,* like synecdoche, can be divided into two groups: the particularizing (miniature models), which concentrate and limit the meaning of the fiction; and the generalizing (transpositions), which give the context a semantic expansion beyond that which the context alone could provide."[33] Though the *mise en abyme* fits into the referential (and mimetic) fabric of the novel, its semantic investment is entirely out of balance with the rest of the text, making it, in its capacity to mean, more like the rhetorical figures of poetry.

As for processes of totalization or synthesis, this condensation/expansion of semantic potential in the reflexivity of the *mise en abyme* presents two possibilities. Initially, "although they are microcosms of the fiction, they [transposed fictional *mises en abyme*] superimpose themselves semantically on the macrocosm that contains them, overflow it and end up by engulfing it, in a way, within themselves."[34] The Master's novel, for example, is an interpolated text within *The Master and Margarita* that superimposes itself on the larger novel, eventually supplanting the larger text in both a literal and a figurative sense.

What is more, *mises en abyme* may also "engulf" the larger text of the novel by way of duplication. The potentially infinite duplication of *mises en abyme* of the enunciative type can subsume the novel by adding layers, so to speak, to the narrative onion of the text. I have already mentioned the structure of *The Gift* in this respect. In both kinds of *mise en abyme,* the paradox is that what is contained by the novel appears, in retrospect, to have contained the novel itself. In terms of the novel's totalizing or synthesizing function, therefore, the *mise en abyme* provides, at least theoretically, an array of nonmimetic strategies, what Fredric Jameson might call "strategies of containment."[35]

There is often a literary-historical dimension to these nonmimetic strategies that allows the *mise en abyme* to describe a unique solution to the problems of literary evolution. Like metaphors and other rhetorical figures, *mises en abyme* are both part of the referential fabric of the narrative and something else. Generic and other markers indicate differences between the *mise en abyme* and the rest of the text. The Master's novel is stylistically as well as physically separate from the rest of the novel. In terms of style, the Master's novel recalls an earlier era of literature, one that was more realistic and less metafictional. The effect achieved is that, through the *mise en abyme* of the Master's novel, *The Master and Margarita* smuggles a literary historical past into the present.

Without pushing the comparison too far, one could say that certain novels approximate the famous evolutionary theory of recapitulation, that ontogeny recapitulates phylogeny. In other words, by describing their own genesis, some novels also tell a story of the development of the novel itself. When novelists like Bulgakov, Pasternak, and Nabokov account for the evolution of the novel, they choose their own precursors and, to some extent, create their own tradition.[36] By smuggling in the past, they may also reestablish contact with a tradition lost or alien to modern sensibilities (for example, religious literature), or perhaps with a tradition that is forbidden (as was modernist and avant-garde literature after 1934). In short, the *mise en abyme* creates narrative potentials that could address the problems of the novel's synthesizing function and its role in redefining literary evolution.

How Bulgakov, Pasternak, and Nabokov actually used the *mise en abyme* to formulate new models of selfhood, contain a comprehensive vision of the world, and reconstitute the Russian novelistic tradition is the focus of this book.

The Author as Hero

Chapter One

Mikhail Bulgakov's *The Master and Margarita*

> The more I wrote the stronger the desire grew in me to be a contemporary writer. But at the same time I saw that it was impossible both to depict contemporaneity and to find myself in that highly tuned and tranquil state of mind necessary for a work of great and harmonious effort. The present is too alive, too moving, too exasperating; the writer's pen imperceptibly turns to satire.
>
> —Nikolai Gogol (quoted by Bulgakov in a letter to Stanislavsky)

THERE ARE, perhaps, as many ways to compare Bulgakov to Gogol as there are works in Bulgakov's oeuvre.[1] Especially in *The Master and Margarita,* Bulgakov shares Gogol's uncanny ability to gesture toward the spiritual void beneath a comic, satirical surface. As both Gogol and Bulgakov discovered, satire sometimes becomes its own obstacle. According to popular legend, Gogol did not complete parts two and three of *Dead Souls,* because he was unable to overcome the talent for satire that served him so well in the "Inferno," the wasteland of part one. In *The Master and Margarita,* Bulgakov also undertakes this challenge of combining the comic and the serious, the superficial and the essential. "Art would like to stop being pretence and play," says Leverkühn in Thomas Mann's *Doctor Faustus,* "it would like to become knowledge."[2] Satire is all surface and pretence, knowledge is depth and sincerity. Yet in spite of its satire, *The Master and Margarita* is consumed with this desire that art "become knowledge," that literature reveal the truth. In *The Master and Margarita,* Bulgakov seems to long for a time when essential truths about people and about the universe were the exclusive trade of the author.

Themes of selfhood and tradition are detectable even in the epigraph to *The Master and Margarita:* "Say at last, who are you? / I am part of that power / Which wills forever evil / And does forever good."[3] The question asked here is not only one of identification—*who are you?*—but also one of identity—*give an account of yourself.* Riddles of personal identity and the self thus initiate a novel in which the central hero is both eponymous and anonymous. Even the paradoxical response of Goethe's Mephistopheles, who is unnamed in the epigraph, is relevant, for one of the great paradoxalists of Russian fiction is Ivan's devil in *The Brothers Karamazov*.[4] Thus a second, hidden identity for the epigraph's respondent is produced, one that is bound closely to the Russian literary tradition. Identity in *The Master and Margarita* often emerges through the novel's dialogue with tradition.

Bulgakov's attitude toward tradition in *The Master and Margarita* suggests, moreover, that there is a therapeutic potential in the literary past: one enters into a dialogue with the past in order to heal the self that has been lost or become meaningless in the vagaries of modern reason. By revealing the truth and healing the self, authorship in *The Master and Margarita* becomes an especially privileged and broad concept, at times as much a model of human personality as a profession or calling of the literati.

In his book *Truth and Method*, Hans-Georg Gadamer describes the human experience of the tradition of art as an opportunity both to gain knowledge of the self and to gather oneself into an integral whole by means of the artwork's aesthetic structuring.

> Our experience of the aesthetic too is a mode of self-understanding. Self-understanding always occurs through understanding something other than the self, and includes the unity and integrity of the other. Since we meet the artwork in the world and encounter a world in the individual artwork, the work of art is not some alien universe into which we are magically transported for a time. Rather, we learn to understand ourselves in and through it, and this means that we sublate (*aufheben*) the discontinuity and atomism of isolated experiences in the continuity of our own existence . . . The binding quality of the experience (*Erfahrung*) of art must not be disintegrated by aesthetic consciousness. This negative insight, positively expressed, is that art is knowledge and experiencing an artwork means sharing in that knowledge.

In the broadest sense possible, authorship in *The Master and Margarita* means sharing in a knowledge of the past that restores wholeness to the self and bestows meaning on the present. This complex process is, for Bulgakov, a search for truth.

THE SELF AS AUTHOR AND HERO

> The author's position of being situated outside the hero is gained by conquest, and the struggle for it is often a struggle for life, especially in the case where the hero is autobiographical, although not only there.
>
> —Mikhail Bakhtin, "Author and Hero in Aesthetic Activity"

In *The Master and Margarita* subjectivity is examined through a dialectical relationship to the literary past, which may be characterized by three stages.

First, novelistic reliance on introspection and on the inherent rationality of the mind as the bases of understanding the self is subverted. Without the subjective and epistemological certainty produced by this reliance on introspection and rationality, however, identity is repeatedly depicted as in danger of becoming alien to the self and radically contingent—a matter of mere faith, rather than logic. Finally, Bulgakov compensates for this contingency and alienation by privileging the concept of authorship. An author in this novel is one who, by speaking to the literary tradition, also describes a stable and meaningful horizon for self-interpretation; he is the "hero" of his own literary history.[5]

The undermining of rational subjectivity takes place in the Moscow story of *The Master and Margarita,* and may be considered in light of a fairly common modernist attack on Enlightenment rationality, in which reason-centered concepts of subjectivity are often the favored (if not the sole) targets of criticism.[6] The Russian tradition has Dostoevsky's Underground Man as its leading representative. The Master's apartment is below grade, of course, and while he lives there he is (like the Underground Man) brilliantly insane—writing a novel and subsequently losing his mind. But the antirational work of the novel is more substantial than vague allusions suggest, and shares in broader insights deriving from Dostoevsky's famous work.

In *Dostoevsky's Underground Man in Russian Literature,* Robert Louis Jackson identifies several twentieth-century prose works that draw on the antirationalistic insights and destructive impulses of Dostoevsky's famous antihero. Among them, Jackson isolates a number of postrevolutionary novels: Zamyatin's *We* (1920), Olesha's *Envy* (1926), Pilnyak's *The Volga Falls to the Caspian* (1930), and Voinova's *Semiprecious Stones* (Самоцветы; 1930), along with shorter works by Ilya Ehrenburg and Leonid Leonov. All are products of the twenties and thirties and thus directly relevant to any discussion of how *The Master and Margarita* itself evolves out of the literary questions of that period. The reason for the prevalence of the "underground" theme, according to Jackson, is clear: "It is not accidental that the 'underground' portrait of man as morally and spiritually crippled, as irrational, as distorted in his craving for freedom, nihilistic in his rebellion, should have been produced in a country which traditionally denied to the individual the right even to recognition."[7]

The tale of Woland's visit to Moscow plays satirically on the tyranny of degraded reason in Soviet society and makes a comic subtext of Cartesian (and, of course, Marxist) epistemology. Both reader and characters are hindered by a skepticism that results from this attack on rationality and from the deceptive participation of an "evil genius" in the world of the novel.[8] The loss of epistemological certainty produced by this skepticism parallels a loss of personal identity by the main characters in the novel, for both interpretation and self-interpretation proceed within the framework of ideologies that are repeatedly acknowledged as partial and impoverished. Knowing and being are intimately related in the novel. "The right even to recognition" is an appropriate guidepost for *The Master and Margarita* in both senses of the phrase.

Whereas the epistemological skepticism of the Moscow story might be said to prevent the subject from "knowing," and to indicate the self's alienation within the world, a usurpation of free will and the loss of other traditional properties of personal identity (such as embodiment) prevent the subject from "acting" of its own accord. The self is not sovereign but contingent, it seems, when the devil is in town. Certain passages in the novel (Woland's conversation with Berlioz's decapitated head, for example) suggest that individuals are themselves the architects, or "authors," of the world in which they make judgments and are judged. Thus contingency itself might be creatively authored by the self. It is in order to understand and perhaps overcome the conventional structures of this creativity that an author addresses tradition.

When one considers the Master's literary achievements in the novel, it becomes evident that authorship has great currency as a symbol of metaphysical investigation. It is the author who sees beyond the phenomenal world, obscured to other characters by the novel's skepticism.[9] The author perceives in his contingency and loss of identity a larger purpose or worldly design that can explain the partial nature of his self-understanding. Ultimately, it is the author who, by speaking to the historical structures of creativity, awakens a dormant but responsive tradition. Just as the tradition requires a continuous supply of authors to sustain it, so too does the author need tradition in order to authenticate his search for meaning. This process makes significant demands of the author, who is ultimately the main beneficiary of his relationship to the past.[10]

Inasmuch as the author perceives a noumenal reality or hidden truth, the articulation of an identity for the self uses an ethically charged idiom of language. In *The Master and Margarita,* the possibility of true knowledge implies a risk of purposeful ignorance, and free will engenders personal responsibility. The way an individual articulates his perception of the truth, what makes his life *meaningful,* reveals the framework within which he evaluates beliefs and behavior; indeed, there is some doubt as to whether the self can generate an identity outside such evaluative, moral frameworks.[11] Authorship, in the broadest sense in which it is implied by the novel, is therefore also a "claiming" of, or taking responsibility for, values that may be at odds with political reality. It is not surprising, then, that individuals in *The Master and Margarita* often question themselves in terms of honor or "courage."

This authorial transcendence in *The Master and Margarita* of the phenomenal world toward a moral, constitutive reality may seem, perhaps, like no more than resurrected romanticism. There is a strong sense of the romantic here: even the intimation of an unknowable world may inspire myths of revelation and salvation. In a world of degenerate reason, the self resorts to madness and to myth, and finds alternate structures governing meaning in the "other" of reason. Thus the Master simply remythologizes the Passion and retreats into the safety both of the psychiatric clinic and of his illness. Yet the events of the novel also clearly take us beyond such a version of the romantic, beyond such self-satisfaction with the marginalia of rational discourse, which is sometimes found in romanticism.

First, the Master's perception or vision of the truth is intensely personal. He alone is capable of being transformed by his knowledge—he recaptures his own self at the end of the novel, he does not re-create a myth of human salvation. (This is one of the ways that *The Master and Margarita* deflates its own apocalyptic subtext.[12] Ultimately Moscow *does not* burn, an earlier resolution of the plot that is significantly absent from the final redaction.[13]) Moreover, the Master is not even "saved." In one of the more famous passages in the novel, we find out that he earns "peace," not "light." Thus, in *The Master and Margarita* art is unable in the end to transform or unite society, as it does, say, for Schiller, who reserves this capacity for art alone: "only the communication of the Beautiful unites society, because it relates to what is common to them all."[14] There is apparently no transformative, common sensibility of the Beautiful in Soviet Moscow.

The Master and Margarita is more deeply antisocial(-ist) than even Bulgakov's Soviet critics would have characterized it. It is useful here to compare his early novel, *The White Guard* (1924). Set in Civil War-era Kiev, that novel looks inward to how the (extended) family of the Turbins makes its own meaning and narrates its story. The intimate history of inside jokes and sketches inscribed on the family stove contrasts with an apocalyptic history threatening civilization outside the home. Outside the home there is a violent convergence of mysticism, communism, nationalism, and bloody pragmatism; but for the Turbins this upheaval is primarily a tragic and personally transformative event. Likewise, *The Master and Margarita* follows the lead of its heroes and seems to abandon Soviet society to its numbing blindness.[15] What is ultimately at stake in this novel is not society but the individual and, in addition, the individual's ability to conceive of a self in terms of the tradition he shapes and which shapes him.

Although the Master's constitution of self in this regard is achieved within a moral and highly personal space, his articulation of that vision places him in a world of discourse, as one author among other authors. And the discursive intertextuality that is at the heart of the novel is remarkably complex—now disguised, now revealed with dizzying rapidity by the author.

Because literary tradition is, in an important sense, the relationships among literary texts, establishing the basic structure of intertextuality in

The Master and Margarita is crucial. At the center of the novel is the interpolated text of the Master's story of Pontius Pilate and Yeshua. Although it makes a claim on the truth (i.e., that it is not "textual" at all) by retelling the Passion, the Pilate story is perhaps the most intertextual segment of the novel. Outside the context of the rest of the novel, it is connected with all other versions of the Christ-Pilate story: the Gospels, the Apocrypha, lives of Christ (such as Renan's), Marxist-Leninist debunkings of religion, and so forth. In addition, in style and in its attempted representation of divine goodness, the Pilate story is related to a number of nineteenth-century novels, especially Dostoevsky's *The Idiot* and *The Brothers Karamazov*.[16] Within the context of the rest of the novel, the Pilate story is connected with other works of fiction in the novel—Ivan Bezdomny's antireligious poem, for example—and with the interpolating text of the novel itself. Nevertheless, the Pilate story is devoid of the obvious metaliterary play that reminds the reader of its intertextuality, or even textuality. The Pilate story attempts to conceal its literariness by making a claim on the truth. An early redaction of the novel reads: "'Listen to me, Master,' said Woland, 'In your novel you [have guessed] have written the truth. Everything was exactly as you told it.'"[17] The Master's story is not a story, it's the truth.

By contrast, the interpolating text, the Moscow story, contains numerous obvious allusions to other literary works. Among the authors alluded to in *The Master and Margarita* are Pushkin, Gogol, Dostoevsky, Tolstoy, and Mayakovsky, not to mention Goethe and Gounod. What is interesting about the intertextuality of the interpolating text, as opposed to that of the interpolated text, is that the Moscow story revels in its literariness, in its comic ability to cite so many different works of literature. It is no surprise, then, that the literariness of the Moscow story, which continually announces its status as fiction, accompanies the attack on epistemology and personal identity. To know and narrate reality transparently would be to contradict the irrationality that besets the subject in this fictional world.

The relationship between these two texts in *The Master and Margarita* is particularly important because one finds here a mediation of the present and past of literary tradition. Structurally, this metafictional relationship of interpolating to interpolated text is similar to that of parody to its target text, with the unusual and significant exception that in *The Master and Margarita* the target text, the interpolated Pilate story, is actually present and stands on its own within the larger novel. It is not discredited by the parody—thus my use of "parody" extends the ordinary sense of the term.[18] When viewed as one of the defining characteristics of this parodic structure, the *stylistic* diversity of the two stories betrays a marked concern for the dilemma of literary evolution—bridging the gap between the present and an exceedingly remote but constitutive past.[19] In *The Master and Margarita* there is an unsuccessful attempt to carry the literary past and its untroubled rendering of the self into the present through the retained integrity of the target text, the Master's novel. Preserving the Master's novel means preserving a traditional, and perhaps unrealistic, way of understanding the self.

The novel relates to itself as a work of literature through the *mise en abyme* of the Pilate story, which is, in Dällenbach's terminology, a reflection of the utterance of the narrative.[20] In its resemblance to Bulgakov's novel, the Master's novel suggests itself as a kind of duplication of the former. The similarity of the two stories indicates that the reader may take certain facts about the Master and about his novel, its genesis and its fate, as remarks about "Bulgakov" and about *The Master and Margarita*. Behind the novel's skepticism and attack on personal identity is the author's, Bulgakov's, complex epistemological position vis-à-vis his creation. He is at once the subjectivity that conceives of the world of the novel and at the same time, through the *mise en abyme*, an object within that world—the Master. As both the "author and hero" of the novel, Bulgakov is thus involved in a dialectic of self-reflection that transforms him from subject to object over and over again.[21] In this dialectic, the author posits an objectification of himself, only to discover that what is missing from that objectification is precisely the inner, subjective, and creative self he sought to know.

One can interpret Bulgakov's depiction of the Master's literary creativity as an attempt to retrieve the subjectivity he has relinquished by writing himself into his own novel; that is, he illustrates his hero's subjectivity and implicitly asks the reader to compare it with the author's subjectivity. Yet inasmuch as the hero embodies the author's alienation, he also goes through the same, potentially misconceived, objectifying motions: the Master in turn identifies with *his* heroes, viewing himself sometimes as Yeshua, at other times as Pilate. In this circularity, authorial subjectivity merely continues its retreat, and knowledge of self is deferred time and again.

Perhaps the problem of retrieving this lost subjectivity might be overcome through an interrogation of the past of literary tradition. When one considers the author's, and thus the novel's, relationship to tradition in this way, one encounters a dilemma similar to that which emerges in reflective self-knowledge. Here, too, there is contradiction and circularity. In order to apprehend the underlying, historical structures of literary meaning as they act to define the self as author, the novel incorporates a reexamination of literary tradition and, to some extent, an "education" on how to understand the novel. Thus in *The Master and Margarita*, the metaphysics of authorial creation are viewed through a Faustian glass. Could the Master have written his novel without the "evil" presence of Woland somehow attached to it? To what extent does Margarita's deal with the devil place her in the position of coauthor? Moreover, the theme of the "role of the poet in society" echoes throughout Bulgakov's allusions to Pushkin and Mayakovsky. Ryukhin's realization that his poems are worthless, for example, is told in the context of his shaking his fist at Pushkin's statue, an action which is itself saturated with literary historical significance. Finally, the question of whether truth and beauty may be rendered communicable by literature is hidden in a Dostoevskian subtext. In spite of his other failures to create a Christlike figure, in *The Brothers Karamazov* Dostoevsky recognized the effectiveness of representing Christ via a story told by one of the novel's other characters, rather than directly. The Christ of "The Legend of the Grand Inquisitor" is certainly Dostoevsky's most compelling depiction of supreme goodness. Though Bulgakov's examination of literary tradition reveals the foundation of the novel's comprehensibility, however, it also creates that foundation in an obvious way. *That* self-awareness is manifest in the literariness of the Moscow story, in the narrator's need to reveal as fiction the story's status and its reconstruction of tradition.

The novel thus dramatizes the perceived struggle of literature with its own epistemological groundlessness. For the novel creates an idealization of a literary past in which the truth is allowed to dwell in a story (as in a sacred text) and in which the subject of that story knows itself transparently through its objectifications (as in a saint's life). Both the interpolation of the Pilate story and its apparent synthesis with the Moscow story are attempts to smuggle that past into the present, to transcend the epistemological dilemmas of modern literary artifice and conventionality. The ultimate failure of these attempts is attested to by the novel's epilogue. There the novel succumbs to the Moscow story, to the playfulness of its narrator, and to the vacuity of Ivan Bezdomny's life. Ivan never writes a "continuation"; the events and the telling of the Master's novel leave almost no trace on either the literature or people of Moscow.

This apparent failure of the novel is, of course, relative to the goals by which it is evaluated. If, ultimately, *The Master and Margarita* does not escape the reflexivity it sets in motion, it does manage to reconfigure significantly the way fiction is used to interpret the self as author and inheritor of literary tradition. Whereas much of modernist fiction, and especially avant-garde fiction, attempts to escape or overcome the literary past in parody or "trans-rational" language, *The Master and Margarita* uses the parodic structure to seek out equal ground on which to engage the past and preserve an open dialogue with it. The novel responds in this way not only to the "futurist" element of modernism, which throws the past "off the steamship of modernity,"[22] but also to the Sovietization of Russian modernism, which rewrites literary history, and thereby effaces the past. It is partly because of this double-responsiveness that *The Master and Margarita* has become an important model for contemporary Russian, postmodern fiction, which, at the end of fifty years of socialist realism, has been seeking ways to reconnect to the great Russian literary tradition.

SCHIZOPHRENIA

> "Say at last, who are you?"
> "I am part of that power which wills forever evil and does forever good."
> —Epigraph to Bulgakov's *The Master and Margarita*

> "Now we can talk. Who are you?"
> "I am no one," replied the master with a lopsided smile.
> —*The Master and Margarita*

The paradox of Mephistopheles' account of himself in the epigraph[23] is remarkable, and exemplary in *The Master and Margarita,* because the devil's answer splits self-interpretation down the middle into thought and action, intention and result, the volitional and the pragmatic; the incommensurability of these pairs is weighed out by the syntactic balance of the last two verses themselves.[24] The devil becomes, in effect, the first of many "schizophrenics" in the novel whose attempts to explain themselves or articulate an identity result in paradox or contradiction.[25]

Schizophrenia is an obvious and useful metaphor for describing the novel's general attack on the integrity of the self. It is equally useful, I believe, to describe the fractured plane of narration in the novel. This fractured narration in *The Master and Margarita* attests to more than the division of the text into Moscow and Pilate stories. For there is often tension in the novel between the presumed logic of narrative emplotment, on the one hand, and the narrative depiction of psychological instability, on the other; between supposedly rational form and irrational content. This instability is especially evident in Bulgakov's novel because not only are some passages within the novel illogical, but so too are the thought processes of the writer who produces them. Such is the case in Ivan's fruitless attempt to describe on paper his encounter with Woland at Patriarch's Ponds. Stravinsky uses this paradox of logical form and illogical content to convince Ivan he needs psychiatric care. For rational people in a rational world, we are led to ask, what kinds of events could be unnarratable?

Mephistopheles' paradox, his schizophrenia, has a somewhat different function: it initiates a fissure between self-perception and personal truth in the novel that can be sealed when the individual is redefined in light of an ultimate purpose or design. The apocalyptic subtext in the novel, for example, seems to relate mostly to the fate of the individual. As one unravels the epigraph, the motivation for this kind of personalization of teleology becomes more comprehensible—it resolves a problem of self-referentiality or circularity in the articulation of identity. Mephistopheles is part of "that power," which is in turn constituted only through him, through his "willing"

11

and "acting." That his assertion of identity undercuts itself in this way is not surprising, for Mephistopheles is also, infamously, the spirit of negation.[26] A larger purpose or worldly design may substitute for such a mode of self-interpretation in order to forestall the circularity, in order to provide a second, more fundamental ground from which to view the self. The teleological individualized in this way is a means of projecting finitude onto the subject, of marking off the boundaries of the self. It is a matter of the framework in which the problem is viewed, for a contradiction may be resolved when viewed in a broader context.

Failed narratives in the novel engage these broader contexts. The contradictions of Ivan's poem, for example, provoke Woland's story about Pilate and Christ—the existence of God also resolves the contradiction between Berlioz's thinking he is in control of his life and yet not even being able to plan a single night. That Bulgakov is trying to prove the necessity of God here also explains, at least initially, why a far-reaching skepticism enters into the novel, especially in the Moscow story: only through God is certain knowledge of the world and of the self possible. This necessity is deeply intertwined with the metafictional dimension of the novel. If the novel narrates the author's encounter with his own creativity, one must at some point ask along with the author, whether narrative—as the net result of this authorial encounter with creativity—is capable of rendering an acceptable account of subjectivity, of the self as author. Do the same problems of self-referentiality that turned up in the epigraph lead to riddles here too? What evidence, moreover, does one have that a proof of the necessity of God's existence can unfold within the same fictional space as a novelistic investigation into the dilemmas of selfhood?[27]

Inasmuch as this proof of God is clearly announced as *one of many narratives* within the novel, it also proceeds within the scope of a reinterpretation of the self as author. The overlap is evident from the first chapter of the novel, in which Berlioz and Ivan are arguing with Woland about the existence of Christ. Woland insists that He did exist and that it is not a matter of opinion.

> "But one must have some proof . . . ." began Berlioz.
> "There's no need for any proof," answered the professor, and he began in a low voice, his accent disappearing for some reason: "It's very simple: early in the morning on the fourteenth of the spring month of Nisan the Procurator of Judea, Pontius Pilate, in a white cloak lined with blood red . . ." (19)

The final ellipses indicate the transition from the Moscow story to the first chapter of the Pilate story (from chapter 1 to chapter 2 of *The Master and Margarita*). Arguments and logical proofs of Christ's existence or nonexistence are not met by further argument or proof; they are *supplanted* (with the exception of the "seventh proof") by a narrative that, though it claims to be the simple truth, does indeed have an author—as it turns out, the Master.[28] Thus the narrative proof of Christ's existence also transports the reader into the heart of the novel's examination of the self as author.

The relationship between narrative and subjectivity as such is the central aspect of authorship in the presentation of the Pilate story in the larger novel. Yet there has been some debate as to whether the Master is in fact the author of the very text we have in our hands. The presentation of the Pilate story, after all, is varied: Woland tells it, Ivan dreams it, and Margarita reads it. Although I do not think we are meant to understand the story as it appears in these presentations to be different from the Master's novel, questions about the Pilate story have spilled over to the larger novel itself. Who is the narrator/author of that text? Woland and Ivan Bezdomny have been proposed as candidates.[29] The more important point as I see it is that these texts are meant to deform the identities of their authors, just as the narratives themselves deform rational argument.

To use narrative in place of rational argument is not Bulgakov's invention. As is well known, Dostoevsky believed that Zossima's autobiographical story in *The Brothers Karamazov* would be the victorious answer to Ivan's indictment of God in the previous chapters, which include both stories and logical arguments. More contemporary to Bulgakov is the case of Daniil Kharms's absurd stories, or "incidents," as he called them, from the 1930s. Though many of Kharms's stories are plainly philosophical, the rational argument contained within them is displaced onto various odd narratives.[30] In "Blue Notebook No. 10," for example, the connection between stories and personal identity is explored to a totally absurd conclusion: by the end, there is so little of the red-haired man left that it is impossible to continue telling the story about him that was begun thus: "There once was a red-haired man." In another story, "A Sonnet," the narrator has forgotten which number comes first, 7 or 8. This philosophical argument ends not with a solution but with a violent injury to a little boy that distracts the narrator. In both of Kharms's stories, the logic is the narrative, which dispenses with the logic. In *The Master and Margarita* a logical dispute over the existence of God ends with Woland telling Pilate's story.

Twin facets of the Pilate story—as a narrative that proves Christ's existence and as an objective instance of authorial creativity—form the sharpened point of the novel's initial attack on the hegemony of degraded reason in Soviet society. Narrative is "victor" over rational argument twice in the first chapter of the novel: first, when Ivan's antireligious poem mistakenly depicts a Christ who really lived rather than proves that He was entirely mythical (as in the epigraph, another intention at odds with the result), and, second, when Woland launches into the Pilate story to prove Berlioz and

Ivan wrong about Christ's existence. Simultaneous therefore with the discourse on God's necessity is an assault against the mind's essential rationality, against this rationality as the basis of selfhood.

Echoing the reflective split in the epigraph between intention and result, Woland asks Berlioz: "But this is the question that disturbs me: if there really is no God, then who, one wonders, rules the life of man and keeps the world in order?" (14). Berlioz answers that man rules his own life, and he gives the example, when prompted, of his own certain schedule for that evening. He thus sets himself up to be defeated by what Woland calls the "seventh proof" of the existence of God: namely, that Berlioz will not attend a meeting that evening as planned, because he will be decapitated by a streetcar.

Any novel that contains as much of the supernatural as *The Master and Margarita* could be said to undermine reason as the basis of selfhood. Therefore, further substantiation of such an attack on rationality is required. There are no philosophical tracts embedded in this novel as there are in *War and Peace*, and *The Master and Margarita* is no treatise robed in the guise of fiction, like Chernyshevsky's *What Is to Be Done?* Like Dostoevsky, Bulgakov continually works with material that is recognizably philosophical; and he asks questions that are patently philosophical—"who . . . rules the life of man?"—even if one is hard put to formulate cogently his answers to these questions.

In spite of initial allusions to Kant in *The Master and Margarita*, certain clues indicate that the primary model of consciousness in the novel is Cartesian.[31] I purposely ignore Marxist models of consciousness, because even though the satire in *The Master and Margarita* is ruthless when it comes to Soviet ideology, Bulgakov does not take its philosophical underpinnings seriously. Marxist philosophy as it is manifest in the novel is completely degenerate, an unworthy opponent. Yet the novel pays close comic attention to the exaggerated rationalism of Soviet ideology and to its belief in man's total domination over the natural universe. Within this context of total knowledge and utter certainty, the spark of supernatural doubt may produce a conflagration of skepticism.

This skepticism is also produced by the novel's play on Descartes. The only specific allusion to Descartes's philosophical arguments that I am aware of, though by no means the only reference to his ideas, occurs toward the end of the novel in chapter 30, after Azazello has poisoned the Master and Margarita:

—А, понимаю,—сказал мастер, озираясь,—вы нас убили, мы мертвы. Ах, как это умно! Как это вовремя! Теперь я понял все.

—Ах, помилуйте,—ответил Азазелло,—вас ли я слышу? Ведь ваша подруга называет вас мастером, *ведь вы мыслите, как же вы можете быть мертвы?* Разве для того, чтобы считать себя живым, нужно непременно сидеть в подвале, имея на себе рубашку и больничные кальсоны? Это смешно!

"Ah, I understand," said the Master, gazing round, "you have killed us. We are dead. How clever! How timely! Now I understand everything."

"Oh, come," replied Azazello, "do I hear you correctly? Isn't it true that your beloved calls you Master, *aren't you thinking—how can you be dead?* In order to consider yourself alive, must you sit in a basement wearing a nightshirt and hospital pajamas? It's ridiculous!" (360)[32]

Azazello is poking fun at the famous *cogito ergo sum,* that thinking, or thought, is the most certain sign of one's existence. The standard Russian translation of the *cogito* is: Я мыслю, следовательно, я существую.

The path to epistemological certainty that follows from the *cogito,* as it is developed in the *Meditations,* is directly relevant to my consideration of selfhood in *The Master and Margarita.* Descartes is concerned here with establishing "first foundations" for knowledge, and thus introduces into his meditations a method of doubt, by which he intends to rid himself of all non-certain opinions. One of the most famous strategies in this method of doubt is his supposition of an "evil genius":

> Thus [in order not to fall back into old prejudicial habits of thinking] I will suppose not a supremely good God, the source of truth, but rather an evil genius, as clever and deceitful as he is powerful, who has directed his entire effort to misleading me. I will regard the heavens, the air, the earth, colors, shapes, sounds, and all external things as nothing but the deceptive games of my dreams, with which he lays snares for my credulity. (First Meditation)[33]

Though nothing, it would seem, could henceforth provide grounds for certain knowledge—neither imagination, senses, nor intellect—Descartes finds that if he can doubt and be deceived, he must exist. "Then there is no doubt I exist, if he deceives me. And deceive me as he will, he can never bring it about that I am nothing so long as I shall think that I am something."

We may relate two elements of these passages in the *Meditations* to *The Master and Margarita:* the "evil genius," and the reduction of experience by means of introspection to purely mental phenomena. One need not stretch the imagination too far to detect some of Descartes's evil genius in Woland.[34] It has often been remarked that Woland lacks the malevolence of a proper devil.[35] The Faust tradition proposes more of a trickster Mephistopheles than a killer. In fact, Woland's role in the novel is *primarily* that of "the deceiver." From the antics at the "Variety," and in the "unclean apartment," to the "final adventure of Koroviev and Behemoth," Woland and his unholy troupe mostly create illusions and play tricks. Aside from Baron Maigle, no one is killed, and Moscow is essentially the same after they leave as before they arrived. Moreover, just as Descartes introduces his evil genius in order to prove, eventually, the existence of God, so too does

Woland paradoxically assist in proving the necessity of God in *The Master and Margarita.*

While Woland and his gang are in Moscow, however, nothing is *certain,* and there is good reason for characters to adopt a thoroughly skeptical attitude toward the outside world. Most of the supernatural antics in the novel can be reduced to this epistemological dimension: in the context of exaggerated Soviet rationalism, they raise seemingly insurmountable doubt. Simply put, a series of events transpires for which there is no rational explanation: Woland's prediction of Berlioz's death, Likhodeev's mystical transportation to Yalta, Nikanor Ivanovich's possession of foreign currency, the tricks at the Variety, and so forth. Yet these supernatural events would not be connected with the novel's skepticism were they not consistently attached to fundamental issues of personal identity.

One can start with the varying connections between mind and body that are problematized in the novel, recalling that this dualism is a central feature of Cartesianism. Who could forget Lastochkin's visit to the Theatrical Commission, where the Chairman's body seems to have disappeared: "Behind the huge desk with its massive inkwell sat an empty suit. A dry pen was hurrying, unheld, across a sheet of paper. . . . The suit was hard at work and oblivious of the uproar surrounding it" (184). The Chairman, Prokhor Petrovich, can still be identified by his behavior, his voice, and his clothing, but his body is missing. His *body* seems to be the locus of memory, however, because his clothing has forgotten about his affair with the office secretary. The "empty suit" fails to recognize her when she affectionately addresses it as Prosha.

Play like this on familiar themes of personal identity is common in the novel, and, as in the above passage, dualism can sometimes be easily reduced to the absurd. A second, more significant example is the decapitated head of Berlioz, once a firm believer in materialism. Woland reminds Berlioz (or perhaps just his mind) of his former beliefs as he holds the completely conscious head in his hands and speaks to it:

> Вы всегда были горячим проповедником той теории, что по отрезании головы жизнь в человеке прекращается, он превращается в золу и уходит в небытие. Мне приятно сообщить вам, в присутствии моих гостей, хотя они и служат доказательством совсем другой теории, о том, что ваша теория и солидна и остроумна. Впрочем, все теории стоят одна другой. Есть среди них и такая, согласно которой каждому будет дано по его вере.

> You were always a fervent proponent of the theory that when a man's head is cut off his life stops, he turns to dust and passes into nonexistence. I am pleased to inform you in the presence of my guests that, despite the fact that their presence here is proof of an entirely different theory, your theory is both sound and intelligent. However, one theory deserves another. Among them there is one in which each will be given according to his belief. (265)

And Woland transforms Berlioz's head into the goblet from which he drinks the blood of Baron Maigle.

Two points need to be made about this passage. First, there is obviously a connection between this scene and the scene with the Master and Azazello. Both make clear reference to the novel's dualism—there is supposed to be more to existence than the merely physical. Second, Woland's "other theory," that each will be given according to his belief, belies this first point by suggesting that the relationship of the mental or spiritual to the physical is merely relative. He thus ironically paraphrases Christ in Matthew (9.29): "And Jesus said to them [the blind men], 'Do you believe that I am able to do this?' They said to him, 'Yes, Lord.' Then he touched their eyes, saying, 'According to your faith be it done to you'" (Matt. 9.28–29). Although the Russian word вера is best translated as "faith" in the biblical passage, the context in which Woland uses it indicates "belief" (beliefs often differ from person to person). Thus the mental or spiritual side of existence may indeed supersede the physical, but, as Woland suggests, this is the consequence of one theory among many. In the end, Woland does not prove or disprove this or that theory, he offers and proves a theory about theories.

I said of the ethical dimension of the author's perception of truth that inasmuch as the individual perceives a transcendental truth, or a true vision of cosmic order, the articulation of self in the novel seems to use an ethically charged idiom. Woland's statement about each "according to his belief" exemplifies the responsibility called forth by authorship—that creativity implies responsibility. The act of claiming responsibility for one's beliefs thus appears to be as much a step in authorship as it is in the constitution of a self. If narrative supplants rational argument in the novel, then so too does authorship replace the profession of faith.

The novel undermines traditional concepts of self, partly by emphasizing problems of self-referentiality and circularity (as in the epigraph), partly by introducing the basis for skepticism (as in the supernatural antics). Overcoming this sort of self-referentiality and skepticism leads to narratives that describe a higher purpose or design at work in the world. This activity is a kind of authorship; it also generates a fiction, or a creative interpretation of the cosmos,[36] for which some *one* must assume responsibility. Thus Bulgakov teases the theoretical, speculative "belief" out of "faith," especially in the passage with Woland and Berlioz; but selfhood still lacks an *essential* grounding in the author's cosmological vision.

Personal identity is not always undermined with such subtlety in the novel. Free will, another modern touchstone for the self, is often impeded by supernatural obstacles. For example, after his unsuccessful visit to the Theatrical Commission, Lastochkin sets off for its branch office. There he finds that the entire department has been mysteriously hypnotized to break into song, in perfect unison, at specific intervals of time. Taken outside the whole range of facts in the novel that relate to personal identity, this loss of free will might not be significant. But it is significant in the context of:

1. The epigraph—"who are you?"
2. The hero's renunciation of his name and his life—"I no longer have a name . . . I renounced it, just as I renounced altogether everything in life" (134)—not to mention the novel's more general subversion of names as indicators of identity.[37]
3. The play on the relationship between mind and body.
4. Ivan's loss of memory and assumption of a new identity at the end of the novel.

This list could be lengthened, but I think the main point is clear: properties of the self are consistently the focus of the novel's critical attention.

Nowhere does the rationality of the mind as the basis of selfhood and introspection as the vehicle of self-knowledge come under attack as insistently as in the chapter entitled "The Doubling of Ivan." This chapter is comprised, more or less, of two events: Ivan's attempt to provide an account of what happened at Patriarch's Ponds and, shortly thereafter, his attempt to account for his own behavior, which leads to his doubling. When he is unable to write out logically—or simply rationalize—what happened to him and Berlioz, a new Ivan is born. This Ivan just wants to know more about the story of Pilate and Ha-Nostri, and he wishes he had behaved more intelligently with Woland. Ivan thinks to himself, "Wouldn't it have been more intelligent to ask politely what else happened with Pilate and the arrested man, Ha-Nostri?" (115). The same antirational movement of chapter 1 is repeated here: a demand of logic is met by a narrative response. The new Ivan wants the story, not a rational explanation.

No less important in this chapter is the mutation of personality that accompanies introspection. For a novel that delves so deeply into the reflective, creative side of selfhood, *The Master and Margarita* contains few passages that depict the inner mental world of its characters. They occur much more frequently in the Pilate story and indicate the close ties of that story with Russian realist novels of the nineteenth century. In her study of psychological prose, Lydia Ginzburg uses the term "causal conditionality" for the nineteenth-century narrative practice of showing how individual behavior derives from one or several (possibly contradictory) sources. The free-indirect discourse used so often in scenes of introspection frequently allows for manifold causality because, as a paraphrase of the character's thoughts, it puts together the language of the mind with the narrator's linguistic depiction of social, historical, or even physical or psychological contexts.

The Pilate story is precisely the kind of psychologically explanatory text that the Moscow story usually is not. Pilate has headaches for physical, psychological, and perhaps spiritual reasons. The narrator's paraphrase of his thoughts illustrates a variety of causal combinations:

> Все было кончено, и говорить более было не о чем. Га-Ноцри уходил навсегда, и страшные, злые боли прокуратора некому излечить; от них нет средства, кроме смерти. Но не эта мысль поразила сейчас Пилата. Все та же непонятная тоска, что уже приходила на балконе, пронизала все его существо. Он тотчас постарался ее объяснить, и объяснение было странное: показалось смутно прокуратору, что он чего-то не договорил с осужденным, а может быть, чего-то не дослушал.

> It was all over, and pointless to say more. Ha-Nostri was leaving forever, and there was no one to cure the procurator's terrible, vicious headaches; from them there would be no relief, save death. But it wasn't this thought that now struck Pilate. It was that same incomprehensible anguish that came over him on the balcony, that pierced his whole being. He immediately tried to explain it, and the explanation was odd: the procurator vaguely realized that he had not finished saying something to the condemned man, and perhaps, he had not finished listening to something. (36–37)

Clearly the language of this passage is meant to follow Pilate's thoughts; the passage is psychologically explanatory in essence. Certain words and phrases, "it was all over" and the "terrible, vicious headaches," for example, belong to Pilate's speech patterns and diction. The narrator depicts them but does not quote them, and they are thus double voiced, to use a Bakhtinian term— we hear Pilate's voice together with the narrator's. That there is no escape from the headaches, save death, is an approximation of Pilate's attempt at stoic fatalism. This sentiment belongs with his outcries for poison, and it is comprehensible against the background of Pilate's belief system, such as it is. His incomprehensible feeling, or "anguish" (тоска), is also incomprehensible to us as readers; we puzzle over his motivations and behavior together with him in a kind of sophisticated psychological process that hints at the broader philosophical questions in the novel. Bulgakov takes his satirical and philosophical interests from Gogol and Dostoevsky, but when he turns to this sort of realistic psychological analysis, he seems to draw on Tolstoy.

"The Doubling of Ivan" is an important exception to the lack of introspection in the Moscow story. Here Ivan carries out an interrogation of himself, concerning the way he has reacted to, and thought about, his encounter with Woland. His doubling into an "old" Ivan and a "new" Ivan is a function of his "thinking about thinking." The dynamics of such reflexivity are often literally fleshed out in the novel: the Master is a double of Bulgakov; this is a novel about a novel; thus there are two authors for two books. But Ivan's doubling is also characteristic of *The Master and Margarita* in another way. It turns rational introspection into a dialogue carried on not only between Ivan's two selves, but also between the novel and the literary tradition; for Bulgakov alludes in this chapter specifically to Dosto-evsky's famous doubles and thus continues to associate selfhood with liter-ary tradition.

Bulgakov recaptures the way that Dostoevsky first used the device, that is, not as a means of introducing another character as the alter ego of the hero (as, say, Svidrigailov is of Raskolnikov), but in order to show a split produced by/in the very psyche of the hero. Golyadkin in Dostoevsky's early novel *The Double* represents this earlier function of the device.[38] The dou-ble in that novel is generated, one presumes, by the degenerating mental health of the hero; he represents the hero's fears, is simply a figment of the hero's neurosis. No doubt Ivan's doubling, and the Master's elsewhere, is meant to approximate the effect of such borderline madness. As in Ivan's chapter, in *The Double,* the narration is saturated with Golyadkin's con-sciousness. Golyadkin seems to embody his fears in Golyadkin Junior—self-objectification produces an other. Similarly, when considered as an instance of the novel's more far-ranging theme of schizophrenia, Ivan's doubling is just one example of several in which a subject generates multiple objectifications of itself. As I have argued, the novel creates heroes out of its authors and vice versa. Were it not for the eventual appearance of an actual hero, the novel might not get beyond its satiric consideration of rational self-consciousness.

By the end of chapter 13, "Enter the Hero," it has become clear that the central personality of *The Master and Margarita* is, at long last, one of the novel's eponyms. Although his name appears in the title, the Master himself does not turn up for nearly 130 pages. Yet he is still the most im-portant and most complex figure in the novel—at once Bulgakov's hero and a reflection of the author himself (not to mention an author in his own right). Through the Master, the novel's query into the dilemmas of selfhood plainly overlaps with its metafictional investigation of authorship. Even the chapter's ironic title points us in the direction of this fusion. Not only is this meek person a disappointing "hero," he is hardly a person at all. He has given up his past life and identity and does not ever want to leave the safety of the psychiatric clinic, not even for the sake of his love for Margarita.

The Master is the central figure in the novel because it is through him that personal identity is most insistently associated with authorship; in fact, it is through him the novel reinterprets the self as "text." More than once the Master directly equates his life with his novel, and he speaks of the one as if it were the other: "'At least tell me about your novel,' Ivan asked tact-fully. 'All right. *My life,* I should say, has been a somewhat unusual one,' be-gan the visitor" (emphasis added, 134–35). What Ivan really wants to know here, the reader recalls, is what happens next in the Pilate story—the new Ivan has taken over. But the Master speaks of the novel in terms of the story of his life, and later he refuses outright to tell Ivan what happened afterward with Pilate and Ha-Nostri. To think at all about his novel makes him wince.

The opposite also holds true: the Master speaks of his life in terms of his novel. The hour finally struck, he tells Ivan, when the novel was finished, and he had to "go back out into life": "'When I did go back out into life, clutching the novel, then my life came to an end,' whispered the master; and he hung his head and for a long while wagged the black cap with its embroidered yellow "М"'" (140; —И я вышел в жизнь, держа его [роман] в руках, и тогда моя жизнь кончилась,—прошептал мастер и поник головой, и долго качалась печальная черная шапочка с желтой буквой "М"). Whereas at first it seems in this passage that the Master conscientiously separates "life" from his novel, he ends up associating the two even more strongly. When he says, "then my life came to an end," he means that this was the end of his novel—it was savaged by the critics and rejected by the publisher. More significant, the reader's attention is specifically drawn here to the "M" on the Master's hat. The Master's anonymity, his loss of identity, and the ruination of his novel are thus carefully juxtaposed and equated, and, perhaps, even further emphasized by the swaying, ternary rhythm that dominates the final clause of this sentence (и долго качалась печальная черная шапочка с желтой . . .).

This equation of an individual with a work of literature, or the characterization of the self as text, implies certain undesirable consequences, such as the inherent interpretability of texts. Consider the Master's encounter with the publisher, who considers knowledge of the author's biography tantamount to textual exegesis: "The questions he asked me seemed insane. Without saying anything about the substance of the novel, he asked me who I was and where I came from, had I been writing for long, and why had nothing been heard of me before" (140). The publisher is, of course, both giving the Master an ideological litmus test and checking his personal connections. Biographical detail is significant in this respect only to the degree it can establish an identity, especially a political identity, contrary to the one that can, and will, be construed from the text itself.

It is a truism of the era of high Stalinism that political control of the literary process allowed bureaucrats and cronies to deform an author's identity. Zhdanov's ideological disfigurement of Zoshchenko and Akhmatova in 1946, signaling the end of the moderate ideological thaw present in Soviet culture during the Second World War, is well known and symbolic of the era. Akhmatova's refined and sophisticated lyric poetry seemed particularly vulnerable to mischaracterization, as it marshaled little or no political defenses capable of fending off Zhdanov's crude depiction of her work and, thus, of her authorial—and political—identity.

Bulgakov emphasizes that the Master has no biographical defense at his disposal. The events of the creation of his novel constitute the story of his personal effacement.[39] "I am now no one" (277), as he tells Woland; the novel's demise is his demise. Thus, as the Master finds out, to take one's identity as textual means to run the risk of interpretation and misinterpretation, not just of one's novel but of one's self. Indeed, the critics publish reviews that say little about the Master's novel but, as often happens, a lot about its author. The Master is now recast in the papers as a "Pilatist" and a "militant Old Believer." He eventually goes insane, having "struggled with himself like a madman" (143) until he had burned the manuscripts of his novel.

Why does he burn the manuscripts? The Master explains to Margarita, "I grew to hate that novel, and I am scared" (144). Of course, the novel has by this time already caused him a good deal of trouble and promises to cause more, namely his arrest. More important, though, by pouring his whole soul into the novel, by identifying what is essential about himself entirely with the product of his creativity, the Master has emptied himself of all that belongs exclusively to him. In writing his novel, the Master has rendered himself completely objective and equivalent to his work, but still he is shocked in the end to find that he can no longer recognize himself in it. Or rather, that part of him that is recognizable in the novel is no more his true self than the warped persona made of him by the critics.

The meaning of texts in *The Master and Margarita* invariably eludes their authors' intentions; in terms of the self, the objectifying gaze turned inward does not fully grasp what is essential in creativity. This noncoincidence has troubled all four of the texts from the novel that I have discussed. In the epigraph there is a paradigmatic incongruence between intent and result. Ivan's poem about Christ provides a version of this same incongruence—against Ivan's wishes, his Christ comes out as if He really existed. And Ivan's attempts to describe his encounter with Woland not only fail to explain what happened, they also lead to his doubling. Finally, by rendering himself equivalent to his novel, the Master seems not to assert control over his identity, but to relinquish it.

The main point of this elusiveness of meaning is not that the language of fiction is essentially and totally indeterminate. The radical relativism of such a conclusion is alien to the spirit of the novel. Rather, readers must confront meaning on a level where it is constituted by forces that transcend the individual—in the interpretive process. The activity of interpretation, which is fundamentally the interaction between texts and people, itself serves as a guide to interpretation in the novel.

Two interpretive problems emerge in *The Master and Margarita*, both of which are connected with the broader theme of authorship. The first concerns the reader. Texts, even those defined in terms of selfhood, must be validated or made meaningful by the interpretive activity of some other. Reaching an audience is for both the Master's novel and Bulgakov's novel a problem that extends beyond the bounds of how individual readers create their own meanings in individual texts. Carol Avins has argued persuasively that the novel is shaped by a need to overcome the limitations of print and thus circumvent the sociological and political barrier erected between author and reader.[40] An extreme view of this dependency on the other as reader, one should keep in mind, could be taken to warrant the construal of the Master's novel as "Pilatism" and the Master himself as a "militant Old Believer." The Master's novel, however, is not a tabula rasa into which meaning is inscribed from without.

Some balance or version of sympathetic readership is necessary because clearly the meaning is neither completely inside nor completely outside the text.[41] But herein lies the second problem. Is there a reader who is *capable* of such a sympathetic understanding or reading of *The Master and Margarita*? Bulgakov was genuinely worried whether contemporary readers could even understand his novel. In her biography of Bulgakov, Marietta Chudakova characterizes the reactions of listeners to his reading of one of the versions of the novel: "The pragmatic efficiency of some listeners or the confusion (no less pragmatic in provenance) of others spoke to the same—a sort of destruction of ties between the novel being completed or already completed and the contemporary audience of readers."[42] What is required for a sympathetic reading? How does an author respond to a potential failure in reader competency?

Bulgakov does not presuppose a reader who will understand the novel sympathetically; he endeavors to create that reader. The complex literary allusiveness, the intertextuality of the novel, provides the interpretive framework for reading the novel at the same time as it sifts through and reshuffles the literary tradition. The account of the Master's loss of self, of the misinterpretation of his novel, and of the appropriation of his identity by the critics in the chapter "Enter the Hero," for example, forms a historical and metafictional background to the main action of the novel. With *this past* also in mind, one may view the intertextuality in the present action of the novel not only as an education for the sympathetic reader but also as the preparation for the Master's recovery of self. Both processes are translated into a dialogue with tradition.

PARODY AND TRADITION

> To be situated within a tradition does not limit the freedom of knowledge but makes it possible.
>
> —Hans-Georg Gadamer

> "In Savva Potapovich's masterly interpretation we have just heard the story of 'The Covetous Knight.' That knight saw himself as a Casanova; but, as you saw, nothing came of his efforts, no nymphs threw themselves at him, the

23

> muses refused him their tribute, he built no palaces and,
> instead, he ended miserably after his hoard of money and
> jewels was plundered. I warn you that something of the
> kind will happen to you, if not worse, unless you hand
> over your foreign currency!"
>
> —*The Master and Margarita*

From a late-twentieth-century perspective it is easy to see *The Master and Margarita* as a link between the high modernism of the teens and twenties—pre-Sovietized Russian literature—and the myriad postmodernisms of the eighties and nineties that lie in its distant wake. But the novel seems to regard its own position differently, as one caught between the contradictory aesthetic goals of romanticism and nineteenth-century realism, on the one side, and symbolism and 1920s satire, on the other. From either perspective the novel assumes a mediative position—it links together time periods that are philosophically, stylistically, and historically distant from one another. The novel is involved, more deeply than is at first apparent, in a project of recovery or rehabilitation of the past.[43] *The Master and Margarita* has itself been rehabilitated and its author mythologized, much as the novel retrieves the Pilate story and (re)mythologizes the Passion.

Given that the recuperative projects within the novel often spill over into critical approaches taken toward the novel, it is all the more important that one fully understand the pitfalls of such a project. We must consider not only how and why the Master's manuscript is returned to him but, more important, why the Moscow and Pilate stories go together. *Do they go together at all?* One might justifiably echo Dr. Johnson and call *The Master and Margarita* a sort of stylistic *discordia concors*—the most heterogeneous styles are yoked by violence together. Whereas this kind of stylistic disruption is something readers expect from other more modernist authors, such as Bely or Nabokov, Bulgakov's *The Master and Margarita* is unique in the way it protects and privileges its realist allegiances while at the same time it attacks and dethrones them. Bulgakov is, as Andrew Barratt has aptly put it, "disarming" in his "ability to mock the very things he holds dear."[44]

Whereas the Pilate story is told by a relatively sober narrator who neither impedes the development of the plot nor undercuts the reader's belief in the story's truth, the Moscow half of the novel is told by a narrator who continually interrupts his story and allows it to degenerate into rumor and confusion. His trustworthiness is undermined from the first pages of the novel, where he describes Woland:

Впоследствии, когда, откровенно говоря, было уже поздно, разные учреждения представили свои сводки с описанием этого человека. Сличение их не может не вызвать изумления . . . Приходится признать, что ни одна из этих сводок никуда не годится.

Afterward, when it was frankly too late, various institutions produced their reports with descriptions of this man. Put together, they can only generate amazement. . . It must be admitted that not one of these reports succeeds in the least. (10, my ellipses)[45]

Not only does this narration tastelessly foreshadow the story ("it was too late") and slip into an idiom of "bureaucratese" ("various institutions produced their reports" [разные учреждения представили свои сводки]), it also devolves into rumor, into a series of approximations of the truth, away from the truth itself or what could be accepted as a faithful representation of it. Like doubling, rumor is a device Bulgakov borrows from Dostoevsky (and Gogol) to serve the attack on epistemological certainty; but it is also a consequence of this attack. The narrator points out the falsity of the different descriptions of Woland in the passage above, but his own is equally dubious. By ending his description with "In a word—a foreigner," the narrator takes on the xenophobia of the novel's characters and thus suggests his description is no better: in a word—untrustworthy.

If the Pilate story were excised, *The Master and Margarita* might fit in nicely with other political satires coming out of the 1920s, perhaps as a Faustian version of Ilf and Petrov's *The Golden Calf* (1930). In fact, Ilf and Petrov actually read a version of the novel and said that if Bulgakov removed the "ancient" parts of it they would undertake to publish it. Bulgakov's wife reports that upon hearing this, Bulgakov "went pale."[46] Readers are confronted first and foremost with the *very existence* of the Pilate story, the fact of it, "the most stubborn thing in the world," as Woland says (265). This story makes claims on the truth both stylistically, as sober realism, and rhetorically, as when we read that the Master "created that which he had never seen but which he knew to be true" (355). This truth claim needs to be evaluated within the context of the rest of the novel, but it largely serves to underscore the novel's schizophrenia: one part claims to be true, while the other continually reveals ways in which it is not.

It is easy to accept the assertion that *The Master and Margarita* uses modernist literary devices (especially in the Moscow story) to play out traditional novelistic concerns (especially in the Pilate story). Even though the novel often playfully dramatizes its fictiveness, it inevitably circles back to themes of good and evil, love and infidelity, and artistic freedom, all of which were well tested by the romantic and realist novels of the previous century. What may be less obvious, and therefore less easily accepted, is that Bulgakov designs the novel to be a self-reflexive transmitter of literary tradition; a mediator between nineteenth- and twentieth-century literature from one perspective and between pre- and post-Soviet literature from another. To patch the rended fabric of history and literary tradition—this is one of the reasons *why* the novel fits together the way it does. What significantly remains is to describe *how* it fits together the way it does.

There are three ways that the novel attempts to carry the past into the present: through the Master's novel alone, through a convergence of narrative parallels between the Pilate story and the Moscow story, and through the parodic structure of the novel. Parody, as I use the term, is a form of imitative citationality that does not necessarily seek to discredit the work it targets but always engages the values present within that target.[47] By emphasizing the parodic *structure,* I mean to bring to the fore the way the Moscow story relies upon the reader's acquaintance with the particulars of the Pilate story to generate full textual meaning.[48] Though parodied, the Pilate story thus retains an element of hermeneutic priority over the Moscow story. This metafictional relationship between the Moscow story and the Pilate story may in fact reverse common assumptions about texts within texts.

One usually takes for granted that an interpolated story is, at least ontologically, dependent on its interpolating novel. When *The Master and Margarita* parodies its interpolated story, however, this hierarchy is seemingly reversed, and the way the novel relates to the past and literary tradition is likewise significantly changed. The Russian formalists observed that a parodic work is really in debt to the text that is the object of parody.[49] In order to be fully intelligible, the parody must be interpreted in relation to its target text. In principle, parody also functions as a vehicle of literary evolution. It takes a literary past, creates new meaning for it, but never genuinely breaks ties with it. The past which is the target of a parody is favored and emphasized in a special way.[50]

Like a parody, *The Master and Margarita* targets a work of literature—the Pilate story—without which the novel would be incomprehensible. What is more, the target story is physically manifest within the novel itself; and, therefore, unlike most targets of parody, the Pilate story maintains a formidable independence from the interpolating novel. It is present not as an already-interpreted text but as a primary text within another text. This relative autonomy of the Pilate story, especially when considered in conjunction with the hermeneutic priority of the Pilate story, gives credibility to the reversed hierarchical relationship between novel and interpolated text in *The Master and Margarita.* Such a reversal raises questions that go to the heart of the novel's basic structure. For example, why does Bulgakov not simply allude to the Master's novel, Woland's story, and Ivan's dream, paraphrase and take excerpts from these texts, or provide notebooks as Gide does in *The Counterfeiters?* Why the insistence on what appears to be a word-for-word *reproduction* of the Pilate story instead of a *representation* of it?

There are at least two reasons, and they are connected with the truth claim of the Pilate story. First, not only *The Master and Margarita* but also a great deal of modern literature derides traditional representations of reality as a means of conveying the essence of experience. Often, modernist authors seek an alternate way (mythopoesis, for example) or the idea of conveying truth in a work of literature is discarded.[51] Consider three representations of the Russian Civil War, all of which seek to reveal some sort of essence of the time. Victor Shklovsky's *Sentimental Journey* (1924, 1929), with its factographic tendencies and antiliterary approach to memoir, attempts to reveal reality in a new way. Bulgakov's own *The White Guard* is not an *un*realistic novel, to be sure, but his use of several organizing symbols (the stars, the Dutch stove, the lampshade, and so on) and mythopoetic scenes, such as Nikolka's descent to a netherworld-like cellar after Nai-Tur's body, make for a less realistic representation of the Civil War, even on the surface. Pilnyak's novel *The Naked Year* (1921) is the least realistic portrayal of the three examples; but his discordant, ornamental prose, fractured plot(s), and forest of provocative rhetorical figures (for example, the leather jackets) broadly reflect the tumultuous, contradictory, and violent time of the Civil War. All three novels, each in its own way, suggest something about how representable Soviet history is perceived to be.

The second reason the Pilate story is reproduced rather than represented is that, even though the novel uses a parodic structure, it does not yield to the destructive or discrediting power usually attributed to parody. The concept of truth the novel develops depends in large part on metafictional tactics: the more visibly a literary text is intertextual—in other words, something that represents reality rather than reproduces it—the less true it is, the less perfectly it translates experience. Accordingly, the Moscow story flaunts the intertextuality the Pilate story conceals. That does not mean the Pilate story is not intertextual; it clearly is. But the Pilate story does not continually remind us with metafiction that it is.

I want to make two preliminary observations about the examples of imitative citation I will discuss here. First, with these examples the effect of the imitation is not always comic; it varies from the comic to a mixture of the comic and the serious, to the serious. Second, one must not confuse the parallel narrative structures of the interpolating and interpolated texts with the parodic structure that obtains between them. Parody has a different function in the novel than parallelism.[52]

The title of the chapter in which Ivan first meets Dr. Stravinsky in the psychiatric clinic is "The Duel between Professor and Poet." If nothing else, the rich literary tradition of "the duel" heightens the reader's sensitivity both to the chapter's intertextual nature and also to the codified behavior that dueling requires.[53] Just a few chapters previously the reader has witnessed a "duel" between Ha-Nostri and Pilate. Here the meeting between accused and judge meets the definition of a duel precisely because Ha-Nostri transgresses implied rules of conduct. When Ha-Nostri calls Pilate "my good man" instead of "hegemon" he merely breaks juridical conventions. But when he refuses to defend himself and to deny that he spoke against

Caesar, the reader detects intimations of the code of conventions governing (anachronistically) the duel, which, with its highly formalized behavioral conventions, was frequently a subject and narrative symbol in eighteenth- and nineteenth-century literature. This infraction in conduct is what initially really bothers Pilate—Ha-Nostri has refused to fight for his own life and behaves as only an "insane" man could.

Ivan's duel—another duel between an insane man and his judge—and his failure in that duel have thus been prefigured by the first chapter of the Pilate story, and a structurally similar context for parody has been established. Specific parodic allusions to the meeting between Pilate and Ha-Nostri begin with Stravinsky's entrance with his colleagues into Ivan's room. The doctors' white robes and the inordinate attention and respect paid to Stravinsky remind Ivan of Pilate: "The whole retinue showed [Stravinsky] signs of attention and respect, and his entrance therefore came off very solemnly. 'Like Pontius Pilate!' thought Ivan" (87). Ivan is obsessed with Pilate in general, but it is Stravinsky's specific (parodic) entrance and, moreover, his knowledge of Latin, that shakes and saddens Ivan. The imitation of the scene between Pilate and Ha-Nostri by Stravinsky and Ivan is clearly comic in tone, and the comedy suggests an attempt to trivialize the tragedy of the meeting between Pilate and Ha-Nostri.

This comic aspect is further intensified by an unexpected twist in the parodic structure. Parody itself doubles when the reader recognizes in the description of Stravinsky and his "retinue" (свита) a reference not only to Pilate but also to Woland, whose fellow troublemakers are often called his *свита*. Thus the word *свита* indicates a doubling of parody for the reader; the word "schizophrenia" is what connotes Woland for Ivan: "Suddenly a word made him [Ivan] shudder. It was the word 'schizophrenia,' which the sinister stranger had spoken yesterday at Patriarch's Ponds. And today Dr. Stravinsky was repeating it" (88). The doubled parodic structure in Ivan's meeting with Stravinsky thus confirms the devil's famous claim that he was with Pilate in the garden. Unfortunately for Ivan, the calling to mind of Pilate also recalls the devil, disrupting further his already fragile state of mind.

Of the many memorable things Pilate says, "O gods, gods" and "Poison, I need poison" are especially significant in the novel. The currents of paganism and classical tragedy running through Pilate's exhortation of the gods and calls for poison set into motion a conflict of generic codes. Like Dostoevsky's *The Brothers Karamazov*, *The Master and Margarita* is essentially a Christian work of literature. Yet Pilate is both the fated tragic hero and à great sinner at once. Either his lack of courage is a "tragic" flaw or it is his "most terrible sin" (310), as he says in his dream. When the narrator and the Master repeat Pilate's words, they import this conflict into the larger novel. Part of Bulgakov's rehabilitation of Pilate is to make him a liminal figure. Caught between two systems, he sees himself as a victim of both, as well as the cruel author of his own and others' misery.

In the chapter "The Affair at Griboedov," the narrator cries out "O gods, my gods, poison, I need poison" (61) in mock horror at the bacchanalia that has broken out in the restaurant. The repetition of Pilate's words here suggests either that the narrator is also the author of the Pilate story, which is unlikely, or that he too has read the Pilate story, which reveals his potential role as parodist. This role as parodist is further evidenced in the chapter by an imitation of the conflict between Christian and pagan that I associated with Pilate. Again, similar contexts are available for parody. The party begins with a shout of "Alleluia," but the jazz and the dancing indicate a patently Dionysian atmosphere, not a Christian one. The Dionysian adds a pagan overtone to the apocalypticism of the novel, because the cult of Dionysus also awaits the "return" of a god.[54]

As in Ivan's meeting with Stravinsky, the parody in "The Affair at Griboedov" is twofold—that is, it cites both the Pilate and Moscow stories. This party is undoubtedly also a version of the party in "Satan's Great Ball." Griboedov's Archibald Archibaldovich resembles the devil; both parties begin at midnight; the partygoers at Griboedov are as spiritually dead as the condemned are truly dead. The important conclusion to draw from these examples is that the narrator is established early in the novel (the scene at Griboedov is chapter 5) as probable reader and possible parodist of the Pilate story.

The Master's situation as parodist is somewhat different from the narrator's. Though both repeat Pilate's words, the narrator is aware of his role as parodist and the Master is not. To call the Master a parodist of his own story would be inexact. His repetition of Pilate's words alludes to a narrative similarity between the interpolating and interpolated texts, but can one really call this similarity—or parallel—parody? The Master's reaction to the magical return of his manuscript, for example, is simply that of a deeply troubled man: "Even by moonlight there's no peace for me at night . . . Why do they torment me? O gods, gods . . ." (ellipses in original, 279). The phrase beginning "even by moonlight" refers directly to the issue of cowardice, recalling the context in which Pilate first uttered it. As in previous examples, similar contexts are available for generating parody. The Master, like Pilate, exhorts the gods out of the sense that it is too late to repair what has been done. He tells Woland "I am now no one" (277) and whispers to Margarita "No, it's too late" (280) in response to a secret proposal of hers.

This theme of the irreversibility of fate ties the Master to Pilate. For his part, Pilate acts the part of a murderer who kills again because he knows he is already going to jail; yet he is also aware of the meaninglessness of these actions: "It was clear to him that this morning he had irretrievably lost something and now he was striving to compensate for that loss with a trivial substitute, which took the form of belated action . . . But in this attempt the Procurator had little success" (my ellipses, 301). Pilate and the Master conceive the morality of their behavior similarly. They combine the freedom implicit in the idea of sinning—even as an act of cowardice—with a concept of worldly fate and irredeemability, blending elements of Christian and pagan worldviews.

By this point in the novel, the reader has heard Pilate's words repeated a couple of times, and though the Master's repetition of them undoubtedly carries faint comic echoes of the narrator in "The Affair at Griboedov," they now sound more serious than comic. In order to account for this shift in tone within the parodic structure, one may imagine a sliding scale of imitative citation, with burlesque at one extreme and pastiche at the other—both burlesque and pastiche are subsets of parody, as I have been using the term. In the examples of Ivan and the narrator, the comic element predominates, and the balance tips toward the burlesque. In the case of the Master the tendency is toward pastiche, a more solemn form of imitation.

This solemnity is more marked in a third example of the novel's parodic structure: the Master's farewell visit to Ivan in the chapter "Time to Go!" In this scene the Master tells Ivan to write the continuation of the story: "That's good, that's good. You must write the sequel to it" (362). His final words, "Farewell, disciple" (Прощай, ученик; 363), remind the reader of Matthew, who in a failed plan to stab Yeshua before his crucifixion intends to cry out: "Yeshua! I shall save you and depart with you! I, Matthew, your faithful and only disciple!" (Иешуа! Я спасаю тебя и ухожу вместе с тобою! Я Матвей, твой верный и единственный ученик!; 173). The imitative citation in this later scene between the Master and Ivan thus derives primarily from the Master's calling Ivan "disciple" (though a parody of *this* scene is present in the epilogue).

There are, however, other more obvious *narrative parallels:* the coming storm, the deaths of both Yeshua and the Master, the fact that Matthew and Ivan give up their respective professions, and so forth. Though related to parody, these parallels serve a different purpose. One must take care not to blur the distinction between imitation, which produces a form of parodic citationality such as burlesque or pastiche, and parallelism, which produces like narratives. To be sure, the parallelism one finds here is the result of a temporal movement maintained throughout the entire novel toward the convergence of the separate story lines.

Yet there is no narrative parallelism governing the examples of parody evident in Ivan's meeting with Stravinsky or in the party at Griboedov. Those two scenes do make parallel narratives with other scenes in the interpolating text, but they parody the interpolated text, the Pilate story. The Master's farewell to Ivan, however, contains little of the imitative citationality that marks parody, but the narrative itself becomes strikingly similar to that of the Pilate story—even the time of this parallel between stories is significantly similar, as both events occur on the eve of Passover.

The parody of the Pilate story is neither resolved nor dissolved by the synthesis or convergence of the two narratives in the penultimate chapter of the novel; it is temporarily replaced by this synthesis. To begin with, the parody is sustained until late in the novel, as when the salesman in the hard currency store uses a knife like Matthew's: "With a long sharp knife very like the knife Matthew the Levite stole, he was easing the snakelike skin away from the fat, juicy flesh of a pink salmon" (338). Moreover, the novel does not in fact end with the fusion of the two stories—thus exchanging parody for narrative convergence. Rather, it goes on with the Moscow story and parody in the epilogue. But what then is the significance of this difference between parodic and parallel structures of the novel?

Texts that seem to run parallel to one another reinforce each other's authority: the one text finds validation in the other. I have mentioned several times that the Pilate story in *The Master and Margarita* makes a strong claim on the truth. One could argue that inasmuch as the outer novel runs parallel to, and at one point completely merges with, the Pilate story, it therefore also has a claim on the truth. The conclusions I have been drawing from the parodic structure of the novel need not invalidate that argument, but they do complicate the novel's attempt to transcend its own fictiveness, thus recalling questions pertaining to the epistemological status of fiction.

It helps to redefine the argument about fictiveness versus truth in terms of the novel's rehabilitation of the past; for the truth claim really amounts to no more than a desire that narrative translate experience flawlessly and render the subjective utterly transparent. The past that *The Master and Margarita* is smuggling into the future is the Pilate story in form, nineteenth-century realism in style, and the origins of Christianity in content—a three-sided treatment of literary tradition as the history of revelation and pure experience. As I have mentioned before, the intertextuality of this interpolated story remains hidden. The tale of Pilate and Yeshua is presented within the larger text of the novel as *primarily an experience* and only *secondarily a text*. Accordingly, one chapter is heard, another is dreamt, and the third and the fourth are read to us by Margarita. Though they almost certainly correspond word for word with the Master's text, the "textual" nature of these chapters recedes into the background as their "experiential" nature comes to the fore.

In a similar manner, Leskov, Zoshchenko, and others adapted storytelling techniques, such as the first-person narration of *skaz*, in order to foreground the relationship between a character's language and his or her personality—without the author getting in the way, as it were. Zamyatin's remarkable 1926 story, "Comrade Churygin Has the Floor," for example, uses the curious mistakes of Churygin's political speech to create an image of ideological syncretism in the early years of the Soviet state. Art as experience—*art into life*—was a goal of the avant-garde as well, and its proponents tried to break down the barriers separating aesthetic experience and ordinary experience. Anyone who has seen suprematist designs on cups and saucers knows what I mean, though their presence in museums obviously *re*-aestheticizes them. If the Pilate story were written today, it might be cast as a kind of virtual text on the Internet—seemingly authored by everyone who experiences it, and belonging to no one in particular. *The Master and Margarita* text tries to establish and take advantage of this *non*-textual nature of the Pilate story.

The convergence of narrative parallels that takes place in the chapter "Absolution and Eternal Refuge" is only one of three attempts in the novel to bring the past of the Pilate story into contact with the present. The first is the Master's completion of his novel and his struggle to have it published; the convergence of narrative parallels makes up the second; and the third takes place through the parodic structure that I have been describing.[55] The first attempt, though inspired, transforms the past into an object. It is something to be written, rejected, burned, magically restored, and so forth. The Master's failure in publishing the novel, the literary institution's philistine incapability of understanding it, and the (not so) final destruction of the novel in the Master's stove all point to the failure of this first attempt to bring the past to bear meaningfully on the present.

The second attempt, the fusion of the two stories, though it does not fail, imposes significant restrictions on how the past is conceptualized. Here the novel interprets the past in its own image, as a narrative that shares in its sense of the imminent convergence of time and events. Though the chapter "Absolution and Eternal Refuge" ends with the very words that the Master has promised as the ending to his novel ("the fifth Procurator of Judea, the knight Pontius Pilate" [пятый прокуратор Иудеи всадник Понтий Пилат]), *The Master and Margarita* cannot end at this point. Though the convergence of narrative parallels seems to suggest an equality, a give and take, between past and present, this openness to the validity of the past does not really exist. The interpolating novel ultimately always "knows" more about the story than the story itself—"your novel has still more surprises in store for you" (284), says Woland presciently. The Master cannot really know the end of his story, because its true ending encloses him within it as the hero who sets Pilate free. (Notice how the Master flips here from author back to hero within the novel.)

The novel's third attempt to bring together past and present, through parody, *does* create a genuine openness between the two, because the past is manifest in the novel as a text that can answer the parodying voice of the present. This dialogic relationship to the past is, in a sense, smuggled in through the backdoor of the novel.[56] Often, parody is interpreted as a limitation, something that points to the sterility of literary convention and to the dead end of literary tradition. As Leverkühn says in *Doctor Faustus:* "Why does almost everything seem to me like its own parody? Why must I think that almost all, no, all the methods and conventions of art today *are good for parody only?*"[57] But the parody in *The Master and Margarita* is no ordinary parody. There is an overwhelming difference between a target of parody that exists and has a voice only inasmuch as it is alluded to within the parody itself, and the parodic target that retains its integrity and independence in spite of the parody.

Thus one needs to take a closer look at the epilogue, where *The Master and Margarita* returns to the style and practice of the narration of the Moscow story. The convergence of the two stories has left little trace on present-day Moscow, save for Ivan's perambulations and troubled sleep during the springtime full moon. Yet the parodic spirit that encompassed so much of the earlier novel is maintained, and the narrator's self-consciousness reemerges: he interrupts himself, berates the rumormongers and repeats their rumors, and mimics Woland's talk about "facts." He even mocks the Pilate story's romance with the truth by referring to himself as "the writer of these truthful lines himself in person" (373).

The metaliterary play and parody of the epilogue extends the dialogue between past and present, between Pilate and Moscow stories, by comically reenacting the novel's entire chain of events—the "history" of the novel returns as parody. When the narrator tells of the Muscovites' attempts to explain rationally what happened during Woland's visit, the whole of the novel is repeated in short form. This second time around, there are also black cats and tricksters and people with names sounding like Koroviev who are sought by the authorities. More important, the reader discovers that every year in a spring moon trance Ivan retraces his steps to Patriarch's Ponds, grows disturbed, dreams executions and conversations between Pilate and Yeshua, and then bids farewell to the Master and Margarita. In the end, the "professor," Ivan, is basically a parody of his former self (and of others), restored to his true self but once a year. He now "knows and understands everything" (381), the narrator tells us ironically. Bits and pieces of other characters are now fused into Ivan's new parodic persona. He is a historian like the Master, and he repeats the words of Pilate (Gods, gods) like the narrator and the Master.

The epilogue ends with the very words that were promised by the Master and given a second time in the false ending of "Absolution and Eternal Refuge." The tone and syntax of these final lines recapture the solemnity of the Pilate story and reassert its independence and moral validity. These words have now appeared in the novel a total of three times, and their repetition on each occasion has confirmed the three relations to the past outlined above: first in the context of the Master's writing ("Enter the

Hero"), second in the convergence of the novel's narrative parallels ("Absolution and Eternal Refuge"), and third in the novel's conclusion and reaffirmation of parody in the epilogue.

"THRICE ROMANTIC" AUTHORSHIP

> "Are you a writer?" asked the poet with interest.
> The visitor frowned, threatened Ivan with his fist and said:
> "I am a master."
>
> —*The Master and Margarita*

For the most part, writers fare poorly in *The Master and Margarita,* and worse if they are associated with Soviet institutions of literature. Thus there is more than a small catharsis involved when Koroviev and Behemoth burn down the MASSOLIT headquarters at Griboedov. But if this symbolic destruction of the bureaucrat writer is going to fit in with the broader themes of the novel, one needs to appreciate just what kind of writer is to replace him. Clearly the novel redefines and broadens the concept of authorship—so much so that it is rewarding to discard the singular and discuss the variety of authorships in *The Master and Margarita.*

An idealization of authorship constitutes the "peace" with which the Master has been rewarded: "Oh, thrice romantic master, wouldn't you like to stroll under the cherry blossom with your love in the daytime and listen to Schubert in the evening? Won't you enjoy writing by candlelight with a goose quill? Don't you want, like Faust, to sit over a retort in the hope of fashioning a new homunculus?" (371). Opposed to the philistinism of Soviet Moscow, the pastoral vision described here promises a highly cultured and tranquil life. And, not surprisingly, the identity Woland offers to the Master is both literary and retrospective—literary tradition in *The Master and Margarita* heals the self, recaptures the identity that has been lost or become meaningless.

In the passage above, the Master's lost identity is finally restored, and this reward is a function of his becoming a hero *in* the Pilate story rather than remaining the author *of* it. When he speaks the words that set Pilate free, he is acting a role which he has neither envisioned beforehand nor could have imagined as the novel's ending. As author, the Master could not be rendered definitively by the totalizing vision of the novel, for he was one of the shapers of that vision. Thus in his recovery of a meaningful identity, he is consummated aesthetically for the first time as an individual. He appears at long last as a finite figure against the larger horizon of the novel, and this finalization is simultaneous with his becoming a hero.

Such narrative operations work because of what Bakhtin calls the author's (here, Bulgakov's) "excess" or "transgredient" vision. In order to achieve a determinate and stable image of the hero, the author must first and foremost know more about the hero than he knows about himself or could know about himself:

> The consummating moments are transgredient not only to the hero's actual consciousness but also to his potential consciousness—his consciousness extended in a dotted line, as it were: the author knows and sees more not only in the direction in which the hero is looking and seeing, but also in a different direction, in a direction which is in principle inaccessible to the hero himself; it is precisely this position that an author must assume in relation to a hero.[58]

Bakhtin's analysis here is predicated on his belief that one cannot know the position of the self in world completely without the complementary activity of an other. This line of thought derives from his interest in the phenomenology of vision: that is, we actually see only half of the world and require another to see behind us to complete, literally, our worldview. In terms of the author's relationship to the hero, then, the more the hero shares the author's vision, the less complete or consummated that character may be—he shares in the author's limited knowledge of his own future, of the other half of the world around him, and of those things that move him which are evident to another but hidden from the self. For Bakhtin, there is potentially an inverse relationship between an author's proximity to his hero and the determinateness and stability of the hero's image: the more an author identifies with his hero the less determinate the image of the hero is.

This inverse relationship can contribute to the analysis of *The Master and Margarita* because it allows one to speculate on the position Bulgakov takes vis-à-vis his hero in that moment where the Master recovers his lost identity. It is easy to imagine the Master as a version of Bulgakov throughout the entire novel, and particularly easy to imagine that the pastoral of the author amidst cherry blossoms listening to Schubert represents Bulgakov's own ideal identity. On the contrary: this is the moment in the novel when Bulgakov may be furthest from the Master, when he severs the relationship between himself and his hero.[59] Thus it is also a defining moment for authorship in the novel—it is marked, metaphorically speaking, only by the silence Margarita asks the Master to listen to, which is simultaneous in the reader's experience with the pause before the epilogue.

The silence is important for authorship because the novel is rarely free from both the Master's vision and the narrator's self-conscious, comic behavior. Bulgakov consistently mediates in the novel his knowledge as author, blocking out traces of omniscience that might sneak, like Margarita's compassion, through cracks in the walls. This is one of the touchstones of modernist aesthetics in *The Master and Margarita*. Every creative vision reflects the image of its author as a necessarily limited beholder of that vision. Modern literature often responds to this partial nature of knowledge either by projecting the author as character into the world of the text, or by continually reminding the reader that the text is not the truth but fiction. *The Master and Margarita* employs both of these devices, but there is a difference.

What makes this novel different from many novels is that *The Master and Margarita* would like to have it both ways—literature as a possible truth but also self-aware of the limitations of fiction. I borrow as the title of this section Woland's epithet for the Master, "thrice romantic"—"thrice" to correspond to the tripartite relations to the self and to tradition that were the focus of the two preceding sections, "romantic" to emphasize the privileged position that authorship is accorded in the novel; the hero is, after all, not a "writer" but a "master." In a contradictory attempt both to render the truth in fiction and to remind us that fiction cannot represent experience transparently, Bulgakov incorporates three different views of authorship in *The Master and Margarita.*

The first, a traditional, "realist" view of authorship, can be seen both in Ivan Bezdomny's poem, which was supposed to be about the nonexistence of Christ, and in some aspects of the Master's novel. Here the author is omniscient, absent from the text (like God in the world), and there is an emphasis on literature as mimesis. A strong division between author and text underscores the subject-object epistemology guiding the concept of creativity. In Ivan's poem the author's role as "rational spectator" is exaggerated—his purpose is to debunk the myth of Christ.[60] Language refers unhindered to worldly objects, and the ontological status of these objects is never questioned, which accounts for why Ivan's Christ comes out as if He "really existed."

As a physical text, submitted for publication, burned, and restored, the Master's novel also pays tribute to this realist view of authorship created in *The Master and Margarita.* At this point it is not only representational—depicting the true events of Pilate and Christ—but also reproducible as a physical text.[61] But the rational, dualistic, and material aspects of the Master's novel are undermined in ways that lead one out of the realist view of authorship and into a more strictly hermeneutic view of authorship.[62] By "hermeneutic" I mean that the work of literature is not divorced as an object of the author's creativity from his subjective experience. Instead, it serves as a tool by which the author investigates the nature of creativity and its bearing on selfhood.

This second view of authorship interprets the Master's oscillation from hero to author to hero again as part of Bulgakov's investigation of creativity, whereby the Master's own authorship represents an attempt by Bulgakov to retrieve the subjectivity that was lost when he projected himself into the novel as its main character. The motivation for this hermeneutic investigation of creativity is hinted at by Woland when he says that "each will be given according to his belief." The special privilege of the author is the ability to give life to the world of his belief and project himself into it as one of its characters. It is here that one sees authorship as a potential model for understanding the essence of human personality. Regardless, the author must eventually return from the text, whether it be a literary text or simply the product of the self's creativity, and take back inside what he has learned from his self-objectification, or such an investigation remains incomplete.[63] Ultimately Bulgakov must sever ties with the Master, not only in order to "free" him and grant him his lost identity but also in order to return back into himself and render the experience aesthetic.

Back into the vagaries of modern aestheticism also goes the novel, and here one finds yet another concept of authorship at work. If the first was realistic, and the second hermeneutic, then this third view of authorship might be described as "metacritical." The author as metacritic conceives of himself as neither a rational knower of history (like Ivan in his poem), nor as a self-divided creator of it (like Bulgakov in the Master's novel). He is more like a self-conscious speaker of the strange language called literature. Aware that his ability to speak and be understood depends wholly on the fact that others have spoken before him, the metacritic poses as a parodist who sometimes tries to make fun of and sometimes defers to tradition.

The relationship of the author as metacritic to the work of literature does not create the same *sort* of epistemological problems that were evident in the first two versions of authorship. Authorship in this metacritical sense is least like a model of personality. Here the author suggests that he is not so much the creator of the work of literature as he is created by it. Thus the narrator is not himself a rumormonger, he is merely the product of so many rumors in the novel. Parody is not an authorial device so much as it is the revelation of the inherent dependency of literary texts on one another. (And here we see the postmodern appeal of *The Master and Margarita*.)

Only by recognizing how fundamental the narrator's parodic behavior is to the novel does one fully appreciate the complexity of the novel's relationship to the past it has created. But this relationship to the past is not its sole purpose. *The Master and Margarita* sets rival concepts of authorship against one another. The self-conscious play of modernist narrative strategies alone misses the philosophical capabilities of realist representation; and neither realist nor metacritical authorship can speak to the nature of creativity and its bearing on selfhood as does the dialectic of author and hero in the hermeneutic model.

Three models of authorship develop out of Bulgakov's remarkable sensitivity to the epistemological dilemmas posed by literature. Which concept of authorship he assumes at any given moment depends in large part on the direction of his critical gaze. Sometimes, as when the Master meets Woland in the chapter "The Master is Released," all three concepts are present nearly at once. In one scene, the Master's manuscript is magically re-turned, he describes himself as "no one," and he imitates Pilate, "Oh, gods." The consecutive emphases on the novel as object, on the Master's lost iden-tity, and on parodic imitation correspond to what I have been calling realis-tic, hermeneutic, and metacritical concepts of authorship.

Chapter Two

Boris Pasternak's *Doctor Zhivago*

> Now he feared nothing, neither life nor death;
> everything in the world, all things were words in
> his vocabulary. He felt he was on equal footing
> with the universe.

—Pasternak, *Doctor Zhivago*

CRITICAL APPRAISALS OF *Doctor Zhivago*[1] on the whole may vary, but most readers agree that the exquisite language of description and poetry employed by the novel and its eponymous hero are unmatched in twentieth-century Russian fiction.[2] Perhaps action in the novel merely frames description, and prose provides an excuse for verse. Pasternak himself thought otherwise, of course, and echoed his hero's belief that poetry should lead to prose.[3] Poetry for Zhivago, as he says as a young man, is no more than a series of "sketches for the great canvas [of prose] he had in mind" (67).

Pasternak may have painted his own great canvas in *Doctor Zhivago*, but Zhivago never does complete the work of prose for which his poems are sketches. What we do have and can read is his poetry, which ends the novel and seems a kind of substitution for it. Like the Adam to whom he compares himself, Zhivago has the privilege of naming the unnamed objects of the universe rather than telling their story in prose. And *Doctor Zhivago* does not devise a plot for its hero's life so much as it places like pieces in a puzzle the events that compose a picture of his life. Biography as a sequence of events that shares in historical causality gives way in this manner to the inner logic of language in a "poetic" perception of the self.

In *Doctor Zhivago* history is filtered through the perception of an individual who has no real causal agency in its progression. In his well-known essay on spatial form in modernism, Joseph Frank writes: "What has occurred . . . may be described as the transformation of the historical imagination into myth—an imagination for which historical time does not exist, and which sees the action and events of a particular time only as the bodying forth of eternal prototypes."[4] The eternal prototype in *Doctor Zhivago* is the (romantic) poet, and the myth is the untainted originality of his vision. Hamlet in Zhivago's poem of that name may be right in saying that he "catches the distant echo / Of what will happen in [his] time," but by doing so he thereby produces one more coincidence in a novel of coincidences, and the poem's emphasis is on his passivity in the face of knowledge. One can read *Doctor Zhivago* primarily as a realist work of historical fiction, as a modern *War and Peace,* but to do so misses an essential aspect of the novel's uniqueness: Zhivago's utter absorption in, and sublimation of, his own superfluity.[5]

In *Doctor Zhivago* language is less associated with ideology than in *The Master and Margarita,* and more connected to a narrow sort of poetic perception. Literary analysis of this novel can, and perhaps should, reflect in its terminology a vocabulary more exclusively given, therefore, to poetic perception. In this chapter I will speak generally of figurative language and, more specifically, of Roman Jakobson's theory of the bipolarity in language, the metaphoric and metonymic poles. Jakobson long ago discussed Pasternak's early prose in terms of its tendency toward metonymic figuration; his theory thus offers an early point of entry into the critical debate on *Doctor Zhivago,*[6] and represents an initial attempt to match terminology to Pasternak's poetic prose.

The writing of poetry and the characterization of Zhivago's poetic vision form many of the novel's *mises en abyme,* those occasions when the reader is expected to draw a parallel between individual portions of the novel and the broader novel itself. Zhivago's collection of poetry itself, for example, is a *mise en abyme* in *Doctor Zhivago,* surely the most obvious one. A preponderance of figurative language is the distinguishing characteristic of many of the poetic scenes in the prose, and those scenes *pre*figure the volume of poetry that ends the novel. When one examines metaphor and metonym, therefore, one proceeds directly to the narrative use of the *mise en abyme* in *Doctor Zhivago.* There is a tendency toward metaphor in the novel when the scene is dominated by issues of identity, and there is a tendency toward metonymy when the scene is dominated by historical concerns and philosophical explanation. As Jakobson frequently noted, however, such boundaries between metaphor and metonymy are often blurred, and one figure shades into another.

THE FIGURATIVE SHAPE OF IDENTITY

> The genuine agent has no place in Pasternak's poetic mythology; as a rule the individual has no idea of what "builds him up, tunes him and stitches him together."
>
> —Roman Jakobson, "Marginal Notes on the Prose of the Poet Pasternak"

The opposition of metaphor to metonym interested Roman Jakobson throughout his career. In "Two Aspects of Language and Two Types of Aphasic Disturbances," in particular, he speaks of the two modes of arrangement available for any linguistic sign.[7] The first mode, *combination,* suggests that "any linguistic unit at one and the same time serves as a context for a simpler and/or finds its own context in a more complex linguistic unit" (99). These constituent linguistic units are thus in a state of "contiguity." In broader terms, the tendency in language of the combinative arrangement is to contextualize. The second mode of arrangement, *selection,* "implies the possibility of substituting one [linguistic unit] for the other, equivalent in one respect and different in another" (99). Possible substitution signs are thus linked by their "similarity" or equivalence. In this second mode of arrangement, the tendency in language is to compare and contrast.

Linguistic signs are related to one another by both contiguity and similarity, and this dual relationship in turn points to semantic lines of development in discourse:

> The development of a discourse may take place along two different semantic lines: one topic may lead to another either through their similarity or through their contiguity. The *metaphoric* way would be the most appropriate term for the first case and the *metonymic* way for the second, since they find their most condensed expression in metaphor and metonymy respectively. (109–10)

The metaphoric and metonymic poles may be found not only in discourse but in other sign systems and symbolic processes: verbal art (poetry and prose), painting, dreams (in Freudian theory), and sympathetic magic (as Frazer describes it in *The Golden Bough*).

Three aspects of Jakobson's theory of metaphoric versus metonymic poles are relevant to Pasternak's *Doctor Zhivago*.[8] First, poetry tends to be metaphoric and prose tends to be metonymic.[9] In a well-known formulation, Jakobson states that "the poetic function [of language] projects the principle of equivalence [or similarity] from the axis of selection into the axis of combination."[10] The tendency of verse is thus toward the metaphoric pole, the "axis of selection." By means of rhyme, meter, and other forms of parallelism, poetry foregrounds similarity, "the principle of equivalence." By contrast, (especially realist) prose "metonymically digresses from the plot to the atmosphere and from the characters to the setting in space and time" (111). In a 1935 article on Pasternak's early prose, Jakobson argued that "Pasternak's lyricism, both in poetry and in prose, is imbued with metonymy; in other words, it is association by contiguity that predominates."[11] Whether this metonymy holds in the later *Doctor Zhivago* is a question critics have asked repeatedly.[12]

The second aspect of Jakobson's theory relates to literary history. Jakobson claims that the tendency toward one or the other linguistic pole shifts during various periods of literary history; in other words, such a ten-

dency may in fact define the aesthetic predisposition of one literary movement versus another.

> The primacy of the metaphoric process in the literary schools of Romanti-
> cism and Symbolism has been repeatedly acknowledged, but it is still insuf-
> ficiently realized that it is the predominance of metonymy which underlies
> and actually predetermines the so-called Realist trend, which belongs to an
> intermediary stage between the decline of Romanticism and the rise of Sym-
> bolism and is opposed by both.[13]

Jakobson's theory of metonymy versus metaphor thus potentially offers a
way to detect intertextuality, and therefore specific relations to the literary
tradition, through the figuration of the novel's language itself.[14] Modernist
novels are often highly metafictional, foregrounding the fact that the author
chooses one literary device or another. The chosen predominant mode of
figuration may reflect an attitude toward the literary tradition. One need
not openly allude to Princess Marya's "heavy tread" or Vronsky's teeth, for
example, to call to the reader's mind the prose tradition of Tolstoy: repeated
characterizations by metonymy might achieve the same result. Self-conscious
comparisons of one author to another belong, of course, to the metaphoric
pole.

   One final aspect of Jakobson's theory is of special interest, and that is
the connectedness of language with subjective mental experience. The
main concern of Jakobson's central article on metaphor and metonymy, it is
worth recalling, is to explain by linguistic analysis two types of aphasia. The
inability to generate/recognize figures of metonymy indicates one type of
aphasia, and the inability to generate/recognize figures of metaphor indicates another. This patterning of experience into rhetorical figures (or,
rather, rhetorical figures suggesting patterns of mental experience) leads one
to questions of identity and the representation of selfhood in novelistic prose.
The projection of a self in authorship, in Zhivago's authorship of his poetry,
for example, may rely on rhetorical figures that differ, or do not differ, from
those used in the prose that characterizes him. Thus, there is a semiotic dimension to the authorship of literature and self in *Doctor Zhivago*.

   Doctor Zhivago is a divided novel, at times metaphoric, at times metonymic, and at times both one and the other. Moreover, the metaphoric and
metonymic figuration of language in the novel does not strictly follow the
division of the novel into prose and verse parts.

   Given Roman Jakobson's influence on Slavic studies (and much else)
in the twentieth century, one is hardly surprised to find that other scholars
have taken up the analysis of metaphoric and metonymic poles in Pasternak's prose. Most notable in this regard is Henrik Birnbaum, who has discussed the topic in two articles.[15] Both pieces make the essential point (*pace*
Jakobson) that Pasternak's novel relies on both metaphor and metonymy,

switches between the two, and often slides from one into the other.[16] Birnbaum uses examples of metaphor and metonymy to suggest, among other things, an overlap between Shklovsky's concept of defamiliarization and Jakobson's analysis of literary imagery ranging from one linguistic pole to the other.[17] He considers *Doctor Zhivago* an experiment in new compositional principles, and ultimately an example of a genre for which he coins the term "Gedichtroman," as opposed to the "Romangedicht," which is exemplified by Akhmatova's *Poem without a Hero.*[18] An overarching concern in Birnbaum's articles is the evolution of Pasternak's poetics. *Doctor Zhivago* is served best by comparisons with Pasternak's earlier prose and poetry, especially *My Sister, Life,* and such comparisons confirm that "the writing of the mature Pasternak . . . is marked by an unequivocal turn away from his previous hermetic, introspective style."[19]

While not disagreeing with Birnbaum, I would like to take Jakobson's metaphor/metonymy distinction in a different direction, one that bears on the relation of literary tradition to the self. Interpretation that looks to the *mise en abyme* presupposes figuration—either metaphor or metonymy—because to make an interpretive identification between the local example in the text and the text as a whole is to allow that the metaphoric principle of substitution is at least theoretically possible. Not every case of figuration, however, is a *mise en abyme.* By looking at rhetorical figuration in the novel as an example of Zhivago's failed "signifying processes," I use Jakobson's linguistic analysis in a more psychological examination of the relation of semiotics to selfhood.[20] The novel pushes its interpreters in this direction by continually suggesting that Zhivago's ultimately unhappy love affairs both motivate and replicate his dissatisfaction with, and the untenability of, his poetic vision. Though Birnbaum recognizes that rhetorical figures themselves create a complex image of their author, his overall interpretation of figuration in the novel suggests mainly that their purpose is to defamiliarize.

The general movement of metaphor and metonymy in the novel is complex. Consider the opening sentence: "On they went, singing 'Eternal Memory,' and whenever they stopped, their feet, the horses, and the gusts of wind seemed to carry on their singing" (Шли и шли и пели «Вечную память», и, когда останавливались, казалось, что ее по-залаженному продолжают петь ноги, лошади, дуновения ветра; 7). The principle of metonymic contiguity, rather than of metaphoric similarity, is at work here. As the funeral procession halts, the constituent elements of the procession continue the song. It is typical of *Doctor Zhivago* that the surroundings seem to carry on the action of the main characters, and especially of Zhivago himself, for this sort of figure aims to integrate agency into an organic universe, and Pasternak often presents Zhivago's private, inner world as an integral universe unto itself.[21]

Zhivago has not yet appeared in this scene, however, and a shift in the defining rhetorical figuration will prepare for his arrival. His mother's coffin is lowered into the ground, and shovelfuls of earth fall upon it: "There drummed a rain of clods of earth hastily thrown by four spades into the grave. On it rose a little mound. A ten-year-old boy climbed up on it" (Отбарабанил дождь комьев, которыми торопливо в четыре лопаты забросали могилу. На ней вырос холмик. На него взошел десятилетний мальчик; 7). It is not incidental that the first (mixed) metaphor of the novel, the drumming "rain of clods of earth," prepares for the protagonist's arrival.

Although the novel itself has begun metonymically, contextualizing the funeral procession with contiguous detail, the introduction of Zhivago proceeds metaphorically, fixing his identity by means of an image of a wolf cub:

Его курносое лицо исказилось. Шея его вытянулась. Если бы таким движением поднял голову волчонок, было бы ясно, что он сейчас завоет. Закрыв лицо руками, мальчик зарыдал. Летевшее навстречу облако стало хлестать его по рукам и лицу мокрыми плетьми холодного ливня.

His snub-nosed face became contorted. His neck stretched out. If a wolf cub had raised its head with such a movement, it would have been clear that it was about to howl. Covering his face with his hands, the boy burst into sobs. A cloud flown to meet him began to pour the wet lashes of a cold downpour on his arms and face. (7)

This dense descriptive passage exemplifies the rhetorical complexity that commonly attends the projection of an identity for Zhivago. The reader begins this passage with a metaphor of Zhivago as a wolf cub, which, one might add, also connotes that the orphaned boy Zhivago has been abandoned by his mother to a pack of wolves. Then, the metonymic characterization of atmosphere that started the novel is repeated in the image of the cloud flying to meet him. Finally, as if to suggest (prematurely) Zhivago's mystical poetic power, the boy's tears repeat and realize the earlier metaphor of rain, and a torrential storm ensues.

In the presence of the poet Zhivago, and especially under the influence of his poetic vision, the novel regularly takes a metaphoric turn. One global dimension of the novel's plot—a dimension well characterized as antihistorical, poetic, and metafictional—is formed by this metaphoric turn. (Metafiction and other metalanguages gravitate toward the metaphoric pole because they purport to substitute one set of signifiers for another.) For example, on the first page of the novel the appearance of ten-year-old Yura Zhivago on his mother's grave provokes the following narrative aside: "Only the state of stupor and insensibility which is gradually induced by all big funerals could have created the impression that the boy wanted to speak over his mother's grave" (7). Descriptively, this passage is metonymic: the atmosphere, the torpor generated by the funeral gives rise to the image. As plot, however, this scene suggests a more significant metaphoric dimension. Though the young boy Yura does not in fact speak over his mother's grave, four hundred pages later, in the epilogue, Zhivago does speak *from* the grave, to Gordon and Dudorov when they read his volume of poetry. The point is more fundamental than my play on words suggests: from one perspective, Zhivago's volume of poetry is just as valid a replacement for the novel as it is a culmination of the plot.

In the epilogue, Gordon reflects on a time in Russian history contemporaneous with the novel's beginning:

> Take what Blok says, "We, the children of Russia's terrible years," and you'll immediately see the difference in epochs. When Blok said this, it needed to be understood in a metaphoric sense, figuratively. The children were not children, but the sons, the heirs, the intelligentsia, and the terrors were not terrible but providential, apocalyptic; and they were different things. *Now the metaphoric has become literal,* and children—are children, and the terrors are terrible, there's the difference. (my emphasis, 510)

The metaphoric *has* become literal by the end of the novel, the first term of the comparison leaving only, perhaps, a (metonymic) trace in the reader's memory. The alienation of Yura as wolf cub in a world of noncomprehending humans, or as orphaned child in a world of wolves, has become real, for example, at Varykino, where Zhivago and Strelnikov in turns battle against the wolves that draw closer and closer to the house.

One must be careful, of course, when saying that "the metaphoric has become literal." Metaphor is not mathematical identity; it retains an afterimage, so to speak, of its teleology. When "clods of earth" begin to "rain" in the opening scene of the novel, the reader does not see clods of earth and rain together, nor rain alone, but the one *becoming* the other, as if its propensity to be transformed previously merely lay dormant.

I purposely give metaphor this added "figural" interpretation, in the sense that Eric Auerbach has developed it, because the "metaphoric" plot in *Doctor Zhivago* (as opposed to its "metonymic" plot) contains a teleological dimension that Jakobson's theory of metaphor does not accommodate well. "Figural interpretation," according to Auerbach,

> establishes a connection between two events or persons in such a way that the first signifies not only itself but also the second, while the second involves or fulfills the first. The two poles of a figure are separated in time, but both, being real events or persons, are within temporality. They are both contained in the flowing stream which is historical life, and only the comprehension, the *intellectus spiritualis*, of their interdependence is a spiritual act.[22]

The connection of these events or persons is comprehensible only by reference to a "vertical" Divine Providence, and not by reference to "horizontal," causal, and temporal history.

The vertical and horizontal axes in Auerbach's explanation of figural interpretation may be likened to the metaphoric and metonymic axes in Jakobson's linguistic theory. From Auerbach's vertical axis, Divine Providence, I intend to retain a teleological dimension in my discussion of *Doctor Zhivago.*[23] From Jakobson's metaphoric axis, I mean to emphasize the sense of linguistic selection. "Selection" rightly conveys conscious or unconscious activity in the mind of a speaker, and it is this selectivity in Jakobson's linguistic theory of metaphor that finds its literary correlate in the metafictional use of the *mise en abyme* in *Doctor Zhivago.*

Zhivago's volume of poetry is the "end" of *Doctor Zhivago* in both senses of the word. On the one hand, it chronologically completes the novel; it consoles and provides Gordon and Dudorov with a sense of optimism, that the historical events of recent years really will work out for the best. This is the historical, and causal end of the novel. On the other hand, the end fulfills the novel's poetic (providential) design, is its purpose in a special sense. As readers, we have been waiting for Zhivago to speak, really to speak, since as a boy he climbed up on his mother's grave. This is the poetic, and metafictional end of the novel, and it is also the most obvious *mise en abyme* in the novel.

As *mise en abyme,* Zhivago's poetry stands out as a possible substitution for *Doctor Zhivago.* The novel invites its readers, as it were, to view Zhivago as a fictionalized version of Pasternak himself, to view Zhivago's volume of poetry as a potential version of *Doctor Zhivago. Mises en abyme* thus fit into the figurative dimension of the novel, because they draw attention to the similarities between interpolated and interpolating texts.[24] The *mise en abyme* is, in at least one stage of interpretation, always a potential metaphor or metonym for the entire text. To *end* with the volume of Zhivago's poetry, a relatively uncommon use of the *mise en abyme,*[25] is to suggest that the novel does not necessarily need the prose that led up to the poetry, that the ladder can be pulled up after us.

CHILDHOOD AND AUTHORSHIP

That's how they begin. At two years
They break from their nurse into a cloud of melodies,
They twitter, they whistle,—but words
Appear in the third year.

That's how they begin to understand.
And in the noise of a running turbine
They imagine that mother is not mother.
That you—are not you, that home—is alien.
—Pasternak, 1921

Like Bulgakov's *The Master and Margarita,* Pasternak's *Doctor Zhivago* depicts selfhood in a way that is deeply entwined with the metafictional and literary-historical aspects of the novel. Whereas the Master was a man without a biography, the main characters of *Doctor Zhivago,* especially Zhivago and Lara, have lengthy biographies. The *shape* of the entire life is much more the focus of Pasternak's novel than it was of Bulgakov's, and even though *Doctor Zhivago* is not a biographical novel in the conventional sense, it does gather the significant events in the lives of its protagonists.

For the main characters of *Doctor Zhivago,* there are three touchstones of selfhood in the novel, by which a character's life may be interpreted metaphorically or metonymically. Identity in *Doctor Zhivago* is a function of one's relation to family, history, and poetry broadly construed. Pasternak depicts the family through the prism of the triangular relationship of parents and child, in which the loss of one or both parents motivates the child to seek out substitute objects of affection. History proceeds either "figurally" (metaphorically), in Auerbach's sense, or causally (metonymically); and the relation of the self to history may be either as a fulfilling agent or as an object dissolved into its progression. Finally, poetry in the novel may be an analog of life, which the creative self populates with metaphors of itself, or it may be an explainer of life, which an agent uses heuristically. Here I will primarily consider family and poetry in two of the novel's early *mises en abyme:* the "dumb scene" (немая сцена) between Lara and Komarovsky, and the scene in which Zhivago explains his philosophy of consciousness to Anna Ivanovna on her sickbed.

The first few parts of *Doctor Zhivago* could justifiably be subtitled "The Orphans."[26] Yura, Lara, Gordon, and Dudorov are all deprived of "normal" childhoods. Both of Zhivago's parents die and he lives with the Gromekos; Lara has only her mother, from whom she quickly becomes estranged, and she lives for a time with the Kologrivovs; Gordon feels trapped by his Jewish heritage and, like Zhivago, he too lives with the Gromekos; Dudorov's terrorist father is in exile, his mother has abandoned him, and, like Lara, he too lives temporarily with the Kologrivovs.[27] Of the main characters only Tonia experiences anything resembling a typical or happy childhood. Thus, from the very start of the novel Pasternak draws the reader's attention to the absent side(s) of the family triangle. Affection in such situations, he seems to suggest, is easily transferred to symbolic representatives of the missing child or parent.

On the train, for example, Zhivago's father demonstrates a tenderness toward Misha Gordon that Misha supposes "perhaps was not directed at him" (20). The reader of course knows that Andrei Zhivago sees the son he abandoned in Misha, who is the same age as Yura Zhivago. Another more complex example is Lara, who takes her mother's place as the lover of Komarovsky, a father figure for her and her brother. Finally, Zhivago himself seems continually to transfer the affection he has had for his dead mother to women who resemble her, in both nonromantic (Anna Ivanovna) and romantic (Tonia, Lara, Marina) contexts.

Zhivago's relationships with women may be explained preliminarily by psychoanalytical models in which the love interests of a man are reduced to his attempts to find an object of affection that resembles his mother. In a Freudian model the death of Zhivago's mother might be viewed as an interruption in his libidinal development—crucial to ego formation—at a time when the child takes as his object of affection no longer himself but another, in the traditional view, his mother. I believe that Zhivago's figuration of language may be productively compared to the ways in which he works out his desire for one or another woman in his life.

The most important fact to consider here is that the breakdown of typical family dynamics and the transferability of affection point to potentially ill-formed structures for ego development and the maturation of identity. It does not matter whether one interprets the psychology of the novel's main characters from a strictly psychoanalytical viewpoint or not; what does matter is that one recognize that Pasternak's "orphans" seek *substitute* families throughout the novel. They consequently adopt new structures, or reformulate given structures, for interpreting the self in these new familial contexts. For Zhivago, the project of selfhood is also caught up with his literary endeavors; for Gordon, it involves his anti-Semitism and uncritical adoption of Vedeniapin's theories on Christian personality (личность).[28] Lara's situation, however, is different.

Her path is in many ways easier to trace than Zhivago's (or Gordon's), because unlike Zhivago she is unable to translate her crises and failures into an aesthetic project that sublimates the dilemmas of identity. In other words, Lara's tragedies do not subsequently become episodes in some romantic version of her life that she herself authors. On the contrary, Lara is easily aestheticized or "authored" by others: Komarovsky makes her into a "fallen woman . . . from a French novel" (47), and Zhivago considers her (among others things) a figure from a chivalric fairy tale (362). In fact, in his description of Lara's affair with Komarovsky, Pasternak alludes to several famous women from the Russian literary tradition: Anna Karenina, Zinaida of Turgenev's *First Love,* Olia of Bunin's "Light Breathing," and Katerina from Ostrovsky's *The Thunderstorm.* For Lara herself, of course, this sequence of tragic events represents a rapid loss of identity; for the novel, these events occasion Pasternak's entwining of identity with literary history. Such intersections of selfhood and literary history are central to the *mises en abyme* I have discussed thus far. The frequency of narrative framing techniques in tales of sexual transgression, and the subsequent heightened intertextuality involved in rewriting such a tale, make this scene paradigmatic for Pasternak's approach to literary history through Lara.[29] The affair between Komarovsky and Lara demonstrates as much as any other narrative sequence in *Doctor Zhivago* Pasternak's preoccupation with the reappraisal of nineteenth-century aesthetics. No less, however, does this narrative sequence demonstrate the difference between Pasternak's depiction of Lara's identity formation versus Zhivago's.

Events leading to the dumb scene between Lara and Komarovsky intensify the literary framing of Lara. After the consummation of the affair with Komarovsky, she returns home, where everyone is still asleep. She is wearing a pale dress and a veil, which she has borrowed for the one evening, "as for a masquerade" (47). She then sits down at her mother's dressing table and mirror: "She sat before her reflection in the mirror and saw nothing" (47). She thinks of her mother, of how if her mother finds out about the affair she will kill her and then kill herself; and Lara realizes that now she is a "fallen woman," a woman from a "French novel." Moreover, tomorrow, she thinks to herself, she will go to school and sit next to girls, "who were, compared to her, still little children" (47). She cries out to God, asking how all this could have happened.

This passage demonstrates well both the shape of identity formation in the initial chapters of the novel and the frames that enclose Lara. First, there is the triangle of mother, daughter, and their shared lover. Lara's affair with Komarovsky began, it is worth recalling, when she replaced her mother as Komarovsky's escort to a name-day party. Second, on the evening of the consummation of the affair, Lara's clothing suggests both the loss of her virginity and the effacement of identity that proceeds from her replacement of her mother as Komarovsky's lover. Lara's dress is "almost white," and the veil that she wears "as to a masquerade" intimates both that she has lost her own identity—her face cannot be seen—and that she has assumed someone else's identity, namely her mother's.

But Lara has no more fully assumed her mother's identity than she has completely lost her own; the problem is that she is neither herself nor anyone else. This paradox is the key to the double entendre of her sitting before her reflection in her mother's mirror and seeing "nothing." Both mirror and lover belong to her mother, but Lara sees neither herself nor her mother in the reflection. She is trapped somehow "in between," for she is neither adult nor child, and especially not a child.[30] Her choice of words for her schoolmates, "грудные дети" (meaning literally something like "unweaned children"), is significant in this respect because the idiom suggests in developmental (ontogenetic) terms the psychological break between mother and daughter that is the consequence of Lara's affair with Komarovsky.

This scene can be read simultaneously in terms of narrative framing and its implied pictorial aesthetics. The effacement of the veil and dress suggest a blank canvas, especially when framed by the borders of the mirror in which Lara sees nothing. She in fact later recalls a famous painting in the private room "where it all began" (55) as a metaphor of the loss of her virginity. "When she first saw it she was not yet a woman, she was not yet comparable to such a treasure. That came later" (55). Pasternak associates Lara's objectification (and commodification—she becomes comparable to a valuable work of art) and loss of identity with both pictorial and narrative acts of framing. There is thus a (temporary) collusion between Komarovsky's capitalism and Pasternak's story. Lara's transformation into an aesthetic object by Komarovsky and the text, moreover, prefigures her silence in the dumb scene with Komarovsky.

Pasternak uses this lacuna in Lara's ego development to reinterpret the relation of literary tradition to modern characterizations of the self. Here it is partly a matter of citing and shifting the codes so familiar to the reader of nineteenth-century literature. A comparison should make the point clear.

For Zhivago, identity crises are sublimated into an aesthetic project that continually reshapes and reinterprets the meaning of his personal experience. For Lara, the relation of self to literature might be termed "naive," in the sense that she herself does recognize (what is to the reader) a literary cliché; she does not make it personal and specific to her own life, an exception to the typical, and thereby transcend it. ("Belonging to a type is the end of a man," Zhivago says, "his condemnation" [294].) In Bunin's "Light Breathing," by contrast, Olia's behavior defies literary typification: her transgression serves as an occasion to "speak out," for example, in the diary entry that provokes her murderer. That kind of authorship, or stimulus to authorial productivity, does not cross gender boundaries equally in *Doctor Zhivago* (though in other ways the women in Zhivago's life are all "stronger," less typical, and better suited to the exigencies of postrevolutionary Russian life than he is).

The dumb scene between Komarovsky and Lara also involves Yura's (and Pasternak's) translation of the debauched girl cliché into a modern idiom. Yura and Misha have accompanied Gromeko and Tyshkevich to the hotel where Lara's mother tried to poison herself. While waiting for Gromeko to take them home, the two boys spy Komarovsky and Lara:

> Meanwhile a dumb scene took place between the girl and the man. Not a word passed their lips, only their eyes met. But the understanding between them had a terrifying quality of magic, as if he were the master of a puppet show and she were a marionette obedient to his every gesture . . . Here was the very thing which he, Tonia, and Misha had endlessly discussed as "vulgar," the force which so frightened and attracted them and which they controlled so easily from a safe distance by words. And now here it was, this force, in front of Yura's very eyes, utterly real, and yet troubled and haunting, pitilessly destructive, and complaining and calling for help—and what had become of their childish philosophy and what was Yura to do now? (my ellipses, 63–64)

For Lara this is a scene of utter subjugation and represents the total effacement of her personality and will; for Zhivago it is a lesson that repeats his uncle Vedeniapin's intellectual movement away from Tolstoy; and, lastly, for Pasternak it recasts a clichéd literary treatment into a modernist (perhaps Blokian) rather than a realist literary idiom. The confluence of themes of self, aesthetic/intellectual education, and literary tradition make it an emblematic scene in *Doctor Zhivago* and a central *mise en abyme* in the novel.

The reduction of personality to nothingness initiated by Lara's flawed family structure, and pushed to the brink by her replacement of her mother as Komarovsky's lover, now reaches its completion. Whatever identification with her mother Lara achieved as an adult in an affair with the same man is symbolically vanquished by her mother's attempted suicide. Her mother's capitulation before such a "pitilessly destructive" force leads Lara to believe she has only two options: suicide or a similar capitulation to Komarovsky. There are no other choices within the familial triangle of ego development in which she is first introduced to the reader. There is a third choice, of course; in the very next scene in which Lara appears she appeals to the Kologrivov family. One of the orphans of the first part of the novel, Lara must adopt a new family if she is to maintain a viable, livable personality.

In the scene with Lara and Komarovsky, Yura's uncritical Tolstoyan moralism, marked by his constant reference to the Russian term "пошлость" ("vulgarity"), is transmuted into a Blokian aesthetic appreciation of the terrifying magical force that moves Lara as though she were a "marionette."[31] Earlier in the novel Nikolai Vedeniapin recognized in Yura, Tonia, and Misha's zeal for preaching chastity a stage that all adolescents go through, and he thinks to himself: "'This threesome soaked themselves in *The Meaning of Love* and *The Kreutzer Sonata* and have a mania for preaching chastity.' Adolescence should pass through a frenzy of purity, but they were overdoing it out of all proportion" (42). What for Lara is a real event in her personal demise serves as a lesson in love and aesthetics for Zhivago, when he sees Lara and Komarovsky. Zhivago recognizes this when he speaks of his former, "childish" philosophy.

Like so many scenes in the novel, the descriptive language in this passage is permeated with the uniqueness of Zhivago's *vision*. Both amazing "diagnostician" and poet, Zhivago is characterized in the novel as much by *how* he sees as by *what* he sees and says. In this dumb scene, "Yura devoured them both [Lara and Komarovsky] with his eyes" (63). Pasternak makes the connection between vision and poetry explicit shortly thereafter: "Though Yura qualified only in general medicine, he knew eyes with the thoroughness of an oculist. His interest in the physiology of sight was in keeping with other sides of his nature—his creative gifts and his thinking about the essence of the artistic image and about the structure of the logical idea" (80–81). This passage is an example of what, in some Russian fiction, disturbs admirers of Henry James: Pasternak *tells* us that Zhivago has this gift of vision rather than *showing* us that he does. But Pasternak has other objectives here.

Zhivago's creative perception of events, announced in the later passage, is also implicit in the first passage, and Pasternak's choice of words connects the two passages. Yura knows eyes with the "thoroughness" (доскональность) of an oculist; in the passage describing Komarovsky and Lara, "before Yura's eyes" is the "utterly/thoroughly real" (досконально вещественная) power that is so destructive and magically enchanting. Moreover, the later passage tells us that Zhivago is planning to write an article on Blok (81). This connection between Yura's vision and Blok, though, has also perhaps been in the mind of the Russian reader since the first passage, due to the imagery of the puppet theater that is presented there. In early-twentieth-century Russian literature one of the most famous uses of the puppet theater was Blok's *The Puppetshow Booth* (1906).

In the later passage it occurs to Zhivago that one need not write an essay about Blok, because Blok simply reflects the spirit of the birth of Christ in Russian life, and "all one has to do is paint a Russian version of a Dutch Adoration of the Magi with snow in it, and wolves, and a dark fir forest" (82). Here too Zhivago recalls *The Puppetshow Booth* and the imagery of the scene describing Lara and Komarovsky; for the traditional Russian puppet theater usually performed plays on Christ's birth, the visit of the Magi, or the massacre of infants by Herod.[32]

In short, the scene between Lara and Komarovsky describes a sort of aesthetic tutorial for Zhivago. He moves from Tolstoy to Blok, away from the "safe distance of words," of terms like "пошлость" which mask authentic experience, to what Pasternak calls the "thoroughly real" (досконально вещественная) power of his creative vision. What is shown in the scene between Lara and Komarovsky approximates what is told only three pages later (67)—that Yura is not ready for prose, he writes poetry. And poetry makes an entirely different vocabulary of selfhood available to him.

The scene between Lara and Komarovsky has consequences not only for Lara and Zhivago, but also for Pasternak, inasmuch as it retells a nineteenth-century cliché in a modern idiom. Thus the move from Tolstoy to Blok can also be explained by reference to the metafictional dynamics of the novel. Strictly speaking, since *Doctor Zhivago* leads its prose parts into the poetry that completes the novel, the shift on a metafictional level from Tolstoy to Blok—from Yura's metonymical use of normative language (пошлость) to his metaphorical/poetic vision of images (the puppet theater)—serves as one of several *mises en abyme* in the novel: the scene between Lara and Komarovsky repeats locally the novel's global movement from prose to poetry.

A similar aesthetic shift is visible in the novel's treatment of Zhivago's transition from an orphan to a grown man with a sense of himself and the shape of his life. Again, authorship of personal identity often occupies the same ideational space as the authorship of literary identity. The one form of authorship uses a philosophical vocabulary where the other has recourse to a vocabulary borrowed from the literary tradition. The difference between the two is central to the second *mise en abyme* that focuses the early parts of the novel: Zhivago's conversation with Anna Ivanovna.

Unlike Lara, Zhivago has early in the novel adopted a new family, the Gromekos, who eventually become his in-laws. Part 3 of the novel introduces Zhivago's mature *verbalized* reflections on philosophy, contrasting his *visual* aesthetics in the scene between Lara and Komarovsky. Of consciousness, Zhivago says:

> Applied to oneself, consciousness is a poison, a means for the subject to poison itself. Consciousness is a light directed outwards, consciousness lights the road ahead of us so we don't stumble. Consciousness—it's the headlights in front of a moving locomotive. Turn the light inward, and there'll be a crash. (69)

Consciousness should be directed outward, Zhivago tells Anna Ivanovna, for the self finds meaning only in others; in others, consciousness is sustained and transcends bodily death.

Not solely for the benefit of his dying (future) mother-in-law, this impromptu lecture on life, death, and the nature of consciousness does much to characterize Zhivago himself, who is poised before events that will transform him—from medical student into wartime doctor, from youth into adult, husband, and father. As at the beginning of *Doctor Zhivago* when Yura's mother dies, here a metaphoric turn motivates the novel's plot: the death or loss of a mother figure (metaphor) prepares Zhivago's transition to a new stage in life.

Thus it is fitting that this scene of transition and maturation is chosen by Pasternak to serve his further reconfiguration of a traditional literary idiom; this time it is the literary idiom for consciousness, which, as the reader of Russian novels will recognize, derives, again, from Tolstoy's *Anna Karenina*. Both the "bright light" (яркий свет) that Anna used, first cruelly to analyze others and then tragically to see her own true self, and the oncoming train under which she threw herself are condensed in this passage to produce the image of the "headlights [зажженные фары] of . . . a locomotive"— Zhivago's metaphor for consciousness. The "crash" (катастрофа, also "catastrophe") of consciousness turned inward forewarns one Anna, Anna Ivanovna, of the danger of introspection and unchecked isolation that has undone another Anna—Anna Karenina.

And this scene between Zhivago and Anna Ivanovna is especially Tolstoyan, for Anna Ivanovna's fall against the newly acquired wardrobe is reminiscent of the fall Tolstoy's Ivan Ilych takes while redecorating his new apartment: both "furniture" accidents initiate a deadly illness.[33] The transformation of the "bright light" and "candle" that characterized Anna Karenina's tragic inwardness into the "headlights of . . . a locomotive" recalls and realizes the suspicious attitude adopted in *Anna Karenina* toward modernization in general and railroads in particular.[34] What is more, Zhivago's frequent and rhythmic use of the word for "consciousness" (сознание) in this scene echoes Tolstoy's stylistic idiosyncrasy of relentlessly repeating certain words.

If in the scene between Lara and Komarovsky Zhivago's maturing poetic vision is characterized by a move from metonym to metaphor, here his maturing philosophical self-awareness is characterized by a return from metaphor to metonymy. In the mouth of Zhivago, Tolstoy's metaphor for consciousness is transformed into a kind of metonymy, in Jakobson's terms, "an abstraction [that] becomes objectified . . . overlaid with material accessories."[35] Consciousness is not just a light, it is a light on a train; and the train is moving; and the light is turned inward; and the train crashes. Zhivago's characterization of selfhood to Anna Ivanovna abstracts the "enlightened" quality of consciousness and gives it a life of its own. What I call here Zhivago's "maturing philosophical self-awareness" is partly his recognition that such self-awareness may be impossible: the quest for self-consciousness fails, leads to a "crash," and initiates metonymic digression in its place.

Identity *verbalized* by Zhivago is thus markedly different from identity *visualized* by Zhivago—a contrast that also functioned at the heart of the first *mise en abyme* in the dumb scene between Lara and Komarovsky. In *Doctor Zhivago,* the self told or explained differs from the self imagined, and depending on which structure is invoked, the novel's narration relies by turns on metonymic and metaphoric rhetorical figures: recall, for example, the metaphor of the marionette for Lara. By choosing poetry over prose, Zhivago attempts to avoid summing up life and biography metonymically:

> Ever since his schooldays he had dreamed of composing a book of biographies, into which he would place, in the form of buried explosives, the most striking of what he had managed to see and think. But he was still too young to write such a book; instead, he made do by writing poetry, as a painter would make sketches his whole life for a big canvas he had in mind. (67)

Zhivago chooses the traditionally metaphoric avenue of literary expression, poetry, even when describing his future prose ("buried explosives"); and Pasternak himself turns again to metaphoric characterizations of Zhivago, who is now the painter making sketches for the canvas of his life.

Here, again, the parallel between Zhivago's literary endeavors and Pasternak's makes this passage emblematic of *Doctor Zhivago.* Because Pasternak was known mainly as a poet, this passage can be seen as a comment both on the meaning of the prose work in the author's life and on the poetry that prepared for it.[36] The "book of biographies" that Zhivago dreams of reminds one of Pasternak's *Safe Conduct,* an autobiographical work that portrays the author primarily through his descriptions of the lives of other people he has known. From this perspective, it is true, some of Pasternak's most famous poetry may also be viewed as biographical: the volume *My Sister, Life,* for example, is deeply, if idiosyncratically, biographical.

This passage about the "book of biographies" has some bearing on how one views the volume of Zhivago's poetry at the end of the novel. On the one hand, the volume metonymically serves as the end of the causal series that is the plot of *Doctor Zhivago.* On the other hand, as *mise en abyme* it metaphorically represents the whole of the novel. The passage describing Zhivago's preparation in poetry for prose bolsters this metaphoric reading of the volume of poetry. Since Zhivago writes no large biographical canvas of his life, we are left to view the poetry as a collection of "sketches"— representative of the biography that is told in a different genre by Pasternak but not its logical completion. The summing metaphor of Zhivago's life, the "big canvas," does not exist, and the poetry substitutes, therefore, for that incomplete project.

THE PSYCHOLOGY OF POETRY

Pasternak offers psychological motivation that corresponds to the reliance upon rhetorical figures in his portrayal of Zhivago as artist and person; in other words, one may reconnect the formal to the thematic. In *The Master and Margarita,* Bulgakov's play on different kinds of discourse can be explained by reference to his underlying wish that literature reveal the Truth. By matching realist, hermeneutic, and metacritical discourse to traditional concepts of personal identity and literary history, I described three different, and in some ways opposed, concepts of authorship. There was little need to address psychology per se, because so little of the Master's life was actually represented in the novel. Thus the entire shape of the Master's life influenced the representation of him as author only minimally.

Such is not the case in *Doctor Zhivago,* where certain psychological traits develop early in Zhivago's life, maintain significant influence over his actions, and adumbrate the evolving shape of his identity as author. It is nearly impossible to avoid noticing the profound effect, for example, that the image of Zhivago's mother has on his psyche and aesthetic imagination. The image of Maria Nikolaevna plays an important role in the symbolism of the novel, in Zhivago's metaphoric vision, and in the novel's use of figurative language.

An analysis of recurrent imagery and language is perhaps best initiated by a list of examples. The following entries indicate several references, explicit and implicit, to Maria Nikolaevna.

Example	Part	Chapter	Scene or Passage
(1)	I	1	The funeral of Maria Nikolaevna.
(2)	I	3	Yura recalls his sickly mother and the property that bore the Zhivago family name.
(3)	I	6	Yura faints, having hallucinated his mother's voice.
(4)	III	15-17	Comparisons are made of Anna Ivanova Gromeko's death and funeral with that of Maria Nikolaevna.
(5)	VI	3	Sasha, Zhivago's son, is a "striking copy" of Maria Nikolaevna.
(6)	VII	5	The Zhivagos' final night in their Moscow home; a snowstorm; Zhivago's memories of Maria Nikolaevna.
(7)	IX	5	Zhivago has inherited his mother's poor heart.
(8)	IX	10	Zhivago dreams of a familiar woman's voice.
(9)	XI	7	Zhivago reflects on the childhood image of the forest that has formed his "inward face" and "personality."
(10)	XII	1	A rowan tree is seen by Zhivago as the image of a nursing mother.
(11)	XII	9	Lara is compared to the rowan tree.
(12)	XIII	8	Zhivago has two dreams, one of Sasha and one of Lara.
(13)	XIII	12	Zhivago's second child by Tonia is named Masha, after Maria Nikolaevna.
(14)	XIV	14	Zhivago hallucinates Lara's voice, as he once did his mother's voice.
(15)	XV	2	"Orphaned" fields are compared to thriving forests.
(16)	XV	6	Zhivago's "third marriage," to Marina.

Some of the above sixteen entries are more transparently connected to Maria Nikolaevna than others. Nevertheless, a couple of obvious conclusions may be drawn from the list as a whole.

First, the experiences of childhood, especially those related to Maria Nikolaevna and her death, clearly influence Zhivago's perception of himself as child and as adult. Throughout the novel he seems surrounded by images of his mother: as a small child he hears her voice in the woods (ex. 3), and he perceives her in Anna Ivanovna (ex. 4), in his two children (exs. 5, 13), and in his romantic attachments (exs. 8, 12, 14). Second, it is also apparent that Zhivago's perception of nature, especially of the forest, as vitally maternal begins with his fainting spell at the Kologrivovs' estate (ex. 3); this maternal imagery is also prevalent in the chapters dealing with his experience among the Partisans (exs. 9, 10, 11), where it then becomes further associated with Lara (ex. 14). Later in the novel, the destructiveness of the Civil War on society is opposed in similar terms to a rebirth in nature (ex. 15).

A psychoanalytical interpretation locates many of the operative forces in Zhivago's perception, including the image of his mother, in his unconscious, but nevertheless fully appreciates how Maria Nikolaevna is figured in the novel. The justification for adopting this kind of interpretation is twofold. To start, psychoanalytic theory provides ample ground for viewing certain events of childhood in the triangular family as retaining iconic resiliency for the later, adult mind; and we have seen how crucial childhood in general is for the characters in *Doctor Zhivago*. Second, the same psychological iconicity that psychoanalytic theory attributes to archaic events in the formation of the ego may be related to the rhetorical figures of perception that characterize Zhivago's vision and poetry. Thus, one is able to provide an explanation for the use of figurative language in the novel, while at the same time providing psychological credibility to the sway Maria Nikolaevna holds over Zhivago's adult consciousness.

One may also consider the pertinent aspects of Zhivago's life in a plainer light. Critics have had no problem in discerning the important role of women in Zhivago's life: from his mother to Anna Ivanovna, from Tonia to Lara and Marina, women are always at the crux of the momentous events of Zhivago's life. His relationships to the women share a common denominator: Zhivago's tendency to leave or abandon the women he loves. He leaves Tonia for the war; leaves Lara to return to Tonia; betrays Tonia; is unwillingly separated from both Tonia and Lara; tricks Lara into going away with Komarovsky; and he abandons Marina when he decides to "rebuild his life" in Moscow. Each case is different, to be sure, but this pattern of repeated departure in Zhivago's behavior suggests that in each of his loves, there remains a shortfall, a reserve of psychic investment that prevents Zhivago from identifying himself fully in his love relationships.[37] The decidedly tragic element attributed to the workings of desire in psychoanalytical theory matches well the destined tragedy of Zhivago and Lara's love.

A characteristic passage of Zhivago's perception of himself in and through nature begins chapter 7 of Part 11 (ex. 13):

Юрий Андреевич с детства любил сквозящий огнем зари вечерний лес. В такие минуты точно и он пропускал сквозь себя эти столбы света. Точно дар живого духа потоком входил в его грудь, пересекал все его существо и парой крыльев выходил из-под лопаток наружу. Тот юношеский первообраз, который на всю жизнь складывается у каждого и потом навсегда служит и кажется ему его внутренним лицом, его личностью, во всей первоначальной силе пробуждался в нем и заставлял природу, лес, вечернюю зарю и все видимое преображаться в такое же первоначальное и всеохватывающее подобие девочки. «Лара!»

Ever since his childhood Yurii Andreievich had loved the evening woods seen against the setting sun. At such moments he felt as if he too were pierced by those shafts of light. It was as though the gift of the living spirit streamed into his breast, cutting across his whole being and coming out at his shoulders like a pair of wings. That archetype [first image] of youth that is formed in each person for life and seems for ever after to be his inner face, his personality, awoke in him in all its primordial strength, and compelled nature, the forest, the sunset, and everything visible to be transfigured into a similarly primordial and all-embracing likeness of a girl. Closing his eyes, "Lara!" he half-whispered or thought, addressing the whole of his life, all God's earth, all the sunlit space spread out before him. (339)

I quote this passage at length to demonstrate how a hidden logic of figurative language works in the formative moments of Zhivago's perception of his identity.

The passage begins metonymically, as Zhivago is inspired by the beauty of the forest scenery; he then identifies himself with the forest as the light passes through it, "as if he too were pierced by those shafts of light" (точно и он пропускал сквозь себя эти столбы света), and the light is transformed into a pair of wings, making Zhivago a bird, or perhaps an angel. Here the rhetorical figure changes from metonym—Zhivago as part of the woods—to metaphor, "that archetype ['first image'; первообраз] of youth," which is associated specifically with Zhivago's identity. It is fundamentally associated with identity, first, because the root word is "image" (образ) and, second, because this image is said to form his "inner face" and "personality." The root word "образ" also means "form," "icon," or "iconic image"; thus this "archetype of youth" is suggestive of an "iconic image of youth," forming the basis of Zhivago's metaphoric, poetic vision.

The frame of reference for identity in the passage thus shifts from the metonymic light passing through the forest to the iconic image of Zhivago's personality. It is the power of this image, the power of his poetic vision, that awakens in Zhivago and forces nature to be transformed (преображаться, literally "to take the image/form of") into the "likeness" (подобие) of a girl, Lara. And if there was any doubt as to the spiritual tenor of the passage, it is dissolved by Pasternak's use of the word "likeness," the same word as "in the likeness of God."[38] It is typical of the novel, when it is saturated by Zhivago's poetic vision, to shift from metonymy to metaphor, to a grander myth of human being, often the basis of Zhivago's own strain of Christianity.

Two questions emerge from this reading. First, in what childhood experience is the archetypal, iconic image of identity with nature formed? Where in the novel does one find an origin for the fusion of Zhivago's identity with nature? Second, Zhivago obviously merges his vision of himself and nature into a fantasy that identifies him with Lara. In what way does Lara assume the image of youth that shapes her in Zhivago's creative imagination?

From the first pages of the novel, Zhivago seems to experience nature in all its vitality, and his perception of nature is by and large represented metaphorically. Nevertheless, if we are looking for a *formative* experience of childhood in the novel that fuses Zhivago's image of himself to his metaphoric perception of nature, then we will be drawn to the scene in part 1 where Yura is walking through the Kologrivovs' estate (ex. 3). The sights, sounds, and smells of the grounds recall vacations abroad with his mother, and he hears her calling his name in the sounds of the birds and the bees:

> The specter of his mother's voice hung above the grass like an aural hallucination; it rang out to Yura in the melodic phrases of the birds and in the buzzing of the bees. Yura shuddered, time and again it seemed to him as if his mother were calling him and beckoning him somewhere. (15)

He then crawls down from the wooded area into the dense thicket of branches in the ravine, where he cries out a prayer for his mother, calls to her, and falls into a faint. He awakes with a feeling of lightness he wishes would not go away.

Now, it seems reasonable to suggest that in this scene a vision of connectedness with the maternal in nature becomes iconic in Zhivago's imagination. He correlates his mother's voice calling his name with the sounds of nature, retreats into the closeness of the ravine, where his loneliness becomes that much more poignant, and calls out to his mother as if she were a saint (угодница). In essence, Yura is reenacting a scene of security in identity that he has associated with his mother's voice and his own name; and it is a scene he will repeat again (exs. 8, 13), again choosing nature, but this time calling Lara's name (ex. 13) in place of his mother's. In apostrophe, Zhivago paradoxically turns the "inner face" of his personality *to meet* the object of his love, whether it is his mother or Lara.[39]

In part 12, Zhivago's poetic vision generates a striking metaphor of maternal vitality in nature, the rowan tree (ex. 10); and this time the subsequent connection with Lara is much more direct (ex. 11). Near the partisan encampment a rowan tree alone has maintained its foliage, and Zhivago's attention is drawn to the relationship between the tree and the birds that feed on its berries: "A kind of living intimacy was carried on between the

birds and the tree. It was as if the rowan had seen everything, long remained stubborn, and then, having taken pity on the birds, gave in and fed
them like a nurse unbuttoning her blouse to give breast to a baby" (348). In
itself, this scene does not add much to what we know already of Zhivago's
perception of nature. The image of the nurturing mother in nature is in accord with how Zhivago perceives his own relationship to nature, but, as yet,
there is no identity given to the symbol of the rowan tree (even though the
reader might recall how in the earlier forest scene [ex. 9] Zhivago envisioned the light passing through the trees as a living spirit that, passing
through him, sprouted into a pair of birdlike wings).

The anthropomorphic metaphor of the rowan tree is realized in apostrophe several pages later, when Zhivago escapes from the partisan camp.
He heads in the direction of the tree, telling a guard that he simply wants
to pick berries.

> It was half in snow, half in frozen leaves and berries, and it held out two white
> branches toward him. He remembered Lara's strong white arms, round, and
> generous, and he seized the branches and pulled them to him. In what was
> just like a conscious answering movement, the tree shook snow over him
> from head to toe. Not understanding what he was saying, and forgetting him-
> self, he muttered: "I'll see you again, my picture of beauty, my princess, my
> little rowan tree, my own flesh and blood." (370)

Here again, apostrophe fuses the speaker in his identification with the
metaphor in nature. It is notable too that Zhivago's apostrophe is motivated
entirely by his emotions, which spring from nowhere; he does not "understand," and "forgets himself."

The passages I have examined thus far (exs. 3, 9, 10, 11) suggest that
Zhivago's metaphoric, poetic vision of nature has a basis in the psychology
of personal identity. He creates images of maternal vitality in nature with
which to merge his own self-perception. The channel of Zhivago's identification of himself in maternal images has heretofore been spoken language,
the moment when Zhivago cries out forming an apostrophic climax to each
scene. Other passages in the novel that form similar identifications of the
maternal in Zhivago's lovers need not follow the same chronological series
of nature, metaphor, apostrophe (though in what I would call the emblematic passages of self-identification this is the case).

Boundary states of consciousness of various kinds, for example, draw
the same shape in Zhivago's imagination. In the subsequent part of the novel,
part 16, Zhivago has two bad dreams (ex. 12), one of his son Sasha and the
other of Lara.[40] In the first dream, Zhivago refuses to let his son indoors,
though Sasha begs him desperately. A flow of water raging outside frightens
the boy, but whether it is from a broken water main or from a torrential river
in a mountain gorge Zhivago cannot tell. In his dream Zhivago considers the

boy the victim of "a falsely understood feeling of honor and duty before another woman, who was not the boy's mother" (387). When Zhivago awakens from this dream, he wonders what kind of infection he is battling, that causes him to have such nightmares. One critic has suggested that it is a metaphoric disease, no ordinary typhus, but an apocalyptic "fourth typhus."[41]

In any event, Sasha clearly represents more than himself alone in this dream. To start, he is also in Zhivago's mind (ex. 5) "a striking copy [of Maria Nikolaevna], resembling her much more than all the likenesses preserved of her" (разительная ее копия, похожая на нее больше всех сохранившихся после нее изображений; 172). Metaphorically connected to Zhivago's mother, he is also metonymically connected to his own mother, Zhivago's wife; whereas he is associated with Zhivago himself in a more properly metaphoric sense. Zhivago considered Sasha at his birth to be "a gift from the blue" (105). Sasha is, then, at the very least representative of Zhivago's mother and Tonia, and perhaps he portrays a version of Zhivago himself.

That Zhivago sacrifices Sasha for Lara also suggests that he substitutes Lara both for his own mother and for Sasha's mother. It is telling that in this dream the nature imagery associated with Sasha is threatening rather than nurturing. In place of inspirational sunsets and maternal trees, one finds torrential mountain water carrying with it "the ages of cold and darkness from its caves" (387). In the dream Zhivago's behavior creates a certain amount of anxiety for him, and not on his son's behalf. While he ponders whether to let Sasha in through the door, he worries about Lara, who "might at any moment come into the room from the door on the other side of the room" (387). It is likely that Zhivago's second bad dream, in which Lara rejects him, originates in the anxiety created by the first dream. Either way, Zhivago is forced to choose between competing representatives of Maria Nikolaevna.

More pertinent than his nightmares, perhaps, is the boundary state of consciousness that Zhivago slips into after he has sent Lara off with Komarovsky in part 14. The implicit comparisons of Lara to Maria Nikolaevna are made explicit here and, moreover, the fundamental association of Zhivago's identity with the sound of his name and his poetry rises again to the surface of his consciousness.

> Sometimes, after losing himself in his writing and his work, Yurii Andreievich suddenly remembered with utter clarity the woman who had gone away, and he broke down from tenderness and the sharpness of his loss. As in childhood, when amidst the splendor of summer's nature it seemed to him he heard his deceased mother's voice in the calls of the birds, so now his hearing, accustomed to Lara's and expecting it as part of his life, deceived him. He sometimes imagined he heard the sound of "Yurochka" coming from the next room. (449)

In his reaction to the devastating loss of Lara, Zhivago reenacts one of the central scenes of his childhood. And the most telling sign that Zhivago "slowly loses his mind" (447) after Lara's departure is not that he hallucinates her voice but that he is unable to distinguish this hallucination from others.

Zhivago cannot distinguish the metaphoric identifications he makes in the real world from those he creates in his poetry. After Lara's departure, he spends his days drinking vodka and writing about her, "but the more he crossed out and exchanged one word for another the more the Lara of his poems and notes departed from her living archetype" (но Лара его стихов и записей, по мере вымарок и замены одного слова другим, все дальше уходила от истинного своего первообраза; 447). Notice how the language of the "archetype of youth" (юношеский первообраз; part 11, ex. 9), which formed the substance of Zhivago's identity, has been transformed into an "archetype" (первообраз) of Lara. Inasmuch as Zhivago has invested his self-hood in an image of the "real" Lara, he loses that identification as he writes the poems that figure her aesthetically.

The psychological complexity of this passage nearly prevents the plot of the novel from advancing—until Pasternak makes an abrupt shift to Strelnikov's apotheosis of the young Lara and the early Revolution. Five short sentences after Zhivago hallucinates Lara's voice, chapter 15 of part 14 begins with a psychologically straightforward transition to the "voice of reason": "Here is what happened a day or two later. The doctor finally heeded the voice of reason. He told himself that if he wished to kill himself he could find a quicker and less painful method" (449). The novel shifts back into its historically motivated plot. Pasternak thus seems purposefully to leave unresolved whether the essence of Zhivago's identity is affected by the historical events that contextualize his life.

One can see an attempt to synthesize history and one kind of Zhivago's projected metaphor of self in the Christ poems of the poetic cycle that ends the novel, especially in "Hamlet" and "The Garden of Gethsemane." "Separation," by contrast, functions as a keystone between the novel's prose and poetry. It is a meditation on the role of departure and separation as twin facets of the poet's identity. Zhivago the poet makes his farewells in this poem both to his muse, Lara, and to his Olympus, Varykino, in an intertextual play with Pushkin that signifies the end of his poetic and personal identifications with nature.

SEPARATION

> Since morning there has been
> Some kind of noise in his ears.
> Is he lost in memory? and why
> Are all his thoughts about the sea?
> —Pasternak, "Separation"

As Zhivago writes of Lara, her image departs further and further from its "archetype," signaling, as I have argued, that Zhivago's identification with her also fades. This lost identification is the fate of Zhivago's unconscious desire to re-create a maternal metaphor of ego security. Zhivago repeatedly attempts to fuse his identity in such metaphors to maternal images created by his visual perception of nature and by certain boundary states of consciousness, dreams, delirium, and so forth. When examining Zhivago's poetry, one may for the most part leave these processes of his unconscious behind, and turn to the artifacts of language produced by them.

Zhivago manages to re-create in his poetry the ideal metaphoric fusions that are denied to him in his life. These fantasies of poetry do not eliminate his desire for security of self: the more his poetry departs from the "real" Lara, the deeper he slips into depression and insanity. But such failures are subsequently sublimated into mythic scenes of perfect identification, even when the poetry actually describes loss, as does the sixteenth poem of Zhivago's collection, "Separation." If there is a single poem in Zhivago's collection that crystallizes perfectly his perception of himself in relation to nature and to women, this is the one.

Many readers, it seems to me, mistakenly see "Hamlet," "The Garden of Gethsemane," or both, as the paradigmatic poems of identity in this cycle. These two poems, the first and last in the volume of poetry, link Zhivago's romantic self-perception to his apocalyptic view of history, and therefore synthesize subjective and objective dimensions of his experience. The individual is reintegrated into history. This synthesis and reintegration aim to blend Zhivago's perception of self and nature with the parts of the novel that at once apologize for, reject, and explain the Revolution in terms of an apocalyptic (Christian), deterministic view of history.

"Separation" symbolizes in a single event the departures that characterize much, if not all, of Zhivago's life: his repeated departures from the places and people he loves most. Along with "The Wedding," it is the last poem in Zhivago's notebook, and it serves as both a postscript to, and an idealization of, his relationship with Lara. As in his other crises of identity, Zhivago's meditations on his own identity in this poem also have the effect of reordering his relationship to the literary tradition. The main object of the poem's intertextuality is Pushkin's "To the Sea," itself a highly reflexive poem thematizing Pushkin's Southern exile and self-conscious break with the aesthetics of Byronic romanticism.[42]

My interpretation of "Separation" will focus on two aspects of the poem: its function as a screen for Zhivago's identification of himself in his relationship with Lara, and its reordering of the Pushkinian themes of departure, exile, and evolution of aesthetic orientation.

16. Разлука

С порога смотрит человек,
Не узнавая дома.
Ее отъезд был как побег,
Везде следы разгрома.

Повсюду в комнатах хаос.
Он меры разоренья
Не замечает из-за слез
И приступа мигрени.

В ушах с утра какой-то шум.
Он в памяти иль грезит?
И почему ему на ум
Все мысль о море лезет?

Когда сквозь иней на окне
Не видно света Божья,
Безвыходность тоски вдвойне
С пустыней моря схожа.

Она была так дорога
Ему чертой любою,
Как морю близки берега
Всей линией прибоя.

Как затопляет камыши
Волненье после шторма,
Ушли на дно его души
Ее черты и формы.

В года мытарств, во времена
Несмыслимого быта
Она волной судьбы со дна
Была к нему прибита.

Среди препятствий без числа,
Опасности минуя,
Волна несла ее, несла
И пригнала вплотную.

И вот теперь ее отъезд,
Насильственный, быть может.
Разлука их обоих съест,
Тоска с костями сгложет.

И человек глядит кругом:
Она в момент ухода
Все выворотила вверх дном
Из ящиков комода.

Он бродит, и до темноты
Укладывает в ящик

Раскиданные лоскуты
И выкройки образчик.

И, наколовшись об шитье
С невынутой иголкой,
Внезапно видит всю ее
И плачет втихомолку.

16. Separation

A man looks from the threshold,
Not recognizing his home.
Her departure was like a flight,
Traces of havoc are everywhere.

Chaos is all about the rooms.
He does not notice through his tears
And bout of migraine
The degree of the destruction.

Since morning there has been
Some kind of noise in his ears.
Is he lost in memory? and why
Are all his thoughts about the sea?

When through the window's frost
God's light cannot be seen,
The inescapableness of anguish
Is doubly like the desert of the sea.

Every line of her
Was so dear to him,
As shores, their surf in ranks,
Are near to the sea.

As water's roughness floods
The reeds after a storm,
Her lines and forms
Went into the depths of his soul.

In the years of trial, the times
Of unthinkable ordeal
By a wave of fate from the depths
She was cast up to him.

Amidst innumerable obstacles,
Escaping danger,
The wave carried her, carried her
And drove her close.

And now her departure,
Forced, perhaps.
Separation will devour them both,
The anguish gnaw their bones.

And the man looks around:
In the moment of leaving she
Turned everything upside down
From the dresser drawers.

He wanders, and 'til darkness
Puts back into the drawer
Scattered rags
And sample patterns of cloth.

And, pricking himself on a needle
Left in the sewing,
He suddenly sees all of her
And cries without a word.[43]

In many ways this poem resembles the lyrical prose passages of the novel. To start, there is a familiar tripartite temporal movement in the poem—present, past, present—creating three groups of four stanzas each: "A man looks" (С порога смотрит человек; stanza 1), "Every line of her / Was" (Она была так дорога; stanza 5), "And now her departure" (и вот теперь ее отьезд; stanza 9). The hero's basic passivity is underscored by the choice of verbs in the poem. Verbs describing his unnegated actions appear only six times in the poem, and five of these are in the last three stanzas: "looks" (смотрит; stanza 1), "looks" (глядит; stanza 10), "wanders" (бродит; stanza 11), "puts back" (укладывает; stanza 11), "sees" (видит; stanza 12), and "cries" (плачет; stanza 12). Moreover, three of these five verbs are associated with vision, recalling Zhivago's multiple visual metaphors of identity from the prose part of the novel.

"Separation" has as its overarching theme the inability to recognize the patterns collecting life into a meaningful whole. The man looks, "not recognizing his home" (Не узнавая дома), he "does not notice" (Не замечает) the chaos, "God's light cannot be seen" (Не видно света Божья), and he hears, not his name or a woman's voice, as one would expect from the prose, but "some sort of noise" (какой-то шум). In this theme of loss of recognition the poem traverses the line between being and nonbeing, identity and loss of identity.

Boundaries, lines, and patterns are therefore especially important images: the man "looks from the threshold" (смотрит с порога), compares the lines/traits (черты) of his lover to "all the lines of nearby shores" (близки берега/ всей линией), and picks up "scattered rags and sample patterns of cloth" (Раскиданные лоскуты/ И выкройки образчик). Likewise, the sea and its waves (in stanza 4) present an image of boundless pattern with no closure, an inescapable/hopeless desert: "the inescapableness of anguish / Is doubly like the desert of the sea" (Безвыходность тоски вдвойне / С пустыней моря схожа). Imposing a recognizable pattern of selfhood on experience is the unachievable goal of the poem, and it cannot be accomplished by a romantic projection of self onto passive nature. The frost on the windowpane of stanza 4 traps the poet, as it were, inside a boundless space, whence he can neither see nor project any image of himself.

In order to regain his identity he must give himself over to memory, to the irrationality of the imprint his lover has made on his soul, and ultimately to fate. At the center of the poem, in stanzas 6 and 7, is a record of this mnemonic process. Stanza 6 recalls how her image was impressed upon his soul: "Her lines and forms / went into the depths of his soul" (Ушли на дно его души / Ее черты и формы). The comparison Zhivago makes between this figure in his soul and the flooding of the reeds recalls a tragic sense of human rationality in the face of nature.

Two important allusions are concealed in the first term of the simile: "As water's roughness floods / The reeds after a storm" (как затопляет камыши / волненье после шторма). The first allusion is to Pascal and, in particular, to his image of man as a "thinking reed," an image that has had great resonance in (romantic) poetry. The rhyme between "reeds" and "soul" (камыши/ души) in the first and third lines of the stanza suggest that Zhivago also has in mind Pascal's famous statement: "The heart has reasons that reason does not know." The second allusion is of the same tenor as the first, and collects the themes of the tragic, insanity, and the sea. Leaving aside Pushkin for the moment, one might say that Zhivago also echoes some of the memorable lines of King Lear at the stormy heath: "When the mind's free / The body's delicate; the tempest in my mind / Doth from my senses take all feeling else / Save what beats there" (act 3, scene 4).[44] This nakedness of mind and body, save for the heart, characterizes well the emotional state of the man in the poem, who, after the trauma of his lover's departure, must acquiesce to the tragic fate of his life, before she will be returned to him.

Stanza 7 describes just such an acquiescence and is emblematic of the entire poem. In "times / Of unthinkable ordeal" (во времена/ Несмыслимого быта) she is returned to him by "fate" (судьба). One notes in the Russian of this stanza the pointed lack of agency, the placement of the short-form passive participle at the very end of the stanza, and the presence of the hero as merely an indirect object: "By a wave of fate from the depths / She was cast up to him" (Она волной судьбы со дна/ Была к нему прибита). The hero of the poem has no active role whatsoever in her return; or, rather, his role is to let the water of memory wash over him like the flood that washes over the reeds.

An "active reason" versus "passive memory" dichotomy runs throughout the poem. Even at the end, when he is picking up the pieces of cloth strewn about the room by her, the hero fails to make the metonymic connection between the cloth and the woman. The imprint she has left on his soul is visual and metaphoric. Thus when he pricks his finger on the sewing needle, he "suddenly sees all of her" (Внезапно видит всю ее) without any intermediate ratiocination. Given the series of verbs that detail looking and the failure to recognize, one might characterize this "suddenly" in the poem as an 'aha!' experience, that moment when a pattern, picture, or puzzle becomes clear, where before no image was perceivable. The verbs of perception in the poem tell the reader that he looks, does not recognize, does not notice, looks, and finally *sees* (видит).

He sees "all of her" (всю ее), an integral image derived from the past tense of the poem (stanzas 5–8), in a moment of recognition that commingles physical pain and memory. This last line of the poem is thus cathartic; it reintegrates action with emotion and bodily sensation, when before there was only inaction or failure to act in conjunction with emotion and pain, as, for example, when "He does not notice through his tears / And bout of migraine / The degree of the destruction" (Он меры разоренья/ Не замечает из-за слез/ И приступа мигрени). This cathartic reintegration of self in the last line of the poem stands in opposition to the disintegration of identity in the previous stanzas, signified primarily by the Russian prefix for "division into parts," раз- (разлука, разгром, разоренье, разлука, раскиданные). The whole poem thus follows the movement of stanzas 6 and, especially, 7. In the face of "unthinkable ordeal" the image of the woman who has left him returns. Her form is inscribed upon his soul, giving shape to his own identity when all he perceives within himself is an inescapable desert of waves upon the sea.

Recognition, reintegration of self, and the return of the lover are all the oxymoronic consequences of a poem that purports to be about departure, loss, and disorientation. The first third of the poem depicts departure, loss, and disorientation, and the last third of the poem leads to the former triad of recognition, reintegration of self, and the return of the lover. What stands between the transition from one set of circumstances to the other are stanzas 5 through 8, and, specifically, the predominant image of the sea in these four stanzas. The sea somehow mediates the poem's movement from departure to return, and this centrality of the sea in the journey of selfhood from loss to recovery is what recalls Pushkin's famous apostrophic poem, "To the Sea."

"Separation" is not only a farewell to Lara, it is also Zhivago's farewell to Varykino, a place of self-imposed exile twice within the novel. Thus, aside from their mutual images of the sea (there are, of course, innumerable lyrics about the sea), "Separation" shares with Pushkin's "To the Sea" the function of coda to a discrete period of the poet's life: for Pushkin it is the end of his Southern exile. And for Zhivago Varykino has special associations with Pushkin. He, Tonia, and Alexander Alexandrovich go on reading and rereading Pushkin at Varykino (part 9). Zhivago writes in his notebook of Pushkin's lyrics: "How much depended on his choice of meter!" (281). The simplicity of the iambic rhythm in "Separation" (alternating four and three foot lines of a ballad) and certain other poems of Zhivago's ("Winter Night," for example) bears undoubted affinity with Pushkin's verse (and Blok's). And Zhivago's "exile" rings, in some ways, of the romantic trope of creating one's own world, like "Robinson Crusoe," as he writes in his notebook (275). One suspects, finally, that he has dreams of matching Pushkin's poetic productivity during his own exile.

Stephanie Sandler has written of "To the Sea" that the "farewell that is the poem's subject is diminished in its effects by the poem's own rhetoric."[45] The poem announces itself as a temporal break in the poet's life: "Goodbye, free element" (Прощай, свободная стихия!). But in fact by lingering over the moment of departure in memory and in poetry, Pushkin actually forestalls any such break. And the poem is the "poetic flight" (Мой поэтический побег) written in place of any actual flight from exile. "To the Sea" largely functions as an act of poetic self-definition for Pushkin. He addresses the sea as, "Desired limit to my soul" (Моей души предел желанный!). And in the last stanza, the poet vows to carry away within him the image of the sea: "I, filled with you, will bear / Your crags, your coves, / And glitter and shadow and murmuring waves" (Перенесу, тобою полн, / Твои скалы, твои заливы, / И блеск, и тень, и говор волн).[46] As memory, metaphor, and poem, then, the sea and exile are incorporated into Pushkin's identity.

Both Pushkin's "To the Sea" and Pasternak's "Separation" communicate the poet's desire to follow in poetry and memory the "flight" that cannot be made in real life. "Her departure was like a flight" (Ее отъезд был как побег), Zhivago writes in the first stanza, "Forced, perhaps" (Насильственный, быть может), he adds in the ninth, for Zhivago tricks Lara into leaving Varykino with Komarovsky when he himself will not. Both poems undermine the romantic cliché of freedom the sea offers. Lara's flight is "forced," and Pushkin reconsiders his decision, "What is there to regret? Where could / I have made an untroubled path?" (О чем жалеть? Куда бы ныне / Я путь беспечный устремил?). Except for the image of Lara, in fact, Zhivago's poem sees a "desert" of inescapable anguish in the sea, and thus a metaphor of identity that can only continue to torment him.

If the sea provides a worthy means for the consideration of self-identification in exile, so too does it offer room for reevaluating one's literary identity, one's position in relation to the horizon of literary tradition. The "one object" (один предмет) in the sea's desert that strikes Pushkin is the image of Napoleon and, after him though not named, Byron. Both men, but especially Byron, are identified specifically with the sea. Thus Pushkin's farewell "To the Sea" is often read as his farewell to the romanticism that characterized his Southern poems, though, as Sandler has suggested, it is a prolonged and somewhat subverted farewell.

In "Separation" Zhivago parts ways with Lara, Varykino, and the romantic poetry of nature which has heretofore sustained him, and which he associates in a complex way with Pushkin, Pascal, and Shakespeare, not to mention other Russian poets of "Separation," such as Batiushkov, Baratynsky, Akhmatova, and Tsvetaeva. The last lines of the poem, the reintegration of self with the image of the man's lost lover, also intimate the poet's reduction to verbal silence. The sea's waves which once brought her to him, and do so again in the memory-wrought catharsis of the last lines, ultimately silence the poet's speech: he "cries without a word [quietly, silently]" (плачет втихомолку). If one takes into account the metaphoric experiences of nature from the novel's prose, the "sounds" of Zhivago's identity are reduced from hearing his name, to hearing "noise," to hearing/speaking nothing.[47]

This silence is what ends the final verse, suggesting that the "separation" *enacts* an aesthetic devastation much worse than the emotional one *depicted* by the poem. And in fact we know from the novel's conclusion that after leaving Varykino Zhivago no longer writes about nature with any genuine inspiration—he publishes several booklets on various topics, including his views on medicine, evolution, biology, as well as stories and poems on the countryside. When Zhivago does begin to write with renewed vigor, just before his death, he writes entirely about the city (481).

Pasternak tells the reader at the opening of the conclusion that Zhivago is more or less dead after he leaves Varykino. "It remains to tell the brief story of the last eight or ten years of Zhivago's life, during which he went more and more to seed, gradually losing his knowledge and skill as a doctor and a writer" (459). In a certain sense, then, "Separation," as the last poem of Varykino, is Zhivago's epitaph, sharing with "August" especially, but also with "The Garden of Gethsemane," the themes of preparation and resignation before death.

The "death" of "Separation" completes a cycle in Zhivago's aesthetic being as well, for his metaphoric identification with nature is as much a poetic strategy as it is a psychological one. As the protagonist of the poem "cries quietly," one cannot help but think that the novel, which began with a bang of thunder and Yura's burst of tears, is ending in a sort of failure, a whimper from the man in the poem who never achieves a secure means of self-identification in the figures he creates.

THE "INNER" AUTHOR

I have tried to show specifically how the novel is infused with Zhivago's metaphoric vision whenever the narrative takes an auto-referential turn. In this process of creative self-reflection, Zhivago's childhood is literally and imaginatively constitutive of his adult identity; like other characters, he is profoundly shaped by the disrupted structure of his family, and in his aesthetic perception of the world, the loss of Maria Nikolaevna plays a formative if not key role.

It would seem that Pasternak's conceptualization of authorship in *Doctor Zhivago* could not be more different from the one crafted by Bulgakov in *The Master and Margarita*. In Bulgakov's novel, the author's relation to discourse forms the basis of selfhood, though more than one type of discourse was found to operate at any given moment. The Master lacks a past that could sustain his identity as it is challenged by interpretations of his novel, which is to a certain extent his only means of self-representation. In *The Master and Margarita* personal history is not nearly so important as literary history, with which the novel establishes a rich and complex relationship. In *Doctor Zhivago* it is more important to know the past of Zhivago's life than it is to know the literary past that forms the interpretive background for the novel.

For both novels authorship is defined in certain *mises en abyme* as a triangular relationship to the literary tradition and to the self. In *The Master and Margarita,* one side of that triangle, where auto-reflexive passages address literary tradition, is more prominent than in *Doctor Zhivago,* where describing the author's retrieval of self from childhood is clearly more important. In *The Gift,* by contrast, Nabokov turns in equal measure to the literary and personal histories that shape Fyodor's authorial identity. Thus, however different *Doctor Zhivago* may seem in comparison with *The Master and Margarita* (or with *The Gift,* for that matter), it shares with both works a common strategy of redefining authorship. All three novels fuse authorship, literary history, and selfhood in a way that distinguishes them from other works of the same period.

Nevertheless, I would not push the similarity among these three novels too far. What separates *Doctor Zhivago* from other novels is Pasternak's portrayal of how deeply forms of language may sink into the poet's very being, rendering him utterly unique but simultaneously blind to the forces which move him. This conflict may in the end be responsible for Zhivago's poetry. As Richard Wilbur has said, "One does not use poetry for its main purposes, as a means of organizing oneself and the world, until one's world somehow gets out of hand."[48]

Chapter Three

Vladimir Nabokov's *The Gift*

> But one's own truth is not to blame if it coincides
> with the truth some poor fellow has borrowed.
> —Nabokov, *The Gift*

NABOKOV WOULD NO DOUBT have been annoyed
by my placement of his Russian masterpiece, *The Gift*,[1] adjacent to what he
called "Pasternak's melodramatic and vilely written *Zhivago*."[2] As Mayakovsky complained in his poem *Anniversary* of Nadson, Nabokov might also have
objected that in the alphabet of Russian literary monuments Pasternak stands
between him and Pushkin. Nonetheless, there is much that connects *The
Gift* to *Doctor Zhivago*, and to *The Master and Margarita*. These three novels establish a triangular concept of authorship, in which the auto-reflexive
device of the *mise en abyme* relates the author's vision of selfhood to his
modernist reordering of the literary tradition. Nowhere is this tripartite strategy more in evidence than in Nabokov's *The Gift*.

If the *mise en abyme* is the apex in a triangle of authorship, literary
tradition forms one of the two remaining vertices; and the part played by
literary tradition in *The Gift* has been widely recognized.[3] Nabokov writes
in his foreword to the English translation: "It is the last novel I wrote, or
ever shall write, in Russian. Its heroine is not Zina, but Russian Literature."
The particular beauty of Nabokov's heroine, Russian Literature, betrays the
eye of its beholder, of course. Dostoevsky, for example, does not fit into the
literary canon described by *The Gift*.

An implicit or explicit view of selfhood forms the second vertex in this
triangle of authorship. Selfhood in *The Gift* relies neither upon discourse,
as in *The Master and Margarita*, nor upon metaphor, as in *Doctor Zhivago;*
but Nabokov's view of the self is related to both. Fyodor's articulation of his
identity in *The Gift* is a function of his (metaphoric) "location" relative to
the underlying sources of his valuative judgment. In other words, Fyodor
creates a topography of self in the novel by charting the distance that separates him from Russia, from his childhood, and from his family, especially
his father. It is hardly surprising that identity occupies a central position in
The Gift, since the novel is more or less autobiographical and contains at
least two extensive biographies within it.

My assertion that the novel contains various *mises en abyme* which reorder the Russian literary tradition will probably raise no serious objections. Nabokov's wide-ranging use of metafiction and his desire to define and preserve Russia's literary heritage have been well documented by scholarly criticism.[4] Consequently, this chapter examines several passages in *The Gift* that are familiar in Nabokov criticism. My claim to originality lies in my local interpretations of those passages, in my explication of self-presentation in the novel, and in my particular relation of *The Gift* to *The Master and Margarita* and to *Doctor Zhivago*.

THE STRUCTURAL SELF:
GEOMETRY VERSUS GEOGRAPHY

> My personal I, the one that wrote books, the one that
> loved words, colors, mental fireworks, Russia, chocolate
> and Zina—had somehow disintegrated and dissolved . . .
> One might dissolve completely that way.
>
> —Nabokov, *The Gift*

In the previous two chapters on *The Master and Margarita* and *Doctor Zhivago,* I attempted to discover the critical idiom best suited to each novel's portrayal of selfhood. In Bulgakov's novel, discourse proved the best match; in *Doctor Zhivago* it was the figurative language of metaphor and metonym. The playful, highly metafictional style of Nabokov defies easy categorization, however, and many critics have chosen either to keep close to the structural boundaries of the novel in their analyses of its hero or to see *through* Fyodor, as it were, and identify Nabokov himself in his hero. In both cases, it is as if Fyodor "had somehow disintegrated and dissolved" into the critical background, leaving only Nabokov and his narrative strategies.

As I see it, the great danger is that while reading Nabokov, one is tempted to try to match wits with him, to play his game and, if not beat him at it, at least make a good showing. His novels overflow with riddles, puzzles, word plays, tricks, and illusions that draw the reader into a narrative maze which may or may not reveal an exit. Most notably, Nabokov has suggested chess problems and mimicry as keys for unlocking his complex narrative strategies. *The Defense* provides the clearest example of the chess analogy, but even in *The Gift* Fyodor initially derives his idea for the *Life of Chernyshevsky* from an article he has read entitled "Chernyshevsky and Chess." And later in the novel it is explicitly suggested that *The Gift* itself is based on a "chess idea" (шахматная идея; 327).[5]

In a certain sense, then, the novel contains an invitation to be read as a puzzle, riddle, or problem, and the author intimates that within the closed system of the book there may be a single interpretive solution. Linda Hutcheon terms such invitations, which reach out to the reader beyond any closed system of the novel, part of "the metafictional paradox."[6] A solution is buried within the hermetic structure of the book, but the active participation of a reader is required to unearth it. Nabokov's introduction to the English translation of *The Gift*, for example, contains a characteristically cryptic note: "I wonder how far the imagination of the reader will follow the young lovers after they have been dismissed." The trick here is on careless readers and on Fyodor and Zina. What Fyodor and Zina do not know at the end of the novel is that their plans for an evening of bliss will be thwarted because neither is carrying a set of apartment keys.

Because Nabokov emphasizes the riddle within the novel—not just in the previous local example but also more globally—his interpreters have rightly derived numerous solutions or metaphors that reveal the secret of the novel's structure. Leona Toker aptly entitles her study of Nabokov *The Mystery of Literary Structures*. There truly is a sound textual basis in *The Gift* to initiate this search for a secret structure. In an oft-quoted phrase, Fyodor says that "the most enchanting things in nature and art are based on deception" (364), thereby throwing down the gauntlet to would-be critics: interpret at your own risk, but don't be fooled. Such metafictional taunts and teases have long been a sidelight of Nabokov criticism, occasionally short-changing, in the case of *The Gift*, the importance of the hero and his desire for a degree of self-understanding that will equal his literary skill.

The Gift is full of provocative figures that are suggestive of narrative structure. Most of these figures refer, strictly speaking, to Fyodor's shorter works, but they also seem to characterize the entire novel. For example, Fyodor's poems are models of his future novels (71) and, in a more anthropomorphic turn, they have "the flesh of poetry and the specter of translucent prose" (9). The story of Yasha Chernyshevsky and his friends forms a triangle inscribed within a circle (42); the biography of Chernyshevsky is a "spiral within a sonnet" (English introduction), an apple in one peel (200), an endless ring (204), and, following Chernyshevsky's own plan, a perpetual motion machine (217). Fyodor himself characterizes the intention of his future novel as "beyond the barricades . . . infinity, where all, all lines meet" (329). The problem here is simple: *all* of these metaphors could be used to describe the narrative structure of *The Gift*. Which metaphor, if any, unlocks the secret of the novel is an entirely different question.

Critics have been especially quick to note the recurrent imagery of infinity in the novel: one work gives birth to another, which leads to another, and so forth. This tendency toward infinity appears most vividly in the surprise ending of *The Gift*, where the reader learns of Fyodor's plans to write an autobiographical novel, complete with examples of his previous literary work and structured on the chess moves of fate that brought him together with Zina. This future novel is undoubtedly meant to resemble *The Gift* itself: thus *The Gift* tells the story of how Fyodor comes to write *The Gift*.

The figures of narrative structure suggested within *The Gift* have engendered many critical metaphors outside it to match them. To give a few examples, the novel has been compared to a Möbius strip,[7] a Russian *matryoshka* doll,[8] a series of keys,[9] a spiral,[10] a circle (most critics mention this one), a chess problem,[11] a double fugue,[12] and a "mosaic whose every tile is a perfect cameo."[13] In my opinion, the best of these metaphors fuse the concept of structural repetition and reflexivity with the complex progression of the novel's ideas—they give a geometry to Nabokov's "theme and variations." The image of a spiral, for example, accounts for that sort of narrative "fusion" and has additional resonance for modern literature, though I do not think Nabokov's novel finds any special complement in Yeats's portentous "widening gyre."

This wide range of critical metaphors reflects first and foremost the highly metafictional nature of *The Gift:* the novel is thick with auto-referential narrative emblems, which I have been referring to as *mises en abyme*.[14] In much the same way as the Master's novel and Zhivago's collection of poems serve as *mises en abyme* for *The Master and Margarita* and *Doctor Zhivago*, so too do Fyodor's *Verses*, the story of Yasha, his biography of his father, and his *Life of Chernyshevsky* serve as *mises en abyme* for *The Gift*. The easiest example to adduce is the *Life of Chernyshevsky*. The "apocryphal sonnet" that caps either end of that work, that leads the reader from the beginning of the sonnet (given at the end of the biography) to the end of the sonnet (given at the beginning of the biography), requires a circular reading path. Likewise, the end of *The Gift*, which announces that Fyodor will write a novel similar to *The Gift*, carries the reader back to the novel's beginning, now seen as the result of Fyodor's literary plans.[15]

The Gift is about the writing of *The Gift*, which is about the writing of *The Gift* . . . The infinite regression and potential duplication thus initiated is another kind of *mise en abyme*, one not encountered in either *The Master and Margarita* or *Doctor Zhivago*. *The Master and Margarita* does not turn out in the end to be the Master's novel: there are analogies one can draw between the two works, but the former does not duplicate the latter. *The Gift*, on the contrary, may in fact duplicate the novel Fyodor plans to write. Thus there are two kinds of *mises en abyme* in Nabokov's novel: the first (the *Life of Chernyshevsky*, for example) *resembles* the entire novel in important ways, the second (*The Gift* itself) perhaps *duplicates* the entire novel and initiates a regress when the reader attempts to determine the novel's origin. Following Dällenbach's terminology, I have referred to the former as a *mise en abyme* of the utterance, and to the latter as a *mise en abyme* of the enunciation of the narrative.

The critical metaphors of the circle, the Möbius strip, the *matryoshka* doll, and the mosaic of cameos all capture well the duplicative sense of the enunciative *mise en abyme*. The metaphors of the spiral, the fugue, and the mosaic, however, identify an additional important feature of that *mise en abyme* as it actually appears in *The Gift*—its probable deception. The novel that Fyodor at first proposes to write sounds as if it will be identical with the novel the reader is just completing, but Zina objects to this patent verisimilitude:

> "Yes, but that will result in an autobiography with mass executions of good acquaintances."
> "Well, let's suppose that I so shuffle, twist, mix, rechew and rebelch everything, add such spices of my own and impregnate things so much with myself that nothing remains of the autobiography but dust—the kind of dust, of course, which makes the most orange of skies." (364)

If Fyodor has really shuffled, twisted, and mixed the elements of his life in composing *The Gift*, then the reader stands on yet another slippery slope.

This potential deformation of "the facts" creates an obvious paradox. Fyodor's future novel, which one assumes is *The Gift* itself, might so shuffle the facts that the novel is no longer a true record of his inspiration. This prospect suggests to the reader in retrospect that perhaps Fyodor's comment, not to mention his entire treatment of fate, may be an artifact of the literary structure he has built into *The Gift*. Therefore, the novel does not necessarily present a case of infinite duplication, it presents the possibility of such duplication. Criticism relying on metaphors that describe infinite duplication alone—the circle, the Möbius strip, and perhaps the *matryoshka* as well—do not fully account for the deception that Fyodor may be employing in his narrative.

On a second reading of the novel, the reader recognizes immediately traces of Fyodor's authorial hand. The narrator frequently switches between the first and the third person, for example, though the focus of the narrative remains on the character of Fyodor. The "chess moves" of fate that Fyodor has promised to describe in his future novel are also now readily apparent to the reader, as when Fyodor fortuitously avoids the soirées of Romanov and the Lorentzes, where he would have met Zina. The most telling effect of Fyodor's authorship of *The Gift* may be the way he "remembers" his future works: "It's queer, I seem to remember my future works, although I don't even know what they will be about. I'll recall them completely and write them" (194). These memories may simply demonstrate Fyodor's aesthetic predilection for the important role of fate in life and art. Given all the metafictional traces of Fyodor's authorship of *The Gift*, however, might not his plans for a future novel also be part of the artistic role he has designed for fate to play in his life?

If this dilemma holds true, then the circular paradoxes of the metafiction and *mises en abyme* in the novel seem inescapable. Vladimir Alexandrov, for one, resolves them by drawing a distinct connection between Fyodor and Nabokov:

These parallels between Fyodor and Nabokov are crucial for understanding *The Gift* because they point to a way out of its circular narrative structure . . . Fyodor's pronouncements thus leave open the possibility that everything in the text (and at a minimum, an important dimension of it) is an aspect of his artistic design, rather than a record of actual, lived experience. His forefeeling "future works" could thus be taken as his granting his fictionalized self intuitions regarding his later, authorial self, presumably for the sake of underscoring the metaliterary nature of his interests. By the same token, all forms of patterning in the text could also be read as Fyodor's artistic design meant to underscore the fictionality of his story. What militates against both these interpretations, however, and in favor of the view that Fyodor has quasi-Platonic intuitions regarding his art and life, is precisely that Nabokov does as well.[16]

Alexandrov states in the first line of his study of Nabokov's "otherworld" (потусторонность): "the aim of this book is to dismantle the widespread critical view that Vladimir Nabokov is first and foremost a metaliterary writer, and to suggest instead that an aesthetic rooted in his intuition of a transcendent realm is the basis of his art."[17] If Nabokov is not "first and foremost" a metaliterary writer, however, how does one explain the metaliterary strategies in *The Gift* that have nothing to do with Fyodor's quasi-Platonism? Moreover, a novel in which the parallels between author and hero are repeatedly emphasized is (by definition) constructed on a profoundly metaliterary basis. Rather than "dismantling" the view of Nabokov's metafiction, Alexandrov in this one respect seems to extend it.

By focusing on the project of self-presentation that motivates much of Fyodor's use of metafictional *mises en abyme* in *The Gift*, I will attempt to strike a balance between Alexandrov's dismissal of the centrality of Nabokov's metafiction and criticism that sees only formal play in the novel.[18]

One need not draw a direct parallel with Nabokov himself in order to see Fyodor's authorial activity as a project of self-discovery. Fyodor's metafictional digressions map an orientation toward the Russian literary tradition that informs his own sense of self as an author, émigré, and moral agent in an increasingly hostile environment. By describing elements of *The Gift* in terms of topography, one reintroduces subjectivity as a constitutive element of the novel's structure. Circles, spirals, Möbius strips, and other geometrical figures exclude the purposefulness, the heuristic value, that *The Gift* has for Fyodor, which is that he is writing for some *personal* rather than metaliterary reason.

In *The Gift*, Nabokov uses topography as a metaphor both for one's orientation toward the shape of one's own life and for an author's orientation toward the horizon of literary tradition. This intersection between self and tradition is the identifying feature of the *mise en abyme* as I have been discussing it, and thus topographical orientation will be the thematic or psychological counterpart to my discussion of the structural device of the *mise en abyme* in *The Gift*.

In *Sources of the Self,* Charles Taylor discusses two different aspects of topographical orientation in order to illustrate the necessity of evaluative frameworks in modern articulations of self. His illustration is fitting for my discussion of Nabokov, so I will quote Taylor at length:

> Orientation has two aspects; there are two ways that we can fail to have it. I can be ignorant of the lie of the land around me—not know the important locations which make it up or how they relate to each other. This ignorance can be cured by a good map. But then I can be lost in another way if I don't know how to place myself on this map. If I am a traveler from abroad and I ask where Mont Tremblant is, you don't help me by taking me blindfolded up in a plane, then ripping the blindfold off and shouting, "There it is!" as we over-fly the wooded hill. I know now (if I trust you) that I'm at Mont Tremblant. But in a meaningful sense, I don't know where I am because I can't place Tremblant in relation to other places in the known world.
>
> In contrast, a native of the region might get lost on a trek in Mont Tremblant Park. She presumably knows well how the mountain relates to the Rivière Diable, St. Jovite, Lac Carré. But she has ceased to be able to place herself in this well-known terrain as she stumbles around the unfamiliar forest. The traveler in the plane has a good description of where he is but lacks the map which would give it an orienting sense for him; the trekker has the map but lacks the knowledge of where she is on it.[19]

Taylor speaks of two kinds of lack of orientation. In the first case a man knows where he is at present, but not where he stands in relation to the rest of the known world. Fyodor finds himself in an analogous situation early in the novel after he has published his book of verse dedicated to the theme of childhood. Not only a familiar area of self-analysis but also a well-worn literary topic, childhood in Fyodor's poems emphasizes the discombobulating distance between his present life and land and his former life and land. Only with great difficulty can Fyodor justify/establish the relation of his collection of poems to émigré life and the contemporary literary milieu—his "fame," as he notes at a literary meeting, is still split between the recognition he derives from his authorship and the recognition he warrants as the son of a famous explorer. He may have located a distinctive authorial self in his poems, but he has failed to make it meaningful in his present life. Thus his sense of "disorientation" is not remedied by his authorial activity.

As an example of the second kind of lack of orientation, Taylor depicts a woman who knows the landmarks of the region well but does not know at present her position in relation to those landmarks. Fyodor's failure to complete the book on his father may be likened to this second sort of loss of orientation. Fyodor schools himself well in both the literary and biographical "landmarks" that surround his father's life. His (re)reading of Pushkin and investigation of his father's life provides ample material with which he can begin to place himself—as an author in relation to the central figure in the modern Russian literary tradition and as a son in relation to his father. He loses his way in reference to both and fails to finish his biographical work, partly because he has not yet found his place in the literary tradition (he has overlooked the sociocritical aspect of the Russian tradition), and partly because his continued belief that his father still lives prevents him from obtaining either personal or aesthetic closure. In his biography of his father, Fyodor approaches the problem of selfhood from the other side, so to speak, but he still fails to arrive at a solution.

To be sure, such bald assertions that topographical orientation plays a form-shaping role in *The Gift* can be only of limited value without more complete textual evidence. I would like, therefore, to consider briefly spatiality and plot in the novel before turning to the topography of self, literary tradition, and their intersection in two passages that are emblematic of Fyodor's imaginative process: in his first imaginary conversation with Koncheev and in his biography of his father. I mean to emphasize the necessity of considering the subjective activity of the author in otherwise "sterile" metaliterary play. Metafictional means do not necessarily entail metafictional ends. As Fyodor often reminds the reader, there is not just a sum of devices but a *particular author* behind the text, "the one that wrote books, the one that loved words, colors, mental fireworks, Russia, chocolate and Zina."

Critics have been more or less aware of topography as a metaphor of selfhood in Nabokov's entire oeuvre. Alexandrov treats Vivian Bloodmark/ Vladimir Nabokov's concept of "cosmic synchronization" somewhat similarly, though he is more interested in its "otherworldly" aspects.[20] Consider the first sentence of Nabokov's 1966 foreword to *Speak, Memory*: "The present work is a systematically correlated assemblage of personal recollections ranging geographically from St. Petersburg to St. Nazaire, and covering thirty-seven years, from August 1903 to May 1940, with only a few sallies into later space-time."[21] A less systematic correlation between geography, personal history, and text is precisely what interests me in Fyodor's topography of self in *The Gift*.

IMAGINARY JOURNEYS

> For a long time he had wanted to express somehow that it
> was in his feet that he had the feeling of Russia, that he
> could touch and recognize all of her with his soles, as a
> blind man feels with his palms.
>
> —Nabokov, *The Gift*

The infinite regression of plot initiated by the surprise ending of *The Gift*—that Fyodor will write a novel that resembles *The Gift*—tempts one into thinking that Nabokov's object in employing this type of *mise en abyme* is to undermine conventional novelistic chronology. After all, that is a common strategy in modernist literature. Until the end of the novel, the chronology of the novel's plot more or less fits the simple description, ABC, where A is the beginning, B the middle, and C the end. The surprise conclusion jumbles this deceptive simplicity. Perhaps the chronological terms should now read CAB, since the novel we have just read may in fact emerge from Fyodor's idea to match the development of his literary gift with the chess moves of fate that brought him together with Zina.

That Nabokov drives a deep wedge between *fabula* ("story") and *siuzhet* ("plot") is nothing astonishing to readers familiar with his other novels: in *Pale Fire*, for example, such critical terms become so contorted as to be of little descriptive value. Yet what if it is a mistake to pay too much attention to these divisions of narrative time? Would one not be justified in transferring critical attention away from the novel's conception of narrative time toward its conception of space? Joseph Frank has long since pointed out the primacy of spatial form in modern fiction.[22] Critical metaphors that describe *The Gift* in terms of a structural, geometrical narrative construction *do* in fact make this shift from time to space, treating plot as shape rather than chronology. What they sometimes exclude is how the construction of the novel focuses on the shape of a life, not just on the shape of an artistic text.[23]

Nabokov is quick to dispose of hackneyed spatial metaphors of personal identity in *The Gift*. Following the thought of the apocryphal "French sage" Delalande, Alexander Chernyshevsky thinks to himself (in Fyodor's rendering of his deathbed thoughts):

> And then again: the unfortunate image of a "road" to which the human mind has become so accustomed (life as a kind of journey) is a stupid illusion: we are not going anywhere, we are sitting at home. The otherworld [загробное] surrounds us always and is not at all at the end of some pilgrimage. (310)

In the same way that simplistic chronological plotting is dispensed with in *The Gift*, so too are the common metaphors of a life undermined. "Life as a kind of journey" is the equivalent of a simplistic plot for one's life.[24]

The horizon against which one interprets one's own life shapes and is shaped by a distinct sense of being "at home." What connects Fyodor's perception of himself with his literary production is the way his imagination is stimulated by, and intimately connected to, his surroundings. The basic mechanism of this imaginative process is visible from early on in the novel. He wonders whether there might be a "law of composition," for example, in the sequence of Berlin street shops: "so that, having found the most frequent arrangement, one could deduce the average cycle (ритм) for the streets of a given city, for example: tobacco shop, pharmacy, greengrocer" (5). The distribution of shops may reveal a hidden poetry in the city, its own "rhythm" (ритм). Conversely, a younger Fyodor, like Nabokov, tirelessly used Andrey Bely's idiosyncratic method of charting geometrical, spatial patterns for Russian poems according to their distribution of half-stresses (151).[25]

Fyodor's tours through émigré Berlin have the quality of "wanderings" rather than journeys, and he himself is aware of how intimately, even physically, he feels his surroundings: "it was in his feet that he had the feeling of Russia, that he could touch and recognize all of her with his soles, as a blind man feels with his palms" (63). Fyodor expresses his sense of being "at home" through descriptions of tactile experience. And this association also works the other way around: his reveries about his past life transform the physical world around him, as when the Berlin avenue suddenly widens into a vision of his family estate at Leshino (85).

Topographical metaphors and images of physical position are thus, not surprisingly, intermingled with Fyodor's view of himself as an émigré— a half-resident, half-stranger who feels his own alienation in the city around him. "Home" becomes a psychological point of reference for Fyodor in *The Gift*. He says, "I emigrated seven years ago; this foreign land has by now lost its aura of abroadness just as my own has ceased to be a geographical habit" (17). Neither exotic nor habitual, emigration has little in common with a journey, the more so because one's destination so often turns into a new point of departure.

His moves in Berlin from one apartment to another have often struck readers as indicative of his shifts from one aesthetic paradigm to another. In a famous passage at the end of chapter 2, Fyodor reflects: "The distance from the old residence to the new was about the same as, somewhere in Russia, that from Pushkin Avenue to Gogol Street" (145). Here, the theme of being at home and Fyodor's reflections on his status as an émigré also come into play, and reveal more deliberately than in other passages the intertwining of selfhood and literary history in topographical analogy. Location itself means something for Fyodor's life and work: the places where he has written his poems, biographies, and, presumably, *The Gift* are not interchangeable.

Throughout the novel Fyodor keeps at the forefront of his mind the parallel world of Russia. At one point, for example, he announces his inevitable "return" to his homeland:

> It's easier for me, of course, than for another to live outside Russia, because I know for certain that I shall return—first because I took away the keys to her, and secondly because, no matter when, in a hundred, two hundred years—I shall live there in my books—or at least in some researcher's footnote. There; now you have a historical hope, a literary-historical one . . . (350)

81

Fyodor makes explicit in this passage his dual hopes for authorship: first, that through his books he will resolve the principal dilemma of his self-perception. Literary fame means a return to Russia, or at the very least a metaphorical return. Authorship signifies, second, a "literary-historical hope." *The Gift* and the works that lead up to it clear a space for Fyodor in literary history: he is the rightful heir to the tradition bequeathed by Pushkin, Gogol, and even Chernyshevsky.[26] That is one reason Fyodor claims he has the "keys" to Russia, an image also suggesting a solution that will unlock the novel's riddles.

Coming as it does near the end of the novel, Fyodor's statement represents a culmination of his literary activities throughout the novel: it foretells the rewards he will earn by his authorship of the poems, biographies, and *The Gift* itself. But here, too, Nabokov confronts the reader with a deceptive chronology. Fyodor's return from the journey of emigration and from literary history is deferred until the *future;* yet having already recognized that Fyodor has written *The Gift,* the reader experiences this future as an event in the *past.*[27] Unless provided with some alternative, readers face the prospect of the same paradoxical narrative regress—where is the genuine beginning of the novel? In order to avoid this regress, one may turn to the metaphors of topography in the novel.

Fyodor's first imaginary conversation with Koncheev is one of *The Gift*'s many remarkable passages. Nabokov/Fyodor sustains for several pages the narrative deception that Fyodor is indeed speaking with Koncheev, and only after the fact does the reader learn of the illusion. As they are about to part, Fyodor says to his imaginary interlocutor: "Whose business is it that actually we parted at the very first corner, and that I have been reciting a fictitious dialogue with myself as supplied by a self-teaching handbook of literary inspiration" (76). Two important facts about Fyodor's life and literature surface in this conversation. First, he is deeply concerned with literary schooling, which, for him, means knowledge of the literary tradition. The "self-teaching handbook" is not only for literary inspiration but also for literary history. His conversation with Koncheev relies on mutually comprehensible allusions to Goncharov, Pisemsky, Leskov, Tolstoy, Pushkin, Chekhov, Gogol, Turgenev, Dostoevsky, Aksakov, Lermontov, Tyutchev, Nekrasov, Fet, Balmont, Blok, Rimbaud, and perhaps others. It is this massive number of literary allusions that makes the conversation so amusingly pretentious.

Yet the second important point to draw from Fyodor's conversation supersedes his pretence, for his *imaginary* conversation with Koncheev is paradoxically more authentic or genuine than the drivel of the *real* literary meeting he has just attended. As Simon Karlinsky has noted, in less than four pages "writers and quotations are juggled with bewildering rapidity, but when the passage is finished, a relevant, if minor, point has been made about each of the writers mentioned."[28] In the literary meeting, on the contrary, few if any relevant points have been made.

The entire scene between Fyodor and Koncheev contains a sophisticated web of metaliterary interconnections and images: the topographical theme is represented by Fyodor's walk with Koncheev and metonymically related to the image of his toe-pinching new shoes, which the reader watches him purchase just a few short sentences after he has announced that he feels Russian "with his feet." The shoe-buying scene also initiates a number of poetical verses that Fyodor puzzles over throughout the waning day and that reemerge in his "handbook" exchange with Koncheev.[29] Lastly, Fyodor no doubt intends to echo parodically Pushkin's preoccupation with feet.[30]

After seeing the skeletal structure of his feet in an X-ray machine at the shoe store, Fyodor muses: "With this I'll step ashore. From Charon's ferry" (64). Later on, speaking with Koncheev, he confesses to his poetic preoccupation during the conversation:

> "Even at this moment I am happy, in spite of the degrading pain in my pinched toes. To tell the truth, I again feel that turbulence, that excitement. . . . Once again I shall spend the whole night . . ."
> "Show me. Let's see how it works: It is with *this,* that from the slow black ferry . . . No, try again: Through snow that falls on water never freezing . . . Keep trying: Under the vertical slow snow in gray-enjambment-Lethean weather, in the usual season, with *this* I'll step upon the shore some day. That's better but be careful not to squander the excitement." (75)

This passage is, of course, first a demonstration of the process of Fyodor's inspiration. The literary exercise may be taken from a handbook, and the conversation imagined, but Fyodor's poetical inspiration is genuine, even if the poetry is not first rate. The reality of the imaginary is a theme Fyodor returns to time after time in *The Gift,* as when *real* mountains are reflected in mirages of water in the desert (120), or when the charges against Chernyshevsky are "a phantom," but the phantom is of real guilt (270). Nevertheless, the reflexivity of Fyodor's inspiration is only part of what makes the passage important.

His conversation with Koncheev exemplifies, second, Fyodor's preoccupation with what it means to be Russian. The shoes, the walk, and the metaliterary conversation with Koncheev bring chapter 1 of *The Gift* to a close, and as Fyodor dwells on the theme of death in his verses he accentuates the end of the literary phase in which childhood and the Russia of his youth were his main literary foci. The toe-pinching shoes symbolize the constriction he feels as an émigré and as an author. It is thus not surprising that chapter 2 begins with a flight through time and space to Russia, only now not to the Russia of his youth so much as to the Russia of his father.

To allude once again to Taylor's description of orientation, it is clear from Fyodor's conversation with Koncheev that he knows "the map" of his cultural heritage, all those landmarks in the literary tradition, but he is not yet assured of his own location on that map. His immersion in the émigré literary milieu makes him uneasy about his fate as a Russian author. The time of his literary fame is constantly deferred: Koncheev has not in fact read his poems and no one has written a review of his collection. This deferral is also plainly indicated by a comment about his poems, which Fyodor attributes to Koncheev: "Actually, of course, they are but models of your future novels" (71). The significance of the poetry is not for "now" but for "later"—an age of poetry leads to an age of prose, a transition Pushkin and Nabokov himself made (and that Zhivago was also supposed to make). Even as Fyodor poetically conceives his personal transformation as a "crossing over" (onto Charon's ferry), he stumbles, for the river is not the Lethe but the Styx: he thus makes a faux pas in both senses of the phrase. It is also telling that Fyodor's magnificent imaginary conversation with Koncheev mostly relates his insecurity: he does not have the nerve to approach in reality the only (in his eyes) respectable author in Berlin.

Following closely after the scene with Koncheev, Fyodor's failed biography of his father serves to demonstrate, in spite of its failure, not only the development of Fyodor's literary "gift" but also his continued exploration of selfhood and literary tradition. The image of the father is a remarkable source of inspiration for Fyodor's authorial activity. Throughout the novel Fyodor seems to be seeking, as Monika Greenleaf puts it, "a scene of paternal legitimation."[31] Witnessing Alexander Chernyshevsky's grief, he imagines the story he will never write about Yasha; Fyodor later attempts to write a biography of his own father; his infamous *Life of Chernyshevsky* turns on the critic's role as forefather; and, as Brian Boyd has cogently argued, it is Fyodor's dream of his father that prepares him to write *The Gift*.[32] In spite of wide recognition of the significance of the paternal in the novel, however, not much exclusive attention has been devoted to Fyodor's biography of his father; yet this biography may be the ideological heart of the novel and the source of its creative ethos. Fyodor's biography of his father is more like *The Gift* than the Chernyshevsky chapter or any other interpolated text is, and may therefore have a special iconic resonance within the novel.

We know, of course, that personal as well as literary genealogy was important for Nabokov, as it is for Fyodor. *The Gift* is an autobiographical novel, and Nabokov deems the genre of the paternal biography important enough to rework in *Speak, Memory*. Both works interpolate a version of the father's life as it might read from an encyclopedia. Fyodor's fame as a writer is augmented by his fame as the son of a well-known explorer. His biography of his father unifies this dual aspect of his identity. Although discussions of the biography are often framed by its failure, psychologically the biography is clearly a success. One of the first things Fyodor's father mentions when he returns in Fyodor's dream is that he "was pleased . . . with his son's book about him" (355); he does not say anything, incidentally, about the Chernyshevsky book. Perhaps most important, Fyodor's biography of his father shares many significant features with the larger novel itself: both works are exquisitely multigeneric, disruptive, avoid closure, and highlight the fissures in seemingly complete structures.

Fyodor's biography serves to demonstrate not only the development of his literary gift but also his continued exploration of self and literary tradition. He wanted to accompany his father on his final expedition to Central Asia—his biography takes him on that journey. Most important for Fyodor, this imaginary journey attempts to provide the solution to his father's fate, to answer conclusively whether he is dead or alive. The uncharted territory between life and death serves as the impetus for Fyodor's writing the biography. As Boyd has suggested, the idea for the imaginary journey with his father may derive from Fyodor's friendship with Alexander Chernyshevsky, who has begun to see his dead son's ghost intruding on the real world. Instead of the father imagining his dead son, another son, Fyodor, starts to imagine his dead father's life.[33]

For the reader who has already completed the novel and is reading it a second time, it is apparent from the start that Fyodor may at first be unsatisfied with his account of his father's life. "Life as a kind of journey," one will recall, is an impoverished metaphor of selfhood in the novel (310). But it is precisely in terms of such a journey that Fyodor initially thinks of his father: "Thus had Fyodor, in spite of all logic and not daring to envision its realization, lived with the familiar dream of his father's return" (88). He imagines the conclusion of his father's journey, rather than the conclusion of his father's life. But he is unable to complete the biography. By discovering why he fails, one may unravel the reasons for his later success and for that later successful confluence of life, literary evolution, and narrative structure in the novel. Three facets of the failed biography are pertinent: the influence of Pushkin (which has been recognized by several critics), the multigeneric nature of the biography, and the reflection of self generated by Fyodor's work on the biography.[34]

Fyodor's father loved Pushkin, and Fyodor most likely gets the idea to write his father's biography through that association after he has reread Pushkin's "Angelo" (94) and "Journey to Arzrum":

> Thus did he hearken to the purest sound from Pushkin's tuning fork—and he already knew exactly what this sound required of him. Two weeks after his mother's departure he wrote her about what he had conceived, what he had been helped to conceive by the transparent rhythm of "Arzrum," and she replied as if she had already known about it. (96)

The idea of the journey as a metaphor of life is here intertwined with the idea of recovering the nontraditional from the literary tradition, as Fyodor looks to the works of Pushkin he has bypassed in earlier readings (85). Likewise, in Russian formalist theories of literary evolution, neglected genres of literature are resurrected to replace the worn-out contemporary genres. It also seems probable that his mother's departure for Paris reminds him of the loss of his father, who was leaving on a seemingly ordinary expedition the last time Fyodor saw him.

The multiple allusions to Pushkin in passages that deal with Fyodor's biography of his father provide additional critical clues, above and beyond the concept of the "turn to prose" Fyodor takes with respect to his early volume of poetry. To start, he reads Pushkin's "Angelo," a narrative poem which tells, among other things, of a Duke's false journey; while his subjects believe that he is abroad, the Duke returns to his city incognito to see how life has changed under the governance of Angelo, an upright citizen whom he has left in charge. The Duke "loved novels," the narrator remarks, and perhaps he "wanted to imitate Harun al-Rashid" (part 3, stanza 1), who in *A Thousand and One Nights* walks Baghdad in disguise in order to observe the lives of his subjects.[35] Thus Nabokov may have intended Fyodor's imaginary journey with his father to imitate Pushkin's Duke's imitation of the ruler in *A Thousand and One Nights*. And it is worth recalling, moreover, that Pushkin's *Angelo* is also an imitation—of Shakespeare's *Measure for Measure*. The idea of a potentially infinite number of stories within stories connects these works, as does the idea of a false rather than a genuine journey.

Pushkin's "Journey to Arzrum" is obviously the closer model for Fyodor's narrative of his father's expeditions; both works draw parodically on the tradition of travel literature. Pushkin forgoes descriptions of local culture in order to describe his foray into a bathhouse filled with naked women and his visit to a harem, and Fyodor emulates the anti-ethnographic impulse of his father—"Good marksmanship is the best passport" (122); "Everyone tells lies in Tibet" (123). This last line of Fyodor's models the ironic brevity of Pushkin's prose in "Journey to Arzrum"; it invites comparison with the latter's pithy exclamation, "The Circassians hate us."[36]

The transition from an "age of poetry" to an "age of prose" significantly ties Fyodor, Nabokov, and Pushkin together in their awareness of their own authorial evolution. Both Fyodor in *The Gift* and Nabokov himself in other books thematize their authorial affinity with Pushkin when they abandon the writing of poetry for the practice of prose. Fyodor's reading also follows Pushkin's transition to prose as he moves from "Angelo" to "Journey to Arzrum" to *The History of the Pugachev Rebellion* and *The Captain's Daughter*. And Fyodor makes his reading schedule a metaphor of personal maturation by combining his childhood recollections of Pushkin-like life in Russia with physiological imagery: "Continuing his training program during the whole of spring, he fed on Pushkin, inhaled Pushkin (the reader of Pushkin has the capacity of his lungs enlarged) . . . Pushkin entered his blood" (97–98). The personal and literary maturation deriving from his encounter with Pushkin prepares the way for Fyodor's authorship of the biography of his father: "the rhythm of Pushkin's era commingled with the rhythm of his father's life" (98). The biography "grows," as it were, out of Pushkin's prose. Notice also Nabokov's use of the word "rhythm," which foreshadows Fyodor's turn away from the rhythms of the streets of Berlin that surrounded him on his wanderings through the city toward the opulent rhythms of his father's expeditions through Asia. As if to make the point self-evident, the prose of Pushkin now accompanies Fyodor on his walks: "To strengthen the muscles of his muse he took on his rambles whole pages of Pugachyov learned by heart as a man using an iron bar instead of a walking stick" (97).

Considering the multigeneric nature of Fyodor's biography, one is not surprised to see that he quotes from Pushkin's *Pugachev,* and from his *The Captain's Daughter* just afterward. Especially for the theme of Pugachev, Pushkin realized that telling the story in just one way, either as history or as fiction, would not fully convey the events. As Andrew Wachtel puts it, "for Pushkin, . . . both versions were equally important, and . . . ultimately neither of them can be read adequately without a knowledge of its twin; that is, Pushkin forces his readers to consider these two different encodings of the same events in tandem."[37] Fyodor's problem is that he does not at first understand how to combine the multiply encoded, and sometimes contradictory, stories into a biography of his father; it is as though he were putting together a jigsaw puzzle with too many pieces. Fyodor thus absorbs from Pushkin the idea that stories must be told in no single way but in multiple ways.

Just as *The Gift* tells of how he came to write *The Gift,* chapter 2 is devoted to the story of how Fyodor comes to write the biography of his father, and it also includes portions of that biography. Read another way, however, the various narratives within chapter 2 form a biographical whole, and stitch together perhaps the only literary structure capable of conveying the open-endedness of Fyodor's father's life. Consider the diversity of genres in the chapter. Woven into the imaginative fabric of the narrative are numerous interpolations—a letter Fyodor receives from his mother describing her honeymoon in the Pyrenees, an excerpt from the memoirs of Suhoshchokov, a dialogue between Fyodor's father and his Uncle Oleg, a Kirghiz fairy tale, and Fyodor's own attempt at a conventional biography, which he characterizes as "the general scheme of my father's life, copied out of an encyclopedia" (103), not to mention Fyodor's first-person narratives of the Leshino countryside and of his father's final expedition. The dizzying transition from documentary to creative to documentary material in the chapter seems to reproduce *locally* the oscillation between fictive and autobiographical modes of writing that John Burt Foster identifies in Nabokov's written work more *globally.*[38]

The immediate problem with this sort of generic heterogeneity or diversity is, as Fyodor recognizes, that it makes an awkward structure for an integrated biography, though in a broader sense it is perhaps an acceptable oblique form for Fyodor's autobiography. As he is about to abandon the project, Fyodor writes his mother: "Out of all this I must now make a lucid, orderly book. At times I feel that somewhere it has already been written by me, that it is here, hiding in this inky jungle, that I have only to free it *part by part* from the darkness and the *parts* will fall together of themselves . . ." (my emphasis, 138). In fact, later on, Fyodor does free the biography from the jungle of rough drafts—when he writes *The Gift* itself—by narrating the biography's inception, progression, and near completion. Now structured as a work in progress, the disjointed parts are held together by the inspiration and chronology of their composition and abandonment.

The greater question concerns why it is so important for Fyodor to maintain this heterogeneity at the cost of the biography's completion. The way Fyodor narrates his father's death provides an important clue, as the scene is a microcosm of the whole biography. "Two shaky versions [of his father's death], both more or less of a deductive nature (and telling us nothing, moreover, about the most important point: how exactly did he die—if he died), were entangled in one another and mutually contradictory" (136). But that does not stop Fyodor from going on to tell both versions, undermining the authority of each as he sets them in competition with one another, and wondering all the while whether they both might not be entirely mistaken.

The multiple versions of his father's death accomplish for Fyodor the same task as the multiple genres of the whole biography he has written. The open-endedness of the biography mirrors his father's life: not only is the ending of that life hidden from Fyodor, in which case formulating aesthetic closure would be tantamount to falsifying his father's life, but there is also in his father's persona "a haze, a mystery, an enigmatic reserve which made itself felt sometimes more, sometimes less" (114). This unknown part of his father is what Fyodor can only approximate in his biography, but it is also "perhaps the most genuine" (114) part of his father's personality.

In his biography of his father Fyodor thus uses the dialogue with Pushkin and open-ended structure in order to capture the ineffable character of his father and to thematize his own literary evolution. His perception of himself through his authorship of the biography is no less important. In his first imaginary conversation with Koncheev, he seemed to "stumble" when attempting to conceive of the shape of his own life (and death) in verse, as though his poetry failed to accomplish the task of self-identification he had set for it. Though he apparently fails at the biography of his father, Fyodor is more successful at imagining through this authorship his own aesthetic and personal maturation.[39]

At one point where his writing becomes too effusive, Fyodor exclaims:

> Yes, I know this is not the way to write—these exclamations won't take me very deep—but my pen is not yet accustomed to following the outlines of his image, and I myself abominate these accessory curlicues. Oh, don't look at me, my childhood, with such big, frightened eyes. (109)

This metafictional break in narration is not uncommon in *The Gift*, but Fyodor is speaking not just about his emotions but also about his earlier poetry, which though it dealt with the theme of childhood, explicitly avoided the theme of his father (15, 24). Whereas his volume of poetry contains finely wrought miniatures, Fyodor's biography of his father is lost in an "inky jungle," as he calls the manuscript. By facing the disorder of his father's incomplete life, Fyodor begins to appreciate the paradoxes of authoring biographical and autobiographical works, of aesthetically closing that which is fundamentally open. For the biography of his father mirrors not only his father's life but also Fyodor's. An unproven author on a journey (emigration) from which he will never return, Fyodor resembles his father at this point more than he ever has or ever will.

He makes an aesthetic transition from the closed structures of his poems on childhood to the more radically open structure of his biography on his father in order to accommodate the radical openness in his own life. The closure that one finds in chapter 2, such as it is, is achieved only later, as I have mentioned, when Fyodor translates the biography into the structure of a work in progress. He thereby contains the generic heterogeneity of the biography within the strictures of real, or fabulaic, time: Fyodor begins his biography on such and such a day and abandons it on another. The overall movement is from literature (biography) to life (Fyodor's authorial activity), and back to fiction (since Fyodor's life is a novel, *The Gift*) . . . and so forth. In topographical terms, the chapter begins with Fyodor's imaginative flight to Leshino and ends with his move "from Pushkin Avenue to Gogol Street"; that is, it begins thematically with a journey back to childhood and concludes in Fyodor's identification with his father and with Gogol, one of the more famous literary expatriates of the previous century.

In his volume of poetry Fyodor successfully identified an authorial self, but he was unable to connect that self with his present life. In his biography of his father, Fyodor deals much more with his present life; the bits and pieces of the biography reflect stylistically the myriad forces that pull apart Fyodor's auto-identifications. The distance between these two selves created in authorship is succinctly expressed by Fyodor's description of his fame as a contemporary author and as the son of a great explorer.

When Fyodor hears his name (or imagines he hears his name) repeated at a literary meeting early in the novel, he experiences a special sense of pride at the attention:

It was the forerunner of his future fame; but there was also another earthly fame—the faithful echo of the past: he was proud of the attention of his co-evals, but no less proud of the curiosity of older people, who saw in him the son of a great explorer, a courageous eccentric. (65)

The biography of his father is a failed attempt to make these two selves meet up, to bring the fame of the contemporary author together with the fame he warrants as the son of a great explorer, to plot the fully realized self (as author) in relation to the landmarks of history, genealogy, and literary tradition.

The disjointedness of the biography, which prevents its success in one sense, makes it a success in an entirely different sense. The complex inter-twining of modes of writing in the biography says something about Fyodor not as son or as poet but as thinker. The many different genres, and many different ways of looking at the world, compose an aspect of his gift that need not be related to his authorship, though it is; and that is his "multi-leveled thought," which Fyodor recognizes as a trait that makes him distinct from infinite others. "What he should be teaching was that mysterious and refined thing which he alone—out of ten thousand, a hundred thousand, perhaps even a million men—knew how to teach: for example, multilevel thinking" (163). As Vladimir Alexandrov and others have pointed out, Fyo-dor's multilevel thinking shares much in common with Nabokov's broader concept of "cosmic synchronization."[40]

The biography's generic heterogeneity and open-endedness reflect Fyodor's "habitual dream of his father's return" (79), his inability to believe that his father is really dead. To project aesthetic and structural coherence and completion onto that text would be to admit his father's death. Such an equation between the shape of a life and its rendering in a text is one of the cornerstones of Fyodor's mature aesthetics: in his biography of his father, as well as in the *Life of Chernyshevsky* and in *The Gift* itself, Fyodor makes the non-ending ending the most important form-shaping impulse of the narrative in order not to falsify the unended life.

Since there are so many biographies in *The Gift*—of Yasha, Fyodor's father, Chernyshevsky, and in some ways of Fyodor himself—biography as such has been noted as a theme or topic of consequence by various critics. Usually, but not always, the biography of Chernyshevsky serves as the cen-terpiece of the discussion. Marina Kostalevsky, for example, has made a compelling case for considering Fyodor's biography of Chernyshevsky as a parody of "literary biography," as defined by the formalists, and compares the larger novel to Eikhenbaum's *Young Tolstoy*.[41] And Irina Paperno's daz-zling examination of the sources for the chapter on Fyodor's father extends that formalist heritage; she explicitly says that "Fyodor's creative method is reworking the documentary material with the aid of a series of specific artis-tic devices" (310).[42] Overall, it seems to me reasonable to say that the approach to biography in *The Gift* emerges from a thoughtful interplay of formalist-influenced ideas.

The only potential dilemma involved in a formalist approach, however, is that it can be interpreted as a retreat from knowledge of the person in biography, a complacency before an unseen wall that separates a life from any written appreciation of it. Although Eikhenbaum warns that documentary evidence will never reveal the "nature" of the person, he *does say* it will reveal "his creative consciousness." "The creative relationship to life . . . fuses within itself the personal and the general and makes man an individual."[43] I understand Eikhenbaum to mean here that identity is constituted discursively, inasmuch as language operates to fuse the personal and general for an author. That personal side of the linguistic equation is what may be lost in our pursuit of Nabokov's, and Fyodor's, more general deformation of "the facts." And, in the case of his biography of his father, Fyodor seems to marshal all of his authorial resources, tested and untested, in order to reveal the hidden personal side of his father.

The ability to conceive of one experience simultaneously in numerous ways is the identifying trait Fyodor displays in his authorship of *The Gift*, to be sure, but also in his biography of Chernyshevsky, where radical determinism and freedom are given equal and simultaneous aesthetic form. As a *mise en abyme* that reinterprets the most widely read Russian novelist of the nineteenth century, launches Fyodor's literary career, and proves his brilliant uniqueness, the *Life of Chernyshevsky* must be considered the central chapter of *The Gift*. Here Fyodor inscribes his evolving ideas about the dilemmas of identity into the very style of his authorship, all the while discovering his own position in relation to an aspect of the Russian literary tradition he has previously overlooked.

THE TELEOLOGY OF TRADITION

> A sonnet, apparently barring the way, but perhaps, on the contrary, providing a secret link which would explain everything—if only man's mind could withstand that explanation.
>
> —Nabokov, *The Gift*

Fyodor's biography of Chernyshevsky is different in one important way from other *mises en abyme* in *The Gift*—such as his poems or his biography of his father. Like Zhivago's volume of poetry and the Master's novel, the biography of Chernyshevsky is an *entire* text, interpolated in the same form, the reader presumes, as if it were a work published separately from *The Gift*. As an aesthetically whole, finished text, it tells the reader different sorts of things about its author than do the other *mises en abyme*. For the first time in the novel, Fyodor manages to represent in a work of literature the shape of an entire life, an idiosyncratically perceived life to be sure, but then again the biography of Chernyshevsky is neither a series of cameo fragments of childhood memories nor a disjunctive collage of narrative genres, like Fyodor's volume of poems and his biography of his father. For the first time the idea of how to conceive of an entire life is present in his authorship, and one can detect in the *Life of Chernyshevsky* Fyodor's more and more successful attempts to resolve the dilemmas of his own identity.

Chapter 3 depicts Fyodor's aesthetic transition from the sort of biography he attempted to write about his father to the biography of Chernyshevsky, which he completes and publishes. Aside from his meeting Zina, three steps make up that transition: first, Fyodor reappraises his earlier book of poetry in a less flattering light (155); second, he (again) turns to the literary tradition for inspiration; and third, he reconfigures and reaffirms his relationship to Russia and Russian literature. All three steps proceed against the background of Fyodor's changing perception of himself, which he continues to characterize in terms of spatial or topographical metaphors.

For example, he has moved from Pushkin Avenue to Gogol Street (145), which, as I have previously mentioned, obviously suggests the analogy of literary tradition, and he has shaped his immediate environment, especially his room, to complement his life: "During the past three months [his] room had been completely domesticated and its movement in space now coincided exactly with that of his life" (155). The association between his life as an author and his surroundings is now so close that Fyodor is able to depict in literary terms a lethargic morning in his room: his bed turns into a "parody of a bed" and his pillow is an "anachronism" (157).

The actual reason for Fyodor's decision to write the biography of Chernyshevsky derives from an amalgamation of seemingly chance events, his preoccupation with the Russian literary tradition, and his relationship with Zina and with the Chernyshevskys (Alexander Chernyshevsky once told Fyodor to write of his namesake). After telling Zina in jest that he will write a biography of Chernyshevsky, Fyodor happens upon an excerpt from the radical critic's diary republished in the article "Chernyshevsky and Chess," which he has been reading for its chess problems. The idiosyncrasies of Chernyshevsky's awkward style fascinate Fyodor: "He was so amazed and tickled by the fact that an author with such a mental and verbal style was considered to have influenced the literary destiny of Russia, that on the very next morning he signed out the complete works of Chernyshevsky from the state library" (195). The idea that Chernyshevsky has influenced Russia's literary "fate" spurs Fyodor on to write a biography of him, and to examine a side of the literary tradition that was previously entirely alien to him, yet just as important for literary history.

Rather than to Pushkin or to other favorite poets, Fyodor now turns to forty years' worth of social and literary criticism. "He read a great deal— more than he had ever read" (202), not only by Chernyshevsky but also by Belinsky, Mikhailovsky, Steklov, Lenin, Pomialovsky, Nekrasov, and Herzen. The result is that on the one hand Fyodor recognizes what he calls the "private censorship code of the radical critics" (202), and on the other hand he begins to appreciate the genuine "heroism" of radicals like Chernyshevsky who responded to the abuses of power by the autocracy.[44] This contradiction between the radical critics' own authoritarian habits and their heroic struggle for freedom is one Fyodor will inscribe into the structure of his *Life of Chernyshevsky*.

In the research Fyodor completed for the biography of his father he realized that his father maintained a secret part of himself undisclosed to his family, and that perhaps his father stayed away from home in order to avoid something unpleasant. This and other realizations had the effect of dulling the glow of perfection that surrounded his father. In much the same way, Fyodor's research into Chernyshevsky begins to convince him that his appreciation of the Russia "of old" is misguided or simply naive; and his feelings toward his homeland become more complex and contradictory:

> Gradually, as a result of all these raids on the past of Russian thought, he developed a new yearning for Russia that was less physical [пейзажная] than before, a dangerous desire (with which he successfully struggled) to confess something to her and to convince her of something. (203–4)

In this remarkable passage Fyodor struggles to ward off the paradoxical fever of writers from Chernyshevsky's day: he feels the desire to "convince" or "confess" something to Russia, to be both the rebellious and the repentant child, an "underground man" of sorts. One notices also how Fyodor resists relinquishing the physical/landscapish (пейзажная) yearning for Russia that I have characterized as a tendency to situate his identity "topographically" or as a matter of physical orientation.

In his biography of Chernyshevsky, Fyodor does return to the theme of topography as a metaphor of self. Only now topography serves as an antipode to Chernyshevsky's own vision of selfhood and to Fyodor's method of depicting him, in which total freedom and radical determinism are fused, mirroring the desire to convince and to confess something to Russia. Gogol provides the literary correlate to Fyodor's spatial conception of identity. Thus the phrase "the landscape hymned by Gogol passed [Chernyshevsky] unnoticed" (214) serves a double task of defining Chernyshevsky in stark opposition to Fyodor, both in literature and in life. Chernyshevsky's ignorance of Gogol confirms Fyodor's identification with the latter. The literary structure Fyodor chooses for his biography matches his subject perfectly, but sets his own evolving values into relief. The circle of the biography is an utterly closed structure that suggests an antithetical authorial freedom of infinity, directly contrasting with Fyodor's biography of his father, which used an open structure that led Fyodor into an authorial dead end.

Fyodor encounters certain pragmatic and aesthetic difficulties in the *Life of Chernyshevsky* that were of no concern in his biography of his father. First, Chernyshevsky is such a famous figure in Russian history that everyone knows the basic story of his life. To write a biography of him is not to reveal a hitherto unknown or exotic world. The demands of originality are thus not to be met in the subject matter but in its literary execution. Second, there is the sticky matter of writing about an ideology with which one does not agree. Though Fyodor's portrayal of Chernyshevsky is generous in many respects, he refuses to write his biography in a way that subjugates art to reality, in the manner of Chernyshevsky. The challenge, therefore, is to write of the famous materialist in a way that represents his beliefs faithfully but challenges those beliefs "stylistically."

Fyodor himself describes that aesthetic challenge as the need "to keep everything as it were on the brink of parody" (200) on the one side, and "an abyss of seriousness" on the other. This path between parody and seriousness is certainly well trod by Fyodor in the *Life of Chernyshevsky;* but parody alone is only part of the larger issue implicit in his authorship of the biography, and it represents above all the tendency toward greater freedom of meaning, as opposed to the determinism of fact in rigorous cause-and-effect historiography.

In a second imaginary conversation between Koncheev and Fyodor that takes place later in the novel, Koncheev characterizes Fyodor's use of parody in the *Life of Chernyshevsky:*

> You sometimes bring up parody to such a degree of naturalness that it actually becomes a genuine serious thought, but on *this* level it suddenly falters, lapsing into a mannerism that is yours and not a parody of a mannerism, although it is precisely the kind of thing you are ridiculing. (339)

Here is the more precise definition of Fyodor's use of parody in the *Life of Chernyshevsky.* It is in one sense uncontrollable and liberating, and in another equally valid sense, well regulated and imposing: parody becomes serious, which in turn yields a second order of parody resembling that which it purports to ridicule. The effect is that Fyodor is able to poke fun at Chernyshevsky while representing his life and ideas faithfully—the style of the biography itself bears a multiplicity of divergent meanings. Fyodor's "own mannerism" serves as the line that bisects parody and seriousness.

Fyodor repeats in the *Life of Chernyshevsky* a crucial paradox that also forms the background to his writing of *The Gift.* How does one keep a literary text open enough to depict in proper measure and significance a life that has not yet ended, and therefore not yet acquired the stability of meaning that only closure and wholeness can provide? To echo the first line given of the apocryphal sonnet, is it really "In vain [that] historians pry and probe?" In the *Life of Chernyshevsky* this paradox means posing the author's openness against the deterministic rigor with which Chernyshevksy endeavored to interpret his own life. The paradox that Fyodor battles in his self-representation in *The Gift* on the whole thus shades into a related battle between author and hero in the *Life of Chernyshevsky*.

Fyodor frequently points out, first, the ironic contradictions in Chernyshevsky's life—the surprises in the life of the determinist, the spiritual and mystical sides of the materialist, the dualism of the monist. A brief list of examples from the text will suffice:

1. "Everything [Chernyshevsky] touches falls to pieces" (218). The materialist is unable to use appliances of any sort.
2. "He broke crockery, soiled and spoiled everything. His love for materiality was not reciprocated" (225). More of the same: the materialist cannot work with his hands.
3. A "great expert at plans" (232), Chernyshevsky was easily led into digressions by his students—for example, about the hall where the National Convention of 1791–95 held its meetings. The determinist and expert planner cannot stick to a plan himself.
4. Born one hundred years after Lessing, Chernyshevsky fears his wife will die in childbirth, as Lessing's wife did (234). The believer in deterministic laws of nature is superstitious. (But here Fyodor adds irony of a second order—Chernyshevsky's wife nearly *does* die in childbirth.)
5. Finally, there is the ironic contradiction found in the "dualism of the monist Chernyshevsky's aesthetics—where 'form' and 'content' are distinct, with 'content' preeminent—or, more exactly, with 'form' playing the role of the soul and 'content' the role of the body" (239). You can take the boy out of the seminary, but you can't take the seminary out of the boy.

The reason Fyodor displays so many of the ironic contradictions in Chernyshevsky's beliefs and life is partly to ridicule him and partly to smile at his own authorial project. Fyodor's self-irony reveals the contradictory nature of literary biography, for if the man cannot sum up his own life without contradiction, then biographers (and readers) who reduce Chernyshevsky's life, for example, to a battle cry for one political agenda or another, are doomed to betray themselves. This is one of the reasons that Fyodor's book provokes such divergent reactions—it reveals the ideological baggage one carries into the reading of it.

Fyodor renders down to the finest detail the contradictions of Chernyshevsky's determinism, so much so that a dialectic seems embedded in the very *style* of Fyodor's writing. Where the subject matter implies freedom, he imposes the effects of literary structural control:

1. He writes of the students at the Saratov seminary: "In winter, in the snowy darkness, a rowdy gang used to tear downhill in a huge, horse-drawn, flat sled while roaring out dactylic hexameters" (213). The image of ebullient freedom in the students is countermanded by their recitation of classical poetic meters.

2. "Here the author remarked that in some of the lines he had already composed there continued without his knowledge a fermentation, a growth, a swelling of the pea, or, more precisely: at one or another point the further development of a given theme became manifest" (214). Structure "swells" without the author's knowledge or intent; and not just any structure—for "themes" govern the major part of the text of the *Life of Chernyshevsky*. Notice, too, how this sentence "ferments," "grows," and "swells," as if resisting completion.

3. "And here we find ourselves again surrounded by the voices of his aesthetics—for the motifs of Chernyshevsky's life are now obedient to me—I have tamed its themes, they have become accustomed to my pen; with a smile I let them go: in the course of development they merely describe a circle, like a boomerang or a falcon, in order to end by returning to my hand" (236). Even themes that the author "lets go" return obediently to his pen; again, freedom in structure governs the shape of the biography, just as liberating contradictions enter into Chernyshevsky's deterministic theories.

By following from the first set of textual examples to this second set, one can see how ironic inconsistencies become a model of structural composition in Fyodor's biography. The one set complements the other. Chernyshevsky's life provides numerous occasions with which the author may contradict Chernyshevsky's theories of art and life, but by the same token, those liberating contradictions may be brought into (ironic and temporary) order by the authorial activity of literary structuring.

The next step Fyodor takes in the biography of Chernyshevsky is central to his tentative resolution of the dilemmas of selfhood that have emerged in *The Gift*, making it something of a *mise en abyme* within the *mise en abyme* of the *Life of Chernyshevsky*. Fyodor transforms those seemingly infinite alternations between openness and finitude into symbols of human experience. Again, one can first look to the narrative irony Fyodor uses in describing Chernyshevsky's life. The occasion is Chernyshevsky's speech on Dobrolyubov: "While speaking, he played ceaselessly with his watch chain . . . but, when you think of it, he might have been fiddling with his watch because there was indeed very little free time left to him (four months in all!)"

(267). Always quick to dispose of simplistic symbols or metaphors of life (for example, the road of life), Fyodor creates and then undermines the image of life's time passing away with the sweeping hands of a watch. Chernyshevsky plays with his watch (how ironic!), and those readers who know the details of his life are humorously tempted to see it as a tragic symbol, for he only has four months left of freedom.

On the level of style, which is imbued with the contradictoriness of Chernyshevsky's life in particular and of literary biographies in general, the reader finds the striking image of the perpetual motion machine: a symbol of Chernyshevsky's "materialistic" idealism, the ironic basis (according to Fyodor) for his theory of ethics, and a *mise en abyme* for the *Life of Chernyshevsky*, and for *The Gift*. Fyodor takes the failed plans for a perpetual motion machine as paradigmatic for every sort of idealistic/materialistic plan Chernyshevsky would have in life:

> In this mixture of ignorance and ratiocination, one can already detect that barely perceptible but fatal flaw which gave his later utterances something like a hint of quackery . . . but such was the fate of Chernyshevsky that everything turned against him: no matter what subject he touched there would come to light—insidiously, and with the most taunting inevitability—something that was completely opposed to his conception of it. (217)

Thus the plan for a perpetual motion machine is transcribed as a symbol of Chernyshevsky's life and work taken as a whole: his best and most idealistic intentions turn against him. The passage above demonstrates again Fyodor's use of irony in describing Chernyshevsky's materialism. Chernyshevsky's "material" end, his death, is always present in the author's narration—one can detect "that *fatal* flaw"; "such was the *fate* of Chernyshevsky"; "the most taunting *inevitability*"—as if the perpetual motion machine itself has woven the teleological "pattern in the carpet" of Chernyshevsky's life.

When it comes time to discuss Chernyshevsky's version of utilitarian ethics, the perpetual motion machine is invoked at a structural level. This mechanistic metaphor of the perpetual motion machine reminds one of antihumanistic images Dostoevsky conjured for his Underground Man to use against Chernyshevsky (for example, man as an organ stop).

> Chernyshevsky's ethical structures are in their own way an attempt to construct the same old "perpetual motion" machine, where matter moves other matter. We would very much like this to revolve: egoism-altruism-egoism-altruism . . . but the wheel stops from friction. (282)

The repetition "egoism-altruism-egoism-altruism" mirrors the structural mechanism of Chernyshevsky's thought, in which dualisms of all sorts appear and contradict all of his monistic intentions—disjunctive "intentions" themselves being yet another mentalistic intrusion on his materialism.

The perpetual motion machine is one of the best examples of the way Fyodor inscribes Chernyshevsky's contradictoriness into the very structure of the biography, making it emblematic of the entire *Life*—and thus a *mise en abyme*. Fyodor has placed the beginning of the sonnet at the end of the text, so that one has to reread the beginning of the text in order to complete the sonnet. The biography thereby takes, according to Fyodor's plan, "not the form of a book, which by its finiteness is opposed to the circular nature of everything in existence, but [the form of] a continuously curving, and thus infinite, sentence" (204). The *Life of Chernyshevsky* would perhaps not be a perpetual motion machine in Chernyshevsky's eyes, but the readerly experience of the text approximates that same goal of endless motion.[45] Moreover, this potentially infinite circularity is usually taken as a defining feature of *The Gift,* because Fyodor discloses only at the end that he plans to write a novel similar to *The Gift,* forcing the reader to *reread The Gift* much differently. The perpetual motion machine therefore serves as a *mise en abyme* for both the *Life of Chernyshevsky* and for *The Gift.*

The idea of perpetual motion as an emblem of the *Life of Chernyshevsky* turns on the presentation of the apocryphal sonnet at the beginning and end of the text. That sonnet describes the paradoxical nature of identity in the biography and in the novel as a whole. I have rearranged it below to establish the proper order of stanzas:

> What will it say, your far descendant's voice—
> Lauding your life or blasting it outright:
> That it was dreadful? That another might
> Have been less bitter? That it was your choice?
>
> That your high deed prevailed, and did ignite
> Your dry work with the poetry of Good,
> And crowned the white brow of chained martyrhood
> With a closed circle of ethereal light?
>
> Alas! In vain historians pry and probe:
> The same wind blows, and in the same live robe
> Truth bends her head to fingers curved cupwise;
>
> And with a woman's smile and a child's care
> Examines something she is holding there
> Concealed by her own shoulder from our eyes. (300, 212)

Immediately following the sonnet, Fyodor writes: "A sonnet, apparently barring the way, but perhaps, on the contrary, providing a secret link which would explain everything—if only man's mind could withstand that explanation" (212). In other words, the sonnet may contain an all-encompassing explanation. Does that ambiguous "everything" include the riddles of *The Gift* as well?

It does in the sense that in the *Life of Chernyshevsky,* as in *The Gift,* the reader is often led to believe that interpretation is a matter of revealing what is "concealed." The sonnet figures this buried interpretive gold as Truth, who "Examines something she is holding . . . / Concealed by her own shoulder from our eyes." The idea of concealed knowledge connects the biography to the larger novel that encloses it, and thus the "key" to the novel seems to disappear into ever smaller texts (the novel, the *Life of Chernyshevsky,* the sonnet) until it melts away like Fyodor's identity in the forest (334).

A second aspect of the sonnet's relation to the biography also sheds light on the larger novel. The sonnet advocates a degree of relativity taken toward historical and biographical investigation that is not so obvious in Fyodor's broader self-presentation in *The Gift.* The conditional "if only man's mind could withstand that explanation" recasts "concealed" knowledge as a dubious goal and suggests that *what* is depicted is perhaps not as important as *how* it is depicted. The sonnet echoes this idea in the lines, "Alas! In vain historians pry and probe: / The same wind blows" (in Russian the idea is less forcefully spoken: Увы! Чтоб ни сказал потомок просвещенный, / все так же на ветру). Fyodor's guarded relativism—that how experience is depicted is more important than what is depicted—stands in stark contrast to the attitude taken toward the truth, for example, in *The Master and Margarita,* where it was the capacity of literature to reveal the truth that focused much of the author's metafictional energies.

The sonnet's "secret link," coupled with Fyodor's relativistic doubts about historical and biographical judgment, relate to two of the three aspects of authorship that I have been examining—the *mise en abyme* and depiction of self—for the sonnet may reveal everything that we need to know about *The Gift* and its author. Moreover, the sonnet is imbued with a concern for tradition, the judgment of posterity, and the possibility of understanding across vast stretches of time, making it part of Fyodor's effort to reconfigure literary history. The first line, for example, reads: "What will it say, your far descendant's voice." One presumes that the "you" in the poem refers to Chernyshevsky, whereas Fyodor surely occupies the position of the "descendant" who is about to judge the former's life and work.

To read the sonnet as a *mise en abyme* of *The Gift,* as I have been doing, is to minimize the significance of the real world as the referent of Fyodor's narrative. Granted, by making this move one loses some of the "work in progress" aspects of the novel, that *The Gift* is first and foremost a record of literary inspiration. On the positive side, however, the novel is decisively opened as an imaginative space in which the author charts the boundaries of his own evolving identity; and the illusory *fabula* becomes a suggested means of containing the disparate parts of the novel rather than the basis of plot.

DEATH AND AUTHORSHIP

> Funny that I have thought of death all my life, and if I
> have lived, have lived only in the margin of a book I have
> never been able to read.

—Nabokov, *The Gift*

The idea of overcoming death in and through the authorship of literature is a familiar one. In *The Master and Margarita* the hero authors a story through which he escapes death into another story: by writing and participating in the end of the Pilate narrative the Master is granted the "peace" of a boundless existence in a decidedly more idyllic narrative. Pasternak's version of transcending death through authorship is less ingenious—Zhivago lives on (quite conventionally) in the volume of poetry he leaves behind. In *The Gift* Fyodor is aware, as he often is, of both of these authorial devices, and he uses them at the same time as he discredits them.

For Fyodor, overcoming death is part of the larger authorial project of formulating an identity that does not bind him to the text in which it inheres. His multigeneric biography of his father, for example, is structured in a way that eliminates aesthetic closure and leaves open the possibility that his father is still alive. Literary form accommodates the "enigmatic reserve" of his father's personality, that same reserve which prevents perfect identification of him in the biography.

A similar strategy of undermining the death of closed literary structure is evident in each of the works Fyodor interpolates in *The Gift,* though as originally conceived, his volume of poems may seem an exception to this rule. Fyodor's intention in his *Verses* is to create a perfectly rendered image of himself:

> In fervently composing them, the author sought on the one hand to generalize reminiscences by selecting elements typical of any successful childhood—hence their seeming obviousness; and on the other hand he has allowed only his genuine quiddity to penetrate into his poems—hence their seeming fastidiousness. (9)

In this passage Fyodor does not seem to fear in any way that his identity will be bound to a single text. On the contrary, his stated intentions for the poems are to create an integrated personality: a balanced admixture of the specific and the typical in his self-portrayal.

These very comments, however, also indicate to the reader Fyodor's ultimate dissatisfaction with his poems and the image they create of him, for he refuses to let the poems stand on their own in the text. Their appearance in *The Gift* is accompanied by the author's numerous later interpretations, clarifications, and amplifications of their childhood context. Especially significant in this respect is Fyodor's decision to include a poem in the novel that was not in the original volume of verse. "This poem is the author's own favorite, but he did not include it in the collection because, once again, the theme is connected with that of his father and economy of art advised him not to touch that theme before the right time came" (24). When the decisive moment arrives, there is no "economy of art" that suggests Fyodor reproduce the collection of poems as it was written; whereas with the *Life of Cherny-shevsky,* for example, that is precisely his goal.

The reason for Fyodor's decision to add commentary to his poems may be found in the next text he interpolates into the novel—his failed biography of his father. The biography's generic heterogeneity and open-endedness reflect Fyodor's "familiar dream of his father's return" (88), his inability to believe that his father is really dead. To project aesthetic and structural coherence and completion onto that text would be to admit his father's death. Such an equation between the shape of a life and its render-ing in a text is one of the cornerstones of Fyodor's mature aesthetics: in the *Life of Chernyshevsky* and in *The Gift* itself, Fyodor makes the *"non-*ending" ending the most important form-shaping impulse of the narrative in order not to falsify the unended life.[46]

In chapter 5 of *The Gift,* the last chapter, the relationship of death to authorship is approached from at least four directions. First, like Zhivago, Fyodor will leave a literary legacy, *The Gift,* for future generations in Rus-sia, which he specifies (350). Overcoming death is thus also overcoming emigration. Second, although Fyodor rejects crass psychological approaches to an author's biography, he is not above appreciating the way his father's fame augments his own (65). The intersection of his fame as an author and his fame as the son of a great explorer creates a trans-generational identity that tends, as in the previous example, to subsume his status as merely an émigré author.

The two remaining directions from which Fyodor addresses death and authorship in the novel may be found in the structure and content of chapter 5. Fyodor's first tack, to parody death, may be witnessed through-out the novel. The epigraph to *The Gift* is, in part, "Russia is our fatherland. Death is inevitable," so it is not surprising that the constitution of an autho-rial identity ideally generates a dual transcendence of emigration and death. Russianness and immortality seem to be two sides of the same authorial coin, even in the humorous context of Smirnovsky's grammar textbook.

In chapter 5, death and its transcendence are frequent themes, in both real and figurative senses.[47] Alexander Chernyshevsky dies just as Fy-odor's *Life of Chernyshevsky* is published. His real death is thereby coupled with the figurative birth of a work of literature. Alexander Chernyshevsky thinks to himself on his deathbed that he has "lived only in the margin of a book" that he has never been able to read—perhaps death and access to the "book of life" are related. By writing *The Gift,* a multigeneric autobiographical novel that reflects deceptively back on itself rather than ending, Fyodor creates a "book of life" that does not require his death, in the sense that Fyodor equates aesthetic closure with death. In another context I noted that at the end of chapter 1, Fyodor "stumbled" when he tried to author in poetry his crossing over from life to death.

Fyodor also resolves the contradiction of aesthetic structure and death in two parodies of his own death. The first takes place in the Grunewald forest. Fyodor's nakedness, the disappearance of his "I," his visit to the place of Yasha's suicide, and the procession of hymning nuns all suggest Fyodor's self-conscious parody of his own death. He enacts the thoughts about mortality that he failed to figure poetically in chapter 1 and that he was unable to conjure in himself at and after the funeral of Alexander Chernyshevsky. It is significant that immediately following his "death" in the forest, Fyodor writes his mother, asking her to convey his congratulations to his sister on the recent birth of Fyodor's niece. Death and life go together, as do the death of Alexander Chernyshevsky and the *Life of Chernyshevsky*.

The second parody I have in mind is more properly a pastiche of a death scene, occurring the night after Fyodor's visit to Grunewald. That night Fyodor dreams that his father is alive and that his family is reunited. The dream that his father has "come to life" in itself is not as strange as the way Fyodor awakens from the dream. "And this senseless tangle sent a shiver of panic running through him: I have woken up in the grave, on the moon, in the dungeon of dingy non-being" (355). The premonition of death as he wakes from the dream—his perception of a "dungeon of dingy non-being"—probably derives, as Fyodor believes, from the day's events in Grunewald, but death is also figured in the dream itself. On his way to the Lorentzes Fyodor passes a funeral, and he describes his feelings before seeing his father as "like that of a man before execution" (354).

Fyodor's play with the death/birth opposition creates an obvious structural parallel: the reader approaches the end of the novel, but it is not really an end at all, it is a new beginning. As in Pushkin's *Eugene Onegin,* a circular structure carries the reader back to the beginning—Nabokov's translation of Pushkin's last stanza significantly reads, in part: "Blest who left life's feast early, . . . who never read life's novel to the end."[48] Thus in addition to the three previous strategies of overcoming death (leaving a legacy, reconstituting the author's real biography, and parodying death) there is also a structural strategy in *The Gift*.

Part of this structural strategy is to make chapter 5 reenact many of the scenes from chapters 1, 2, and 3.[49] Places and themes from early in the novel return: Fyodor has a second imaginary conversation with Koncheev; he revisits the Lorentzes during his dream of his father's return; he goes to the place of Yasha's suicide, which he narrated earlier; he attends another literary meeting; and he writes a second letter to his mother. In short, the novel turns back on itself well before its famous auto-referential ending, when Fyodor decides to write *The Gift*, and before the *Onegin* stanza that (deceptively) closes the final chapter: "nor does this terminate the phrase" (366).

The idea of transcending death is a popular one in Nabokov's works. In *Invitation to a Beheading*, Cincinnatus reflects after having read the novel *Quercus:* "and it was somehow funny that eventually the author must needs die—and it was funny because the only real, genuinely unquestionable thing here was only death itself, the inevitability of the author's physical death."[50] In *The Gift* the idea of transcending death can also be metaphorically extended to the author's fear of an end to Russian culture and literature, as well as to the hero's reconfiguration of authorship and death in his own literary works. It is interesting that of the three novels which I have examined only *The Gift* ends with its hero/author still alive and well. It may be that Nabokov conceived of his novel as a transitional work—there is no doubt that he looked back on it as such—whereas Bulgakov and Pasternak viewed their novels with the twilight of their careers in mind.[51]

Psychology and the Russian Novel

> We are entering, obviously, into a new age of
> Russian prose, which seeks new paths—beyond
> the connections with the psychological novel of
> Tolstoy or Dostoevsky.
> —Boris Eikhenbaum, 1921

IT IS REASONABLE to expect that a vital literary tradition will continually outpace itself, trace new paths, and discover overlooked turns in the old. Much of what I have written has been motivated by my desire to show how Bulgakov, Pasternak, and Nabokov reshape the Russian tradition of psychological prose by elevating the figure of the author to hero in their novels. *The Master and Margarita, Doctor Zhivago,* and *The Gift* illustrate a transition in Russian literary tradition from novels that use an "analytical, explanatory psychologism" (Lydia Ginzburg's phrase) to those using a novelistic psychology of selfhood.[1] In all three novels, in other words, the psychological focus shifts from how people understand the world to how authors understand the relationship between their creativity and their identity.

Just as all nineteenth-century Russian novels were not based on explanatory psychologism, so too are there a number of important early-twentieth-century Russian novels that do not reflect any special interest in the psychology of identity. The symbolism of Bely's *Petersburg,* the ornamentalism of Pilnyak's *The Naked Year,* the dystopian in Zamyatin's *We* and in Platonov's *The Foundation Pit,* as well as Ilf and Petrov's use of the picaresque all testify to the remarkably broad boundaries of the Russian novel in the first decades of the twentieth century—and this is to say nothing of the influx of socialist realist novels that find their precursors in Gorky's *Mother,* Gladkov's *Cement,* and Kataev's *Time, Forward!* Each of those novels may be about psychology in some way, but they do not as insistently interrogate names, mind/body problems, childhood memories, and so forth with the focus of Bulgakov, Pasternak, and Nabokov; nor do they suppose that novels are the proper place for considering such themes. Of those novels, *We* is the most psychological: D-503's use of a documentary genre, the personal diary, to re-create his identity follows in the nineteenth-century tradition of using introspection as a primary psychological method for uncovering the roots of personality. In *Petersburg,* Bely also addresses the narrative representation of psychology, but though his novel is maximally intertextual, it is not as obviously about the relation of authorship to identity.

In establishing a psychological ground for *The Master and Margarita, Doctor Zhivago,* and *The Gift,* one must take care to distinguish literary strategies that they share with other twentieth-century novels, strategies making them modernist rather than realist novels, from those strategies that discriminate one form of psychologism from another. Bulgakov, Pasternak, and Nabokov, like Bely, Pilnyak, and Platonov, often emphasize highly subjective perceptions of the world and the self in their novels. Language for them is consequently not always perfectly suited for describing the real world and is just as likely to conjure alternate, solipsistic worlds as it is to represent reality faithfully. For these novelists, as for other early-twentieth-century novelists, the march of historical time is largely at odds with the idiosyncratic time of the self, and narrative must therefore stitch together multiple disjunctive chronologies. These modernist characteristics separate Bulgakov, Pasternak, and Nabokov from conventional definitions of nineteenth-century realism, but as yet do little to define a "new" psychological novel in relation to the old.[2]

Central to any such consideration is the traditional novelistic relation of auto-reflexive psychological methods to autobiographical texts. In her study *On Psychological Prose,* Lydia Ginzburg convincingly demonstrates that the analytical impulse was shared in the nineteenth century between certain kinds of documentary and autobiographical literature—familiar letters, confessions, and diaries—and novels commonly given the epithet "psychological." The same analytical habits of introspection one finds in the diaries of Tolstoy, for example, are aesthetically transformed by him into the psychological basis of character portrayal in his novels. As Ginzburg puts it: "The documentary character of Tolstoi's writing consists of the fact that his heroes not only address the same problems of existence that he addressed, but that they address them in the *same psychological form* and in relation to virtually the same everyday circumstances that he himself was faced with."[3] Though Tolstoy was an ingenious creator of individual personalities, he also sought to portray that which was common to *all* human experience. It is hard to imagine, for example, Fyodor and any other character in *The Gift* perceiving events with the same general psychological similarity that, say, Pierre and Andrei share in *War and Peace.* Nabokov is interested in how Fyodor in particular understands his own creativity; Tolstoy is interested in how people in general understand themselves and their worlds.

The fine alterations of personality undergone by characters as the world affects their perception of themselves and others suggest that the psychological basis of the nineteenth-century realistic novel is experiential or epistemological rather than ontological. In spite of its title, *Anna Karenina* does not fix the identity of Anna any more than *Doctor Zhivago* defines a general, social experience of the Revolution and Russian Civil War. The contrast between these two novels is instructive. Both titles suggest that the novels will primarily depict an individual personality, the novels' eponyms. Tolstoy, however, is relatively complete in his portraiture of at least three entire families, whereas Pasternak can barely keep track of just one—Zhivago's.[4] Like much romantic fiction and poetry, *Doctor Zhivago* focuses primarily on the personality of the protagonist. Zhivago's idiosyncratic perception of his own creative relation to the world, rather than the world's effect on his perception, is the aesthetic imperative that shapes the novel.

The Master and Margarita, Doctor Zhivago, and *The Gift* are not devoid of analytical, explanatory psychology. On the contrary, there are many passages in these three novels that are psychologically realistic, as I have been using that term. Without such passages, one could (theoretically) construe these novels as nothing more than long lyrical poems in prose—but that overstates the case. The crucial difference is that Bulgakov, Pasternak, and Nabokov frame their psychological analysis of behavior so that realistic parameters of interpretation are replaced by a reflexive hermeneutics. A brief set of examples should clarify this difference.

At the psychiatric clinic in *The Master and Margarita* when Ivan attempts (and fails) to explain his behavior at Patriarch's Ponds, to set down on paper the details of the day's events, he becomes, in effect, one of the novel's many narrators; similar to the ironic narrator of the entire novel, the Master, and Woland. In retrospect, it is clear that Ivan's narrative *could not* be any more complete or successful than the novel's other competing narratives. Together they describe a series of events and reveal an identity; alone they are partial and misleading. Ivan's introspection does not create an illumination of his personality, but rather a split in his personality. His schizophrenia is the result of his applying a single kind of narrative logic to an illogical and, by necessity, multiply representable event. This paradox of narration has been an important frame for *The Master and Margarita* from the very start, where Ivan's misconceived poem of Christ comes out as though He really existed.

Similar narrative frames undermine introspective analysis in *Doctor Zhivago.* Lara, for example, implicitly recognizes the role an aesthetics of commodification plays in her seduction when she recalls the expensive painting from the restaurant where Komarovsky brought her. And Zhivago's reflections on his "childish" Tolstoyan morality are framed by the "dumb" scene of mysterious power he has just witnessed between Lara and Komarovsky. For both Lara and Zhivago, self-analysis is impeded by frames that mediate direct access to the psychological basis of their behavior or beliefs. They realize, implicitly and explicitly, that aesthetic preconceptions modulate their self-interpretations. Zhivago is fascinated by the aesthetic arche-type (первообраз) that shapes him.

The framing of analytical, explanatory psychologism is especially easy to detect in *The Gift*, where, for example, in the *Life of Chernyshevsky* Fyo-dor activates multiple frames to mock the naive logic of introspection in Chernyshevsky's diary. One frame is generated by Chernyshevsky's failed attempt to invent a perpetual motion machine, which is an emblem of the structure of Chernyshevsky's ethics ("egoism-altruism-egoism-altruism"), of the *Life of Chernyshevsky*, and perhaps of *The Gift* itself. It is important to note that although *The Gift* follows closely the interior thoughts of its hero, introspection is nearly always supplanted by "aesthetic" observation in the novel; that is, as readers we discover how Fyodor perceives the world as a work of, and a model for, art, but we are not privy to the quotidian undula-tions of his thought. Fyodor is not consumed by the need to uncover his reasons for acting one way or another as, for example, Raskolnikov is in *Crime and Punishment*.

This comparison of Fyodor with Raskolnikov reveals another, albeit generalized, difference between the psychological fiction of the nineteenth and twentieth centuries. Self-consciousness is debilitating, a kind of disease, in many nineteenth-century Russian novels.[5] Raskolnikov's overly reflective personality is part of what is wrong with him, and he himself wonders whether illness causes, accompanies, or follows the perpetration of crime. Fyodor, on the contrary, suggests that his own highly reflective personality is inte-gral to his creative vitality; it is a feature of the "multileveled thinking" that separates him from innumerable others. Nabokov, who detested Dostoev-sky's novels and therefore did not adequately appreciate them, believed that Dostoevsky's depiction of the inner worlds of his characters never tran-scended mental disease and hence failed to develop real personalities for them.[6] Art may, and perhaps must, transcend such diseases of conscious-ness in Nabokov's novels.

When narrative framing techniques in *The Master and Margarita, Doctor Zhivago,* and *The Gift* have served as reflections of the text, its enun-ciation, or code, I have referred to them, following Lucien Dällenbach, as *mises en abyme* within the novel.[7] *Mises en abyme* are not necessarily asso-ciated with a transition from novels of analytical psychologism to novels of a psychology of identity, but clearly they provide a useful means for setting modes of analysis such as introspection off from the text, for putting such passages into interpretive quotation marks.

It goes without saying that not every novel of identity will rely exclu-sively upon the *mise en abyme* device, and not every psychological novel of the analytical type will be without it. One thinks of a number of nineteenth-century texts that seem precursors to the reflexive narratives of *The Master and Margarita, Doctor Zhivago,* and *The Gift:* the tale of Captain Kopeikin in *Dead Souls* and "The Portrait" by Gogol, Lermontov's *A Hero of Our Time*, and Dostoevsky's interpolated texts, iconic images and paintings, especially in *The Idiot* and *The Brothers Karamazov*. Once an author adopts a strategy of self-reflection (such as introspection) as a model form of psychology, subsequent use of auto-referential strategies (such as the *mise en abyme*) as a model form of narration may not be far behind. There is good reason to believe that Tolstoy, for instance, takes this step in the Anna story of *Anna Karenina*. Anna's introspection becomes so insulating that ordinary channels of communication with others cease to be available to her, and she begins to manipulate aesthetic representations of herself in order to fill the communicative void. In other words, both Tolstoy *and* Anna create a work of art out of Anna, and this parallel between aesthetic frames inside and outside the text is a defining characteristic of the *mise en abyme*.[8]

When Bulgakov, Pasternak, and Nabokov thematize the parallel between authoring a text and authoring a self in *The Master and Margarita, Doctor Zhivago,* or *The Gift*, they engage and reorder the literary tradition. Inspiration is still inspiration, of course—the Master, Zhivago, and Fyodor all write in moments of great inspiration—but these authors have exchanged their Aeolian harps for the well-stocked libraries that have helped to define literary Russians from *Eugene Onegin* to Mandelstam's *raznochinets* in *The Noise of Time*.

What any complex novelistic psychology of identity requires, and an analytical psychology can forgo, is the preservation of cultural heritage in literary tradition. Bulgakov, Pasternak, and Nabokov all recognize that the Russian tradition has been jeopardized by a Sovietization of literature, and that authorship itself is therefore also in jeopardy, for there can be no doubt that what threatens the identities of the Master, Zhivago, and Fyodor is as much the disappearing sense of literary history in society as anything else. To shrink away from that society—to retreat to the psychiatric clinic, to Varykino, or to the Grunewald forest—is to escape a world that no longer comprehends the language these authors use to understand themselves. Margarita, Lara, and Zina are thus not just the heroes' lovers, they are addressees for whom literary activity as a form of being is still comprehensible.

In all three novels, but especially in *The Master and Margarita* and *The Gift*, philistinism therefore plays a remarkably significant role. MASSOLIT is not just a crooked bureaucracy; it is also the negative against which the Master's authentic literary activity becomes visible. Shchyogolev's idea for a novel in which a man marries a widow to get at her daughter is philistine, an example of *poshlost'*, precisely because it reveals Shchyogolev's own transparent desire for Zina. Passing through another authorial prism, however, it becomes the plot of one of the twentieth century's greatest novels—Nabokov's *Lolita*. In *The Gift*, reviews of Fyodor's *Life of Chernyshevsky* serve a purpose similar to reviews of the Master's novel: both reveal the chasm of misunderstanding that lies between the author and the literary establishment.

This alienation or isolation from broader society that in part defines the Master, Zhivago, and Fyodor is at the center of a paradoxical circle of authorship in all three novels. For an author to be separated from "the crowd" is of course nothing new to Russian literature. But these three fictional authors compensate for their uniqueness by conspicuously addressing and situating themselves in a literary tradition that can only serve to isolate them further. Fyodor's attack on Chernyshevsky, the Master's indulgence in "Pilatism" (as his critics refer to it), and Zhivago's theories of individualism are not only at odds with socially acceptable forms of thought, they are a means of withdrawing from social forms of self-definition. Thus what prevents *The Master and Margarita, Doctor Zhivago,* and *The Gift* from being subversive literature in a traditional sense is that which also separates them from many nineteenth-century novels: Bulgakov, Pasternak, and Nabokov are more interested in portraying an individual rather than a social identity.

The uniqueness of their portrayal of individual personality—the intersection of auto-reflexive narration and literary history—has been the main subject of my argument and need not be repeated or redefined. Nabokov, whose novelistic endings would themselves make a good subject for study, provides a fitting conclusion and a final example of metaliterary instruction with which to read him: "And to sum up, I would like to stress once more, Let us not look for the soul of Russia in the Russian novel: let us look for the individual genius."[9]

Notes

INTRODUCTION

1. For example, in Russian literary scholarship, see Charles Isenberg, *Telling Silence: Russian Frame Narratives of Renunciation* (Evanston: Northwestern University Press, 1993); Gary Saul Morson, *The Boundaries of Genre: Dostoevsky's "Diary of a Writer" and the Traditions of Literary Utopia* (Austin: University of Texas Press, 1981); David Shepherd, *Beyond Metafiction: Self-Consciousness in Soviet Literature* (Oxford: Oxford Clarendon Press, 1992); Alexander Zholkovsky, *Text counter Text: Rereadings in Russian Literary History* (Stanford: Stanford University Press, 1994). There are many studies of metafiction in English and other disciplines, but see especially Linda Hutcheon, *Narcissistic Narrative: The Metafictional Paradox* (New York: Methuen, 1980); and Robert Alter, *Partial Magic: The Novel as a Self-Conscious Genre* (Los Angeles: University of California Press, 1975).

2. For an excellent examination of authorship in the nineteenth century, see David Glenn Kropf, *Authorship as Alchemy: Subversive Writing in Pushkin, Scott, Hoffmann* (Stanford: Stanford University Press, 1994). Kropf studies several texts by Pushkin, Scott, and Hoffmann in order to answer the question: "Would it be possible for a writer to subvert the workings of the institution of authorship and thereby write and publish in freedom from the socioliterary processes that conflate life and work?" (2).

3. Jurij Striedter's study of Russian formalism and Czech structuralism is an elegant elaboration of this process in formalist and structuralist criticism. See Jurij Striedter, *Literary Structure, Evolution, and Value: Russian Formalism and Czech Structuralism Reconsidered* (Cambridge: Harvard University Press, 1989).

4. See, for example, Gleb Struve, "The Revival of the Novel," in *Russian Literature under Lenin and Stalin* (Norman: University of Oklahoma Press, 1970); and Victor Erlich, "The Novel in Crisis: Boris Pilnyak and Konstantin Fedin," in *The Russian Novel from Pushkin to Pasternak* (New Haven: Yale University Press, 1983).

5. See the introduction by Andrew Wachtel and Irina Gutkin to *What is Art?*, by Leo Tolstoy (New Haven: Yale University Press, forthcoming).

On the influence of nineteenth-century realism in the formation of socialist realism, see Regine Robin, *Socialist Realism: An Impossible Aesthetic,* trans. Catherine Porter (Stanford: Stanford University Press, 1992); and Herman Ermolaev, *Soviet Literary Theories, 1917–1934: The Genesis of Socialist Realism* (Berkeley: University of California Press, 1963). In many respects, the debates of the twenties set the tone for considering prose throughout the twentieth century. Lukács, when he hails Solzhenitsyn's *One Day in the Life of Ivan Denisovich,* casts his comments in terms specifically from the twenties (*Solzhenitsyn* [London: Merlin Press, 1969], 33).

6. V. G. Belinsky, *Selected Philosophical Works* (Moscow: Foreign Language Publishing House, 1956), 83.

7. Борис Эйхенбаум, «О Шатобриане, о червонцах и русской литературе,» *О литературе: работы разных лет.* (Советский писатель, 1987), 367–68. Eikhenbaum makes a similar point in his 1926 preface to *Russian Prose,* ed. B. M. Eikhenbaum and Yury Tynyanov, ed. and trans. Ray Parrot (Ann Arbor: Ardis, 1985). "At present literature occupies a very modest position. Unsure of the significance of his calling, a writer works rather blindly, confusing his readers and becoming confused himself amidst the diversity and contradictoriness of demands laying claim to him. He is importuned to go 'back'—to Ostrovsky, Pushkin, Tolstoy . . . Yet he senses that somehow that misses the point, that *somehow the question itself of tradition must be posed differently.* It is not a matter of going back to this or that writer, but rather of knowing how to view the entire course traversed. We need to recognize the historical dynamics of traditions, for we have forgotten too much and accepted too much on faith" (my emphasis, 15).

8. My emphasis. Georg Lukács, *The Theory of the Novel,* trans. Anna Bostock (Cambridge: MIT Press, 1990), 60.

9. Юрий Тынянов, «Литературное сегодня,» *Архаисты и новаторы,* 150–51.

10. Ibid., 158.

11. Robin, *Socialist Realism.* Katerina Clark refers to a modal schizophrenia of the socialist realist novel in her monograph *The Soviet Novel: History as Ritual* (Chicago: University of Chicago Press, 1985).

12. The concept of "totality" for Lukács has a much more precise meaning in the context of Marxist criticism. In *The Political Unconscious: Narrative as a Socially Symbolic Act* (Ithaca: Cornell University Press, 1981), Fredric Jameson translates Lukács's notion of ideological totality into a tool of literary criticism: "Lukács' critical conception of the 'totality' may immediately be transformed into an instrument of narrative analysis, by way of attention to those narrative frames or containment strategies which seek to endow their objects of representation with formal unity" (54).

13. See, for example, "Critical Realism and Socialist Realism," in Georg Lukács, *The Meaning of Contemporary Realism,* trans. John Mander and

Necke Mander (London: Merlin Press, 1963). Here, Lukács distinguishes socialist realists from critical realists by arguing that the latter are unable to see
the future "from the inside." "In socialist realism, this barrier is removed. Since
its ideological basis *is* an understanding of the future, individuals working for
that future will necessarily be portrayed from the inside" (my emphasis, 95).

14. T. S. Eliot, *Selected Prose of T. S. Eliot,* ed. Frank Kermode (New
York: Harcourt Brace Jovanovich/Farrar, Straus and Giroux, 1975), 177.

15. All quotes from "The End of the Novel" refer to Osip Mandelstam, *Mandelstam: Critical Prose and Letters,* ed. Jane Gary Harris, trans.
Jane Gary Harris and Constance Link (Ann Arbor: Ardis, 1979), 198–201.

16. The demise of this kind of integrated personality is often taken as
one of the defining aspects of modernism. See Eugene Lunn, *Marxism and
Modernism: An Historical Study of Lukács, Brecht, Benjamin, and Adorno*
(Berkeley: University of California Press, 1982), 37.

17. Mandelstam, *Mandelstam,* 200.

18. Michel Foucault, *The Order of Things: An Archeology of the Human
Sciences,* translation of *Les mot et les choses* (New York: Vintage, 1970), 368–69.

19. "We may consider Romain Rolland's *Jean Christophe,* that swan
song of European biography, with its majestic fluency and noble mastery of
synthetic devices [синтетические приемы] reminiscent of Goethe's *Wilhelm Meister,* the last example of the centrifugal biographical European
novel. *Jean Christophe* closes the circle of the novel" (emphasis added; Mandelstam, *Mandelstam,* 200). For a more optimistic view of Rolland's novel,
see Eikhenbaum, "Novel or Biography," in Русская молва (1913), 69. He
argues (entirely correctly from my perspective) that such biographical works
represent the future of the novel. *Wilhelm Meister* provides a famous use of
the *mise en abyme* device in the puppetry shows early in the novel.

20. Emphasis added. Mandelstam, *Mandelstam,* 199.

21. This opposition of "given" versus "created" is also important to
Mikhail Bakhtin's concept of dialogue, where selfhood is achieved through
the agent's linguistic participation in a world of other speakers.

22. My ellipses. Konstantin Fedin, *Cities and Years,* trans. Michael
Scammell (Evanston: Northwestern University Press, 1993), 313–14.

23. There are many structuralist- and poststructuralist-influenced versions of authorship that could provide interesting comparisons with Mandelstam's novella. For example, Michel Foucault, "What Is an Author?," or Roland
Barthes, "The Death of the Author." These and several other essays are reprinted or excerpted in Seán Burke, *Authorship: From Plato to the Postmodern: A Reader* (Edinburgh: Edinburgh University Press, 1995). Foucault
writes, ". . . the function of an author is to characterize the existence, circu-
lation, and operation of certain discourses within a society" (235). Bulgakov,
Pasternak, and Nabokov reject as ethically bankrupt such depersonalized
concepts of authorial identity, as does Mandelstam in his own way.

24. The epigraph that begins this section is from a letter by Tynianov to Victor Shklovsky quoted in the commentary to the Russian edition of Tynianov's "On Literary Evolution," in Поэтика, 525.

25. Astradur Eysteinsson, *The Concept of Modernism* (Ithaca: Cornell University Press, 1990), 67.

26. All citations refer to Jurij Tynjanov, "On Literary Evolution," in *Readings in Russian Poetics: Formalist and Structuralist Views*, ed. Ladislav Matejka and Krystyna Pomorska (Ann Arbor: Michigan Slavic Publications, 1978), 66–78.

27. Striedter writes, "the term *ustanovka* becomes central to Tynyanov's thinking. Jakobson had introduced it as a Russian equivalent to the German term *Einstellung*" (*Literary Structure*, 59).

28. Ibid., 60.

29. Dällenbach's 1977 study, *Le récit spéculaire: essai sur la mise en abyme*, provides a history of the term, a typology of *mises en abyme*, and "diachronic perspectives" on the *mise en abyme* in the *nouveau roman* and new *nouveau roman*. In the last twenty years there have been several criticisms and revisions of Dällenbach's original elucidation of the *mise en abyme*, but his is still the definitive work. See Lucien Dällenbach, *The Mirror in the Text*, trans. Jeremy Whiteley with Emma Hughes (Chicago: University of Chicago Press, 1989).

30. Dällenbach, *The Mirror in the Text*, 51. Metanarratives are not necessarily a feature of the *mise en abyme*, so Dällenbach reduces the properties necessary in the *mise en abyme* to (1) the reflexive character of the utterance; and (2) its intra- or metadiegetic quality (53).

31. Ibid., 36.

32. Ibid., 50.

33. Ibid., 59.

34. Ibid.

35. Jameson, *Political Unconscious*, 53.

36. Harold Bloom's influential theory of the creation of poetic tradition warrants quotation here: "Poetic history, in this book's argument, is held to be indistinguishable from poetic influence, since strong poets make that history by misreading one another, so as to clear imaginative space for themselves" (*The Anxiety of Influence: A Theory of Poetry* [London: Oxford University Press, 1973], 5). The idea that authors reread (misread, according to Bloom) other authors in the literary tradition in order to create their own identities is central to my own thesis.

CHAPTER ONE

The epigraph for this chapter is quoted from М. Чудакова, *Жизнеописание Михаила Булгакова* (Москва, 1988), 349. In the original context of the letter, Bulgakov is asking Stanislavsky for help in obtaining permission to travel abroad. Gogol is discussing *Dead Souls* in his *An Author's Confession.*

1. See, for example, Lesley Milne, "Gogol and Mikhail Bulgakov," in *Nikolay Gogol: Text and Context,* ed. J. Grayson and F. Wigzell (Basingstoke: Macmillan and University of London, 1989); Nadine Natov, "The Supernatural in Bulgakov and Gogol'," in *The Supernatural in Slavic and Baltic Literature: Essays in Honor of Victor Terras,* ed. Amy Mandelker and Roberta Reeder (Columbus: Slavica, 1988); and Marietta Chudakova, "Gogol in the Life and Works of Mikhail Bulgakov," *Soviet Literature* 4 (1984): 433.

2. Structurally *The Master and Margarita* is like a photographic negative of *Doctor Faustus.* Mann's famous novel uses a traditional humanist narrator to "filter and mediate the norm-breaking art and aesthetics of a radical modernist" (Eysteinsson, *The Concept of Modernism,* 35). Bulgakov's novel reverses these roles: a modernist narrator tells the story of a traditional humanist, the Master. Whereas *Doctor Faustus* approaches modernism through the eyes of the traditional, *The Master and Margarita* approaches tradition through the eyes of the modern.

3. All citations of *The Master and Margarita* refer to М. А. Булгаков, *Собрание сочинений в пяти томах,* Том пятый (Москва: Художественная литература, 1992). Throughout this chapter I have benefitted from the commentary contained in it. Translations of passages from the novel are taken from the Michael Glenny translation, though often I have emended them.

4. For a treatment of the connection between the two novels, see David Lowe, "Bulgakov and Dostoevsky: A Tale of Two Ivans," *Russian Literature Triquarterly* 15 (1978): 253–62.

5. The work of three thinkers influences my discussion of self and tradition. (1) Hans-Georg Gadamer, *Truth and Method,* 2nd ed., trans. Joel Weinsheimer and Donald Marshall (New York: Continuum, 1989). See especially his concept of *wirkungsgeschichtliches Bewusstsein* ("historically effected consciousness"). With this term, Gadamer suggests a double relation of consciousness to tradition, as both "affected" and "effected" by history: "at once the consciousness effected in the course of history and determined by history, and the very consciousness of being thus effected and determined" (xxxiv). (2) Jürgen Habermas, *The Philosophical Discourse of Modernity: Twelve Lectures,* trans. Frederick G. Lawrence (Cambridge: MIT Press, 1987). Habermas proposes a communicative model of self for use in the critique of (philosophical) modernism. Mikhail Bakhtin's concept of "dialogue" as the vehicle of thought and basis of consciousness is related to the communicative model of self. (3) The best collection of Bakhtin's work in translation is *The Dialogic Imagination: Four Essays by M. M. Bakhtin,* ed. Michael Holquist, trans. Caryl Emerson and Michael Holquist (Austin: University of Texas Press, 1981). I use the term "dialogue" frequently in this

chapter, particularly in the context of the relationship of the present to tradition. Here, I mean an openness to exchange between present and past that neither objectifies the past nor fuses with it. "In 'a dialogic encounter of two cultures . . . each retains its own unity and *open* totality, but they are mutually enriched'" (quoted in Gary Saul Morson and Caryl Emerson, *Mikhail Bakhtin: The Creation of a Prosaics* [Stanford: Stanford University Press, 1990], 56).

6. In the Russian tradition, Dostoevsky's *Notes from Underground* is often considered the most important literary work in this attack on Enlightenment rationality. On the relation of personal identity to historicism in this regard, see the chapter on *Notes from Underground* in Michael Holquist, *Dostoevsky and the Novel* (Princeton: Princeton University Press, 1977).

7. Robert Louis Jackson, *Dostoevsky's Underground Man in Russian Literature* (Mouton, 1958), 7.

8. I am referring to the "evil genius" in Descartes's *Meditations*. This reference to the evil genius is further substantiated by the parody of the *cogito* in chapter 30 of Bulgakov's novel. See the section "Schizophrenia" of the present chapter.

9. Transcending the ordinary world in this way is often related by critics to the novel's concern with gnosis. See George Krugovoj, *The Gnostic Novel of Mikhail Bulgakov: Sources and Exegesis* (Lanham: University Press of America, 1991).

10. Andrew Barratt makes a comparison of this theme of the demands of creativity in the novel with the ideas of Nikolai Berdyayev. For example, in *The Meaning of the Creative Act* Berdyayev writes: "For creativeness is needed great courage" (in Barratt, *Between Two Worlds: A Critical Introduction to "The Master and Margarita"* [Oxford: Oxford Clarendon Press, 1987], 326).

11. Charles Taylor calls such discriminations cases of "strong evaluation": "What they [questions of what makes life worth living] have in common with moral issues, and what deserves the vague term 'spiritual,' is that they all involve what I have called elsewhere 'strong evaluation,' that is, they involve discriminations of right or wrong, better or worse, higher or lower, which are not rendered valid by our own desires, inclinations, or choices, but rather stand independent of these and offer standards by which they can be judged" (*Sources of the Self: The Making of Modern Identity* [Cambridge: Harvard University Press, 1989], 4).

12. For a treatment of the novel's relationship to apocalyptic literature, see David Bethea, *The Shape of the Apocalypse in Modern Russian Fiction* (Princeton: Princeton University Press, 1989).

13. M. Chudakova, *"The Master and Margarita:* The Development of a Novel," *Russian Literature Triquarterly* 15 (1976): 177–209.

14. Quoted in Habermas, *Philosophical Discourse*, 49.

116

15. Chudakova writes: "The epilogue of the novel is a place of action abandoned not only by Woland and his retinue and not only by the Master. In it the parallel nature of those two temporal planes of human life is lost, the connection between which was accomplished through the creative will of the Master" (М. Чудакова, *Жизнеописание*, 463). I agree that the parallel structure of the novel ends with the epilogue, but the parodic structure—the other structural relationship between interpolating and interpolated texts—is maintained.

16. Lesley Milne writes: "Bulgakov's portrayal [of Yeshua] undoubtedly owes much to Dostoevsky's Prince Myshkin in *The Idiot:* both have what Bakhtin calls 'the penetrating word' that pierces to the core of the interlocutor's being" (*Mikhail Bulgakov: A Critical Biography* [Cambridge: Cambridge University Press, 1990], 231). For an interpretation of Bulgakov that also benefits from Bakhtin's thought, see Nadine Natov, "Structural and Typological Ambivalence of Bulgakov's Novels Interpreted against the Background of Baxtin's Theory of 'Grotesque Realism' and Carnivalization," in *American Contributions to the Eighth International Congress of Slavists* (Columbus: Slavica, 1978), 2:536–39.

17. Quoted by Barratt, *Between Two Worlds*, 248–49.

18. I use the term "parody" and "parodic structure" throughout this chapter in the broad sense of "imitative citation." Later, I will refer to two subsets of this extended sense of parody: burlesque and pastiche. When the imitative citation of parody reveals a comic or subversive intention I will use the term "burlesque," and when the intention is nonsubversive and more solemn I will use the term "pastiche." In Bakhtin's terminology, my interpretation of parody would approximate "double-voiced discourse," and my use of the terms "burlesque" and "pastiche" would fall under the rubric of "active" and "passive" double-voiced discourse. See Mikhail Bakhtin, "Discourse in Dostoevsky," in *Problems of Dostoevsky's Poetics,* ed. and trans. Caryl Emerson (Minneapolis: University of Minnesota Press, 1984).

19. Parody was particularly important for formalist theories of literary evolution. See Striedter, *Literary Structure;* and Victor Erlich, *Russian Formalism: History–Doctrine,* 3rd ed. (New Haven: Yale University Press, 1955). See also my discussion of Tynianov's theory of literary evolution in the introduction to this volume.

20. See my discussion of *mise en abyme* in the introduction. A specific reading of the Pilate story in *The Master and Margarita* as an instance of *mise en abyme* may be found in Georges Nivat, "Deux romans 'speculaires' des les années trente: *Le Don* et *Le Maître et Marguerite,*" *Revue des études slaves* 61 (1989): 269–75.

21. The various "doublings," not only of "Bulgakov" but also of Ivan and the Master, that emerge in this dialectic are discussed in the section "Parody and Tradition" in this chapter. Michel Foucault views the human

"ambiguous position as an object of knowledge and as a subject that knows" as central to the self-contradictory and anthropocentric nature of modernism (*Order of Things,* especially chapter 9, "Man and His Doubles").

22. Bulgakov's feelings toward Mayakovsky are well known. The latter included, in one of the scenes of his play *The Bedbug* taking place in the future, selections from a "dictionary of obsolete words." The name "Bulgakov" is among the obsolete words. For a more detailed look at the relationship between Bulgakov and Mayakovsky, see chapter 4, "Bulgakov and the Futurists (Mayakovsky and Meierhold)," of Kalpana Sahni's *A Mind in Ferment: Mikhail Bulgakov's Prose* (New Delhi: Arnold-Heinemann, 1984).

23. The Russian text of the epigraph (Я—часть той силы, что вечно хочет зла и вечно совершает благо.) is, incidentally, a good translation of the original German of Goethe's *Faust:* "Ein Teil von jener Kraft, / die stets das Böse will / und stets das Gute schafft."

24. Particularly in Goethe, Mephistopheles' answer is ambiguous. To will always evil and do always good may mean to will evil and *therefore* do good.

25. Riitta H. Pittman, in her monograph *The Writer's Divided Self in Bulgakov's "The Master and Margarita"* (New York: St. Martin's, 1991), uses the concepts of schizophrenia and split personality both to describe the distance between the public and private selves of many of the novel's characters (17), and also to characterize a conflict between life and art (95). My use of "schizophrenia" is meant to allude both to the attack on the self's integrity in the novel and also to the novel's fractured narration.

26. The pertinent passage in Goethe's *Faust* is part 1, scene 3.

27. Proofs of God that proceed from the inwardness of the self are usually associated with St. Augustine. Compare Taylor, *Sources of the Self:* "Augustine shifts the focus from the field of objects known to the activity itself of knowing; God is to be found here . . . the activity of knowing is particularized; each of us is engaged in ours. To look towards this activity is to look to the self, to take up a reflexive stance" (130).

28. Some may object, but I see no conclusive reason for doubting that the Pilate story of chapters 2 and 16 is identical with the Master's novel. At any rate, their identity is not really at issue as much as the media through which they are experienced. By hearing and dreaming the Master's novel, Ivan *experiences* it more purely. As experience rather than text, the Pilate story strengthens its claim of the truth.

29. Laura D. Weeks provides a summary of the issue in her introduction to *The Master and Margarita: A Critical Companion* (Evanston: Northwestern University Press, 1996).

30. See Neil Carrick, *Daniil Kharms: Theologian of the Absurd* (Birmingham: Department of Russian Language and Literature, University of Birmingham, 1998).

31. Kantian thought does seem to play into some aspects of the novel. The objectivity accorded to the Master's moral vision, and the sense of responsibility that attends it, has resonance with Kant's categorical imperative, "the moral law within."

32. *The Master and Margarita* has had many textological problems over the years. Here the Glenny translation is inaccurate in two ways. The allusion to the *cogito* is lost in the English, and the sentence by Azazello beginning with the words "In order to consider yourself alive" is missing. The allusion is noted in the commentary of the Russian edition. It is restored in the new translation of *The Master and Margarita* (Ann Arbor: Ardis, 1995) by Diana Burgin and Katherine Tiernan O'Connor, and noted in the annotations by Ellendea Proffer.

33. René Descartes, *Meditations on First Philosophy in Which the Existence of God and the Distinction of the Soul from the Body Are Demonstrated,* trans. Donald A. Cress (Indianapolis: Hackett, 1979), 16.

34. A survey, albeit limited, of the critical literature on *The Master and Margarita* suggests that this facet of Woland's identity has been overlooked. I make no certain claim to originality, of course, but it seems to me that the relation of Woland to Descartes's evil genius cannot be disregarded, especially when one considers Woland's obvious role as "tester" of human reason.

35. There are many opinions on Woland. Here, I agree with A. Colin Wright. See his *Mikhail Bulgakov: Life and Interpretations* (Toronto: University of Toronto Press, 1978); and A. Colin Wright, "Satan in Moscow: An Approach to Bulgakov's *The Master and Margarita,*" *PMLA* 88, no. 5 (October 1973): 1162–72. On this point, I oppose Andrew Barratt, who calls the reader's attention to "the fact that Woland's arrival in Moscow results in a number of scenes of quite horrifying brutality" (*Between Two Worlds,* 151). I do not want to overstate Woland's innocence in the novel, but I believe that Barratt's examples of Berlioz's and Bengalsky's decapitations do not prove Woland's brutal malevolence sufficiently. Berlioz's death is, after all, "in the stars." Why must we see it as punishment for provoking Woland, and thus blame the messenger? Nor is Woland the direct agent in Bengalsky's decapitation. And as for the grotesque description of the decapitations— Woland is hardly responsible for that. Barratt's more central point on this matter, that these scenes dramatize both "the urge for retribution and the urge for mercy" and thus complicate the reader's emotional response, is extremely compelling (153).

36. See Frank Kermode's treatment of "concordance fictions" in *The Sense of an Ending: Studies in the Theory of Fiction* (New York: Oxford University Press, 1967).

37. This play on names ranges from the existence of an anonymous hero, to using famous names for minor characters (for example, Berlioz,

Stravinsky), to referring to individuals by profession (the poet, the chairman) rather than by name.

38. Bakhtin maintains that there is always a "second voice" in the consciousness of Dostoevsky's heroes; in the later novels, however, this second voice is embodied by an independent character. For example, "In its externally formal plan Ivan Karamazov's dialogue with the devil is analogous to those interior dialogues that Golyadkin conducts with himself and with his double; for all the dissimilarity in situation and in ideological content, essentially one and the same artistic task is being solved here" (*Problems of Dostoevsky's Poetics,* 217).

39. Perhaps the objection will be made that the Master's narrative of the novel's creation is also the story of his love for Margarita. In this instance, though, she fares no better than he. The Master tells Ivan: "She impatiently awaited the already promised final words . . . and she said that this novel contained—her life" (139, my ellipses). The allusion to the novel's "final words," which the Master has long since known, plays into the Master's and Margarita's belief that their love was "fated." Here again the biographical is translated into the textual.

40. Carol Avins, "Reaching a Reader: The Master's Audience in *The Master and Margarita,*" *Slavic Review* 45, no. 2 (1986): 272–85. See also the highly influential essay by Walter Benjamin, "The Work of Art in the Age of Mechanical Reproduction," in *Illuminations: Essays and Reflections,* ed. Hannah Arendt, trans. Harry Zohn (New York: Schocken, 1968).

41. I mean to suggest by the term "sympathetic readership" a balance similar to the one Gary Saul Morson and Caryl Emerson find in Bakhtin's concept of "creative understanding": "Unlike alternative forms of interpretation, then, creative understanding demands a double and dialogic activity. In contrast to relativism and modernization, it presumes that the text is truly *other* and contains semantic depths otherwise unattainable . . . it demands what Bakhtin calls the interpreter's own 'outsideness'" (*Mikhail Bakhtin,* 289). This balance lies in between an essentialism of meaning inside the text, on the one side, and a relativism of meaning outside the text, on the other. A similar dialogic balance, between present and past, is part of Gadamer's concept of "historically effected consciousness."

42. Bulgakov, *Жизнеописание,* 462. Bulgakov seems to have been particularly worried about problems of cultural dispersion caused by the Revolution. See the following note.

43. There is reason to believe that Bulgakov was concerned, even outside of his literary work, with the problem of cultural dispersion brought on by the Revolution. In 1922 he began (though did not complete) compiling a bibliography of Russian writers both in Russia and abroad (Чудакова, *Жизнеописание,* 167–68; see also Bulgakov's relationship with the journal Россия, 208). Russian authors, it seems, often make a career out of writing

both literature and history. See Andrew Wachtel, *An Obsession with History* (Stanford: Stanford University Press, 1994).

44. Barratt, *Between Two Worlds*, 250.

45. Again, since I have been loosely following the Glenny translation, I feel obliged to mention to the reader that one or two paragraphs here are missing entirely from the English edition.

46. Чудакова, *Жизнеописание*, 462.

47. Like many other critical terms, "parody" can be construed to mean many things. I am less interested in fixing the meaning of the term once and for all than I am in suggesting what it is not. I agree with Linda Hutcheon when she refuses to grant the parodying text absolute semantic authority over its target (*A Theory of Parody: The Teachings of Twentieth-Century Art Forms* [New York: Routledge, 1985], for example, 50). Here, she directly opposes Gary Saul Morson's definition of parody (*The Boundaries of Genre,* 110). Thus parody, in the sense in which I am using it, does not force the reader to agree with the values of the parodying text and, indeed, may call upon the reader to suspect those values.

48. It is important to make a distinction between the targets of parody that are outside *The Master and Margarita* and ones that are inside the novel. The Moscow story parodies works of literature by Pushkin, Tolstoy, and so on, but it also treats the Pilate story as a target of parody. I dwell on the parody of the Pilate story because the past in this text is allowed an independent voice in the novel, whereas Pushkin's "The Covetous Knight" is allowed a voice only inasmuch as the novel alludes to it.

49. Especially Тынянов, «Достоевский и Гоголь,» *Архаисты и новаторы* (Ленинград, 1929).

50. This kind of formalist analysis of literary evolution is reshaped and extended by Mikhail Bakhtin in the essay "Epic and Novel," in *The Dialogic Imagination.* Here, Bakhtin describes the novel as a form of literature that continually parodies other genres, and he sees the ascendancy of the novel in terms of its parody of traditional genres.

51. See Erich Auerbach, *Mimesis: The Representation of Reality in Western Literature,* trans. Willard R. Trask (Princeton: Princeton University Press, 1953), especially the final chapter "The Brown Stocking" on Virginia Woolf. Needless to say, Bulgakov is not interested in giving up all hope for literature's ability to convey the essence of experience.

52. The distinction may seem difficult to make. For example: "The relationship of the Master to Ivan is not precisely a parody of that between Yeshua and Matvei, but it is certainly a conscious parallel" (Ellendea Proffer, *Bulgakov: Life and Works* [Ann Arbor: Ardis, 1984], 539). I believe that when we do make a distinction between parody and parallelism, relationships that at first seem ambiguous, like the one cited by Proffer, turn out to be unexpectedly significant.

121

53. See, for example, William Mills Todd III, *Fiction and Society in the Age of Pushkin: Ideology, Institutions, and Narrative* (Cambridge: Harvard University Press, 1986). In this scene and others Bulgakov shows that his flair for the satiric and parodic also has a more subtle side. Personal confrontations and parties in *The Master and Margarita* inevitably parody nineteenth-century duels and balls of the *belle monde*, frequent mise en scènes of many of Bulgakov's favorite authors, especially Pushkin, Lermontov, and Tolstoy.

54. See Friedrich Nietzsche, *The Birth of Tragedy*. Available in various editions.

55. My analysis of these three approaches to the past and tradition benefits from Gadamer's description of the hermeneutical experience (*Erfahrung*) of tradition, which he analyzes in terms of three "I–Thou" relationships (not to be confused with Martin Buber's account). The third I–Thou constitutes the "historically effected consciousness": "I must allow tradition's claim to validity, not in the sense of simply acknowledging its otherness, but in such a way that it has something to say to me. This too calls for a fundamental sort of openness" (*Truth and Method*, 361).

56. Andrew Wachtel has reminded me that this is a strategy employed by modern composers, most notably Stravinsky in *Pulcinella* and other works. Music-related motifs are treated by Борис Гаспаров, «Из наблюдений над мотивной структурой романа М. А. Булгакова *Мастер и Маргарита*,» *Slavica Hierosolymitana* 3 (1978): 198–251.

57. Emphasis in original. Thomas Mann, *Doctor Faustus*, trans. H. T. Lowe-Porter (New York: Modern Library), 173.

58. Mikhail Bakhtin, "Author and Hero in Aesthetic Activity," in *Art and Answerability: Early Philosophical Essays*, ed. Michael Holquist and Vadim Liapunov, trans. Vadim Liapunov (Austin: University of Texas Press, 1990), 13.

59. Milne characterizes in a similar way the question of guilt and atonement in the novel: "The question of guilt was one that Bulgakov addressed right at the start of his literary career, with the story 'The Red Crown.' *Flight* gave guilt a dramatic embodiment and took it to the next stage: repentance expressed either as the criminal's suicide or his act of atonement. *The Master and Margarita* develops the latter of these two paths: suicide is enacted on the self by the self, but the fulfillment of atonement, which is remission of sin, cannot be granted to the self by the self: like immortality, it can only be granted by another" (*Mikhail Bulgakov*, 246).

60. With the term "rational spectator" I mean to refer to John Dewey, who dismantles traditional epistemology in *The Quest for Certainty* by arguing that it is based on a model of vision. See *John Dewey: The Later Works, 1925–1935*, vol. 4 (Carbondale: Southern Illinois University, 1988). It is worth noting that in an earlier redaction of *The Master and Margarita*,

Ivan draws in the dirt for Berlioz a caricature of Christ. When the unknown "citizen" (Woland) appears on the scene, he nevertheless immediately recognizes Christ in the drawing (Чудакова, *Жизнеописание,* 301).

61. See Carol Avins, "Reaching a Reader." It goes without saying that realism as a literary-historical movement cannot be reduced to concepts such as the physicality of a book.

62. The fiction of the Pilate story remains realistic, of course, but this need not impinge on the view of authorship implied by its production. A novel could magically appear in one's hands and still be a work of realism.

63. In his essay "Author and Hero in Aesthetic Activity," Bakhtin calls this return from the other the beginning of aesthetic activity, through which self-consciousness is gathered and integrated: "Aesthetic activity proper actually begins at the point when we *return* into ourselves, when we *return* to our own place outside the suffering person, and start to form and consummate the material we derived from projecting ourselves into the other and experiencing him from within himself" (26, emphasis in original). It is by "returning" from his shared experience with the Master that Bulgakov avoids identifying himself completely with his novel; such complete identification left the Master defenseless against the critics.

CHAPTER TWO

1. English translations of *Doctor Zhivago,* though often emended considerably by me, are taken from the paperback edition of *Doctor Zhivago,* trans. Max Hayward (New York: Signet, 1958). Any Russian quotes from *Doctor Zhivago* refer to Борис Пастернак, *Собрание сочинений в пяти томах,* том 3 (Москва, 1990).

2. See Neil Cornwell, "The Critical Heritage: Adulation and Onslaught," in *Pasternak's Novel: Perspectives on "Doctor Zhivago"* (Keele: 1986). See also Munir Sendich, *Boris Pasternak: A Reference* (New York: Macmillan, 1994).

3. Olga Andreyev Carlisle quotes Pasternak: "I believe that it is no longer possible for lyric poetry to express the immensity of our experience. Life has grown too cumbersome, too complicated. We have acquired values which are best expressed in prose" (*Voices in the Snow: Encounters with Russian Writers* [New York: Random House, 1962], 198). Henrik Birnbaum notes of this comment: "Also in his conversation with me, which took place at Peredelkino on August 30, 1959, Pasternak repeatedly emphasized that he now considered prose, rather than verse, the adequate literary form to mirror and interpret the experience of modern man." See Birnbaum, "Further Reflections on the Poetics of *Doctor Zhivago:* Structure, Technique, and Symbolism," in *Boris Pasternak and His Times: Selected Papers from the Second International Symposium on Pasternak,* ed. Lazar Fleishman

(Berkeley: Berkeley Slavic Specialties, 1989), 309. Pasternak may also have in mind here Pushkin's reflections on the path of his own writing career.

4. Joseph Frank, *The Widening Gyre: Crisis and Mastery in Modern Literature* (New Brunswick: Rutgers University Press, 1963), 60.

5. For an excellent comparison to *War and Peace*, see Elliot Mossman, "Metaphors of History in *War and Peace* and *Doctor Zhivago*," in *Literature and History: Theoretical Problems and Russian Case Studies*, ed. Gary Saul Morson (Stanford: Stanford University Press, 1986), 247–62. The comparison of Zhivago to the Russian type, the "superfluous man," has been made by many critics. Zhivago would reject such typology, of course: "Belonging to a type is the end of a man," Zhivago says, "his condemnation" (294).

6. The article is "Marginal Notes on the Prose of the Poet Pasternak," reprinted in Jakobson's *Language in Literature* (Cambridge: Harvard University Press, 1987), 301–17.

7. Coauthored with Morris Halle, and reprinted in *Language and Literature*, 95–114. Though Jakobson had spoken previously of metaphor and metonym, in an article on realism (1921) and in the article on Pasternak (1935), this essay on aphasia (1956) presents most fully his theory of their opposition. Unless otherwise noted, page references in parentheses refer to "Two Aspects."

8. By any standard, Jakobson's theory of the bipolarity in language has had a profound and varied effect on criticism. Claude Lévi-Strauss made use of the theory in his *The Savage Mind* (London: Weidenfeld and Nicholson, 1966), a foundational work of structural anthropology. The opposition of metaphor to metonymy plays a significant role in Jacques Lacan's reworking of Freudian psychoanalysis, for example, in *Ecrits: A Selection*, trans. Alan Sheridan (New York: Norton, 1977). David Lodge provides a comprehensive account of Jakobson's theory in *The Modes of Modern Writing: Metaphor, Metonymy, and the Typology of Modern Literature* (Ithaca: Cornell University Press, 1977), 73–124.

9. For example, in "Marginal Notes," 310, and also in "Two Aspects," 114.

10. The essay I refer to here is "Linguistics and Poetics," reprinted in Jakobson's *Language and Literature*, 71.

11. Jakobson, "Marginal Notes," 307.

12. For example, in *Boris Pasternak and His Times*, see Henrik Birnbaum, "Further Reflections on the Poetics of *Doctor Zhivago*: Structure, Technique, and Symbolism," 284–314; and Elliot Mossman, "Toward a Poetics of the Novel *Doctor Zhivago*: The Fourth Typhus," 386–97. Birnbaum has discussed the question in an earlier article, "On the Poetry of Prose: Land- and Cityscape 'Defamiliarized' in *Doctor Zhivago*," in *Fiction and Drama in Eastern and Southeastern Europe: Evolution and Experiment in*

the Postwar Period, ed. Henrik Birnbaum and Thomas Eekman (Columbus: Slavica, 1980), 27–60. I discuss Birnbaum's articles below.

13. Jakobson, "Two Aspects," 111.

14. For an intertextual approach, see Igor P. Smirnov, *Порождение интертекста: Элементы интертекстуального анализа с примерами из творчества Б. Л. Пастернака* (Vienna: Wiener slawistischer Almanach, 1985).

15. Birnbaum, "On the Poetry of Prose: Land- and Cityscape 'Defamiliarized' in *Doctor Zhivago*" (1980), and "Further Reflections on the Poetics of *Doctor Zhivago:* Structure, Technique, and Symbolism" (1989). Birnbaum has also directed his attention to the question of *Doctor Zhivago*'s genre. See "Gedichtroman und Romangedicht im russischen Postsymbolismus (Zu einigen tiefgründigen Übereinstimmungen und oberflächlichen Unterschieden zwischen *Doctor Schiwago* und dem *Poem ohne Helden*)," in *Text, Symbol, Weltmodell. Johannes Holthusen zum 60. Geburtstag,* ed. J. R. Doring et al. (Munich, 1984), 9–36; and *Doktor Faustus und Doktor Schiwago. Versuch über zwei Zeitromane aus Exilsicht* (Lisse, 1976). I have consulted Birnbaum's excellent remarks on the novel and followed his examples to some passages in the novel that I had previously not considered.

16. Birnbaum, "On the Poetry of Prose," 33; "Further Reflections," 296.

17. Birnbaum, "On the Poetry of Prose," 35.

18. Birnbaum, "Further Reflections," 291. Compare Birnbaum, "Gedichtroman und Romangedicht im russischen Postsymbolismus."

19. Birnbaum, "On the Poetry of Prose," 28; "Further Reflections," 295.

20. By "signifying process" I mean the constitution of the subject's identity in language. I equate this process with Zhivago's repeated attempts to retrieve through metaphor an archaic, secure identity. Compare Julia Kristeva, "From One Identity to Another," in *Desire in Language: A Semiotic Approach to Literature and Art* (New York: Columbia University Press, 1980), 124–47, especially 136.

21. Hayden White, who refers to such figures more correctly, strictly speaking, as synecdoche, sees the crucial difference between metonymy and synecdoche in their reductive (metonymy) versus integrative (synecdoche) capacities. He views the metonymy "fifty sails," referring to fifty ships, for example, as mechanistic and reductive; whereas the phrase "he is all heart," which is still a part/whole relation like that of metonymy, can be read as a synecdoche, "suggesting a qualitative relationship among the elements of a totality" (*Metahistory: The Historical Imagination in Nineteenth-Century Europe* [Baltimore: Johns Hopkins University Press, 1973], 36). The emphasis is on the *qualitative* wholeness intimated by synecdoche.

22. Auerbach, *Mimesis,* 73.

23. By identifying it as a "hidden epic device" in Pasternak's poetry, Ilya Kutik makes a similar teleological treatment of Pasternak's use of metaphor, and suggests, almost parenthetically, that here is the crux of Pasternak's

dualism, "his divarication between poetry and big prose" (*The Ode and the Odic: Essays on Mandelstam, Pasternak, Tsvetaeva and Mayakovsky,* Ph.D. dissertation, Stockholm University [Stockholm: Almqvist and Wiksell, 1994], 109). The teleological dimension should also remind one that the distinction between metaphor and metonymy is tenuous. When "clods of earth" become "rain," when the metaphor is realized, we view a *process* that recalls metonymic contiguity.

24. As I mentioned in the introduction to this volume, Zhivago's volume of poetry is a *mise en abyme* that reflects the utterance of the narrative, in Dällenbach's terminology. It is also a *mise en abyme* of the enunciative type because Zhivago indicates that his poetry is a "work in progress" for a large prose work, which would, one presumes, resemble *Doctor Zhivago* itself.

25. Dällenbach, *The Mirror in the Text,* 61. Dällenbach says of these *mises en abyme:* "If the initial *mise en abyme* says *everything* before the fiction has really started, the final or terminal *mise en abyme* has *nothing* to say save repeating *what is already known* . . . This is a great constraint which, apparently, can only be avoided in one way: by moving on to a higher plane and universalizing the meaning of the narrative" (65, emphasis in original, my ellipses). Such a "transcendental" ending, in some ways a good characterization of Zhivago's collection of poems, also emphasizes how the preceding was *not* transcendent, as Dällenbach later suggests, tongue in cheek.

26. For a comparison to Dickens, see Christopher Barnes, "Pasternak, Dickens and the Novel Tradition," *Forum for Modern Language Studies* 26, no. 4 (1990): 326–41.

27. Pasternak's descriptions of childhood draw heavily on nineteenth-century literary traditions. See Andrew Wachtel, *The Battle for Childhood: Creation of a Russian Myth,* especially chapter 3, "Canonizing the Myths of Russian Gentry Childhood" (Stanford: Stanford University Press, 1990), 82–130. Of the "canonized myths" we could include Zhivago's idealized mother and spendthrift father, as well as the unhappy childhood of the *raznochinets* Dudorov. Though *War and Peace* is the most obvious work of Tolstoy's that Pasternak alludes to in *Doctor Zhivago,* Tolstoy's *Childhood* and other works must also be added to this list. See my discussion below, *passim,* of *Anna Karenina,* "The Kreutzer Sonata," and "The Death of Ivan Ilych."

28. On the question of anti-Semitism, see D. Segal, "Pro Domo Sua: The Case of Boris Pasternak," *Slavica Hierosolymitana* 1 (1977): 199–250. Lazar Fleishman briefly addresses the question in *Boris Pasternak: The Poet and His Politics* (Cambridge: Harvard University Press, 1990), 263–67.

29. Similar uses of narrative framing have been noted by Amy Mandelker for Tolstoy, Charles Isenberg for Turgenev, and Alexander Zholkovsky for Bunin. See Amy Mandelker, *Framing Anna Karenina: Tolstoy, the Woman Question, and the Victorian Novel* (Columbus: Ohio State University Press, 1993); Charles Isenberg, *Telling Silence,* and note especially

his discussion of the dumb scene and *mises en abyme* in *First Love* (22–49); and Alexander Zholkovsky, "A Study in Framing: Pushkin, Bunin, Nabokov, and Theories of Story and Discourse," in *Text counter Text*, 88–113.

30. The "homelessness" of identity befalls characters especially at times of temporal "in-betweenness," for lack of a better term. Pasternak thematizes a similar semiotic interlude in Zhivago's typhus-ridden dream of writing "a poem not about the resurrection and not about the burial, but about the days passing in between the one and the other" (206).

31. Zhivago's youthful moralism in the early parts of the novel is also informed by Solovyov, though I think the Tolstoyan connection is the stronger of the two. Jerome Spencer provides an account of Pasternak's position in the Tolstoy/Solovyov polemic on love in "'Soaked in *The Meaning of Love* and *The Kreutzer Sonata*': The Nature of Love in *Doctor Zhivago*," in *"Doctor Zhivago": A Critical Companion*, ed. Edith W. Clowes (Evanston: Northwestern University Press, 1995), 76–88.

32. Entry for "Puppet theater," in *Handbook of Russian Literature*, ed. Victor Terras (New Haven: Yale University Press, 1985), 356. For more on the Petrushka, see *Petrushka: Sources and Contexts*, ed. Andrew Wachtel (Evanston: Northwestern University Press, 1998).

33. Pasternak's preliminary epigraph for *Doctor Zhivago* from Revelation also served as a starting point for "The Death of Ivan Ilych." Noted by Mossman in "Toward a Poetics," 396.

34. On the symbolism of the railroad, see Roger Anderson, "The Railroad in *Doctor Zhivago*," *SEEJ* 31, vol. 4 (1987): 503–19.

35. Jakobson, "Two Aspects," 309. Homeric, or epic, simile shares these characteristics.

36. See note 3.

37. In Jacques Lacan's reworking of Freudian psychoanalysis, such failures can be explained by reference to the constitution of the infant's identity in a "mirror stage." See "The Mirror Stage as Formative of the Function of the I," in Lacan, *Ecrits*, 1–7. See also, in *Ecrits*, chapter 5, "The Agency of the Letter in the Unconscious since Freud," and chapter 9, "The Subversion of the Subject and the Dialectic of Desire in the Freudian Unconscious." Simply, when a mother speaks the infant's name as she nurses it, she fosters a sense of deeply grounded personal identity associated with the "mirror" of the name. However, that sense of subjective identity is also thereby tragically bound to an unstable signifier (the "I"), forming an "ideal ego," the demands of which can never be met in the real world by the workings of adult desire. For desire functions in specific, metonymic, contexts that do not repeat the metaphoric demands created by the constitution of identity in the mirror stage. In other words, there is no relation to a love object that is able to refoster the deep sense of security in which identity was originally formed. This gloss on the mother's voice and the name is largely

informed by Charles Altieri's reading of Lacan in *Painterly Abstraction in Modernist American Poetry: The Contemporaneity of Modernism* (Cambridge: Cambridge University Press, 1989), 450. Identity, thus conceived, is tied both to language—the name as signifier—and, in language, to Jakobson's metaphoric pole—similarity and substitution as the grounds and object of desire. By taking up the psychoanalytical model in interpretation of *Doctor Zhivago,* one clears a space for discussing in psychological terms the figurative language of the novel. Lacan takes the structure of metaphor/metonym from Jakobson in, for example, "Agency of the Letter," 156. That one should speak of Zhivago's identity in primarily metaphoric terms should surprise no one; after all, the name "Zhivago" is itself a metaphor for the "man of life."

38. See Pasternak's poem "Marburg," where the Russian word for "likeness" is twice repeated: in the first stanza, "... и ветер, как лодочник, греб / По липам. И все это были подобья" and again later in the poem: "Все—живо. И все это тоже—подобья." Ilya Kutik discusses at length the role of "likeness" in Pasternak's poetics in "Boris Pasternak—The Odic as a 'God of Details,'" in *The Ode and the Odic,* 59–109.

39. One also notes a similarity in language between the quoted passage and Pasternak's poem, "Так начинает. Года два," which I quoted as an epigraph to the section "Childhood and Authorship" of this chapter. In *Doctor Zhivago* the passage reads: "ему то и дело мерещилось, будто мать аукается с ним." In the poem, the pertinent lines are: "Мерещится, что мать—не мать. / Что ты—не ты, что дом—чужбина."

40. Compare to Zhivago's dream of Lara's voice (ex. 8) in part 9 of the novel.

41. Elliott Mossman considers that Zhivago's greatest poetic inspirations come from his encounters with death, and that the novel's guiding metaphor is a catachresis, a wresting of one metaphor from another, that is best seen in the metaphorical disease of a "fourth typhus." See "Toward a Poetics."

42. See Stephanie Sandler, *Distant Pleasures: Alexander Pushkin and the Writing of Exile* (Stanford: Stanford University Press, 1989). I use her literal translation of "To the Sea" (59–61), and my discussion of Pushkin benefits from her discussion of the poem in the chapter "Distance in the Lyric Voice" (16–77).

43. The translation is mine. I tried to follow the original Russian closely, but I was not always successful in rendering one-to-one equivalents. Alternate translations of key words are provided in my discussion of the poem.

44. In his translation of Shakespeare, Pasternak renders the lines as: "При бодром духе тело / Чувствительно. Но у меня в груди / Все вытеснено вон душевной бурей." It seems safe to say that Pasternak emphasizes the spiritual storm of the mind in this translation.

45. Sandler, *Distant Pleasures,* 66.

46. Compare Pasternak's "Тема": "Скала и шторм. Скала и плащ и шляпа. / Скала и—Пушкин." The word for "crags" (скала) has reference here to Byron as well as to Pushkin. The image of the "storm" is of course also present in "Separation." A further connection between Pushkin and Pasternak in this regard may very well be in Tsvetaeva's fourth poem of her cycle "Разлука": "Думаешь—скалы / Манят, утесы, / Думаешь, славы / Медноголосый // Зов его—в гушу, / Грудью на копья? / Вал восстающий / —Думаешь—топит?"

47. Compare Akhmatova's "Separation" (Разлука; 1914), which also figures a reduction from spoken language to silence: "Вечерний и наклонный / Передо мною путь. / Вчера еще, влюбленный, / Молил: «Не позабудь». / А нынче только ветры / Да крики пастухов, / Взволнованные кедры / У чистых родников," (*Стихотворения и поэмы* [Ленинград, 1989], 152.

48. Quoted by Christian Wiman in "Finishes: Notes on Ambition and Survival," *Poetry* 169, no. 3 (1997): 223.

CHAPTER THREE

1. English translations and references to the novel under discussion refer to Vladimir Nabokov, *The Gift,* trans. Michael Scammell with collaboration of the author (New York: Vintage, 1991). Any Russian notes to *The Gift* refer to Владимир Набоков, *Собрание сочинений в четырех томах,* том 3 (Москва, 1990), 5–330.

2. Vladimir Nabokov, *Strong Opinions* (New York: McGraw-Hill, 1973), 57. For a discussion of Nabokov's marginal notes to *Doctor Zhivago* (notes for a review he never wrote), see Robert P. Hughes, "Nabokov Reading Pasternak," in *Boris Pasternak and His Times,* 153–70.

3. For example, Simon Karlinsky, "Vladimir Nabokov's Novel *Dar* as a Work of Literary Criticism: A Structural Analysis," *Slavic and East European Journal* 7 (1963): 284–90; and Sergei Davydov, "*The Gift:* Nabokov's Aesthetic Exorcism of Chernyshevsky," *Canadian-American Slavic Studies* 19 (1985): 357–74.

4. For an excellent narratological study of Nabokov's metafiction, see Pekka Tammi, *Problems of Nabokov's Poetics: A Narratological Analysis* (Helsinki: Somalainen Tiedeakatemia, 1985).

5. See D. Barton Johnson, "Nabokov as Literary Chess Problemist," in *Worlds in Regression: Some Novels of Vladimir Nabokov* (Ann Arbor: Ardis, 1985), 79–107.

6. Linda Hutcheon, *Narcissistic Narrative.*

7. Leona Toker, *Nabokov: The Mystery of Literary Structures* (Ithaca: Cornell University Press, 1989); Irena Ronen and Omry Ronen, "'Diabolically Evocative': An Inquiry into the Meaning of a Metaphor," *Slavica Hi-*

erosolymitana 5–6 (1981): 371–86; and Sergej Davydov, *'Teksty-matreski'*
Vladimira Nabokova (Munich: O. Sagner, 1982).

8. Davydov, *'Teksty-matreski.'*

9. The play here is on the different meanings of ключи ("keys," "key moves," "springs"). See D. Barton Johnson, "The Key to Nabokov's *Gift*," *Canadian-American Slavic Studies* 16, no. 2 (1982): 190–206; and his "Nabokov as Literary Chess Problemist." See also Sarah Tiffany Waite, "On the Linear Structure of Nabokov's *Dar:* Three Keys, Six Chapters," *Slavic and East European Journal* 39, no. 1 (1995): 54–72. Waite also provides examples of the many critical metaphors used to describe the structure of *The Gift.*

10. Toker describes a "receding spiral" (*Nabokov,* 161).

11. Johnson, *Worlds in Regression,* 93–107.

12. Karlinsky, *"Dar* as a Work of Literary Criticism."

13. Donald Malcolm, review of *The Gift,* by Vladimir Nabokov, translated by Michael Scammell, *New Yorker* (April 25, 1964): 198, 202–4. Quoted by Waite, "On the Linear Structure," 59.

14. Vladimir Alexandrov (*Nabokov's Otherworld* [Princeton: Princeton University Press, 1991]) is the foremost critic who takes issue with Nabokov's being read primarily (and sometimes solely) as a master of metafiction. I am not the first to discuss *The Gift* in terms of *mise en abyme;* see Georges Nivat, "Deux romans 'speculaires' des les années trente." Tammi (*Problems of Nabokov's Poetics*) does not use the term *mise en abyme,* but his narratological analysis of Nabokov highlights the same metaliterary features.

15. Fyodor/Nabokov pays very close attention to the effect he has on his readers. See Stephen H. Blackwell's insightful *Zina's Paradox: The Figured Reader in Nabokov's "The Gift"* (New York: Peter Lang, 2000), especially chapter 3, "The Structure of the Problematic Reading."

16. Alexandrov, *Nabokov's Otherworld,* 113. My ellipses.

17. Ibid., 3.

18. Leona Toker sees a similar split between critical literature that "either discusses his breathtakingly subtle techniques or explores his humanistic themes (the latter a rather recent reaction to the previously unjust treatment of Nabokov as a cold virtuoso)" (*Nabokov,* ix).

19. Taylor, *Sources of the Self,* 41–42.

20. Alexandrov, *Nabokov's Otherworld.*

21. Vladimir Nabokov, *Speak, Memory* (New York: Pyramid, 1966), 7.

22. Joseph Frank, "Spatial Form in Modern Literature," in his *The Widening Gyre: Crisis and Mastery in Modern Literature.* Alexandrov draws the connection between Nabokov's fiction and Frank's ideas on spatial form (*Nabokov's Otherworld,* 47, 215), as does Tammi (*Problems of Nabokov's Poetics,* 16–17, n. 43).

23. As Pekka Tammi has put it: "the relationship between man's life and its literary representation in the text becomes the dominant Nabokovian theme" (*Problems of Nabokov's Poetics*, 21).

24. Michael Holquist interprets Dostoevsky's *Notes from Underground* as similarly rejecting an Aristotelian plot for one's life. See his chapter on *Notes from Underground*, significantly entitled "The Search for a Story," in *Dostoevsky and the Novel*.

25. D. Barton Johnson discusses this and other aspects of the relationship between Bely and Nabokov in "Bely and Nabokov: A Comparative Overview," *Russian Literature* 9 (1981): 379–402. Alexandrov sees a special connection in this scene with *Petersburg* because Fyodor uses two crucial words from the latter work—рой and ритм (*Nabokov's Otherworld*, 218).

26. Sergei Davydov puts Fyodor's path through Russian literary history concisely: "It is interesting to note that Fëdor's development as an artist loosely parallels the path of the history of Russian literature of the nineteenth century. Chapter 1, which covers the years of Fëdor's poetic apprenticeship and contains his juvenile verse, corresponds to the Golden Age of Russian poetry, the early 1820s. Chapter 2 is Fëdor's Pushkin period. Following Pushkin's example, Fëdor makes his own transition to prose with Pushkin's "Journey to Arzrum" serving as inspiration for Fëdor's imaginary exotic journey to Central Asia. At the end of the chapter, Fëdor informs us that the distance from his old residence in chapter 2 to the new one in chapter 3 "was about the same as, somewhere in Russia, that from Pushkin Avenue to Gogol' Street" (167/157). Chapter 3 brings us to the 1840s, Fëdor's Gogol' period. Reading *Dead Souls* is a perfect exercise in detecting *poshlust*, while Gogol's art of the grotesque sets a stylistic example of how *poshlust* should be mocked. Fëdor applies this new skill in his biography of Chernyshevskii in chapter 4, where he reenacts the literary polemics of the 1860s. Chapter 5 is a recapitulation of all the previous themes, leading to the eternal themes, such as death, religion and immortality, that of Dostoevskii and Tolstoi. By the end of chapter 5 Fëdor's last work is born, *The Gift* itself. With this novel . . . Nabokov/Fëdor makes his entry into modern Russian literature, *The Gift* representing a part of that tradition" ("Nabokov's Aesthetic Exorcism," 359–60, my ellipses).

27. Alexander Dolinin discusses this aspect of chronology in the novel, and he carefully explores the bifurcation of real and imaginary time in *The Gift* and other works by Nabokov. See his "Nabokov's Time Doubling: From *The Gift* to *Lolita*," *Nabokov Studies* 2 (1995): 3–40.

28. Karlinsky, "*Dar* as a Work of Literary Criticism," 287.

29. Shoes and footsteps have drawn several critics' attention. Alexandrov discusses a "footstep motif" as part of the novel's relation to the transcendental (*Nabokov's Otherworld*, 111); Toker notes that Fyodor's "shoes seem to stretch together with the growth of [his] creative experience"

(*Nabokov,* 160); and Davydov views the scene in light of incidents from Chernyshevsky's life ("Nabokov's Aesthetic Exorcism").

30. See Nabokov's commentary to *Eugene Onegin* in Aleksandr Pushkin, *Eugene Onegin: A Novel in Verse,* translated with commentary by Vladimir Nabokov (Princeton: Princeton University Press, 1975).

31. Monika Greenleaf, "Pushkin's Trace in *The Gift," Slavic Review* 53, no. 1 (Spring 1994): 149.

32. Brian Boyd, *Vladimir Nabokov: The Russian Years* (Princeton: Princeton University Press, 1990), 472.

33. Boyd, *Vladimir Nabokov: The Russian Years,* 471.

34. Nearly all critics of *The Gift* say something about Pushkin, but see especially Greenleaf, "Pushkin's Trace"; Karlinsky, "*Dar* as a Work of Literary Criticism; and Davydov, "Nabokov's Aesthetic Exorcism."

35. А. С. Пушкин, *Сочинения в трех томах,* том третий (Минск, 1987).

36. Пушкин, 376.

37. Wachtel, *An Obsession with History,* 66. My ellipses.

38. John Burt Foster, *Nabokov's Art of Memory and European Modernism* (Princeton: Princeton University Press, 1993).

39. John Kopper has reminded me that, as critics have noted, Nabokov frequently creates mundane and fragmented worlds in his fiction which refer to an invisible sphere of purity and beauty (*Ada, Bend Sinister, Invitation to a Beheading, Glory, Luzhin's Defense,* among others). That sphere may be conjured by writing or by death. In *The Gift* Fyodor's study of his father provides both.

40. Alexandrov, *Nabokov's Otherworld.*

41. Marina Kostalevsky, "The Young Godunov-Cherdyntsev or How to Write a Literary Biography," *Russian Literature* 43 (1998): 283–95.

42. Irina Paperno, "How Nabokov's *Gift* is Made," in *Literature, Culture, and Society in the Modern Age: Festschrift in Honor of Joseph Frank,* Stanford Slavic Studies, vol. 4, no. 2 (Stanford: Stanford University Press [1992]), 309–10.

43. My ellipses, Boris Eikhenbaum, *The Young Tolstoy,* trans. Gary Kern (Ann Arbor: Ardis, 1972), 8.

44. Nabokov expands on the "dual censorship" of nineteenth-century Russian literature in "Russian Writers, Censors, and Readers," in his *Lectures on Russian Literature,* ed. Fredson Bowers (New York: Harcourt Brace Jovanovich, 1981).

45. That Nabokov would equate Chernyshevsky's life experience with the same sort of circularity that the reader experiences is perhaps not too surprising. As Alexandrov notes, Nabokov "may have seen the hermeneutics of experience and the hermeneutics of reading as equivalents" (*Nabokov's Otherworld,* 8).

46. Twentieth-century criticism has related death and authorship in two basic ways: there have been two "deaths" of the author. (Svetlana Boym provides a useful overview of theories of death and authorship in the introduction to her *Death in Quotation Marks: Cultural Myths of the Modern Poet* [Cambridge: Harvard University Press, 1991].) According to the first version, literary criticism must not draw direct lines of causation between the author's real life and his works. In their more strident articles the Russian formalists, for example, banned facts of the real author's life to "literary biography." (See Boris Tomashevsky, "Literature and Biography," in Matejka and Pomorska, *Readings in Russian Poetics,* 255–70.) The second version of the death of the author, popularized by French structuralism, relegates subjectivity to the back rooms of the literary process and views authorship as an impersonal linguistic phenomenon (see Barthes's "Death of the Author"). Fyodor would accept some aspects of the first version and reject the second entirely.

47. Blackwell's discussion of Zina as creative reader posits a prior, and more fundamental, novelistic structure for transcendence: "When Zina hears and critiques *The Gift*—when the entire novel is presented through her readerly perspective—we are forced to reconsider the nature of art and the place of human relationships (especially love relationships) in the world. *Reading is presented as a model for transcendence of the isolated self,* a merging of two beings in the artistic sphere, where the triviality and ugliness of daily life in Berlin makes way for an intimation of unfettered existence" (my emphasis, *Zina's Paradox,* 6).

48. Pushkin, *Eugene Onegin,* 1:319.

49. Karlinsky notes the "mirror-image technique" relating chapters after the *Life of Chernyshevsky* to chapters before it (*"Dar* as a Work of Literary Criticism," 286).

50. Vladimir Nabokov, *Invitation to a Beheading* (New York: Vintage, 1989), 124.

51. The whole notion of the death of the author is again taken up by Nabokov with daunting sophistication in *Pale Fire.* In that novel, there is certainly at least one death of an author, perhaps a murder, though it might also be only a metaliterary play of mirrors. Whereas Fyodor lives on at the end of *The Gift,* Shade's daughter has certainly committed suicide in *Pale Fire.* Thus in re-creating aspects of authorship in *Pale Fire* that he had previously considered in *The Gift,* Nabokov forges a far more grim combination of death and metaliterary play.

CONCLUSION

The epigraph for this chapter is from Boris Eikhenbaum's introduction to *The Young Tolstoy* (Молодой Толстой [Петербург, 1922], 9).

1. Lydia Ginzburg, *On Psychological Prose,* ed. and trans. Judson Rosengrant (Princeton: Princeton University Press, 1991), 221. My portrayal of the nineteenth-century Russian psychological novel below is informed by Ginzburg's compelling account.

2. Realism as such is an aesthetic system that coheres more in theory than in practice. For "non-realist" views of Russia's most famous realists, see Elizabeth Cheresh Allen, *Beyond Realism: Turgenev's Poetics of Secular Salvation* (Stanford: Stanford University Press, 1992); Donald Fanger, *Dostoevsky and Romantic Realism* (Cambridge: Harvard University Press, 1967); and Amy Mandelker, *Framing Anna Karenina.*

3. Emphasis in original. Ginzburg, *On Psychological Prose,* 245.

4. Nabokov, who loved Tolstoy's novels above nearly all others, criticized Pasternak/Zhivago for forgetting to mention anything about Tonia and their children at various points in the novel. See Robert P. Hughes, "Nabokov Reading Pasternak."

5. See Andrew Wachtel, "Psychology and Society in the Classic Russian Novel," in *The Cambridge Companion to the Classic Russian Novel,* ed. Malcolm V. Jones and Robin Feuer Miller (Cambridge: Cambridge University Press, 1998).

6. Nabokov, *Lectures on Russian Literature,* 109.

7. See my discussion of Dällenbach's *The Mirror in the Text* and his definitions of the *mise en abyme* in my introduction.

8. See Amy Mandelker, *Framing Anna Karenina;* and also Justin Weir, "Anna Incommunicada: Language and Consciousness in *Anna Karenina,*" *Tolstoy Studies Journal* 8 (1997).

9. "Russian Writers, Censors, and Readers," in Nabokov, *Lectures on Russian Literature,* 11.

Bibliography

Alexandrov, Vladimir. *Nabokov's Otherworld*. Princeton: Princeton University Press, 1991.

Allen, Elizabeth Cheresh. *Beyond Realism: Turgenev's Poetics of Secular Salvation*. Stanford: Stanford University Press, 1992.

Alter, Robert. *Partial Magic: The Novel as a Self-Conscious Genre*. Los Angeles: University of California Press, 1975.

Altieri, Charles. *Painterly Abstraction in Modernist American Poetry*. Cambridge: Cambridge University Press, 1989.

Anderson, Roger. "The Railroad in *Doctor Zhivago*." *Slavic and East European Journal* 31, no. 4 (1987): 503–19.

Auerbach, Erich. *Mimesis: The Representation of Reality in Western Literature*. Translated by Willard R. Trask. Princeton: Princeton University Press, 1953.

Avins, Carol. "Reaching a Reader: The Master's Audience in *The Master and Margarita*." *Slavic Review* 45, no. 2 (1986): 272–85.

Ахматова, Анна. *Стихотворения и поэмы*. Ленинград, 1989.

Bakhtin, M. M. *Art and Answerability: Early Philosophical Essays*. Edited by Michael Holquist and Vadim Liapunov, translated by Vadim Liapunov. Austin: University of Texas Press, 1990.

———. *The Dialogic Imagination: Four Essays by M. M. Bakhtin*. Edited by Michael Holquist, translated by Caryl Emerson and Michael Holquist. Austin: University of Texas Press, 1981.

———. *Problems of Dostoevsky's Poetics*. Edited and translated by Caryl Emerson. Minneapolis: University of Minnesota Press, 1984.

Barnes, Christopher. "Pasternak, Dickens and the Novel Tradition." *Forum for Modern Language Studies* 26, no. 4 (1990): 326–41.

Barratt, Alexander. *Between Two Worlds: A Critical Introduction to "The Master and Margarita."* Oxford: Oxford Clarendon Press, 1987.

Belinsky, V. G. *Selected Philosophical Works*. Moscow: Foreign Language Publishing House, 1956.

Benjamin, Walter. *Illuminations: Essays and Reflections*. Edited by Hannah Arendt, translated by Harry Zohn. New York: Schocken, 1968.

135

Bethea, David. *The Shape of the Apocalypse in Modern Russian Fiction.* Princeton: Princeton University Press, 1989.

Birnbaum, Henrik. *Doktor Faustus und Doktor Schiwago. Versuch über zwei Zeitromane aus Exilsicht.* Lisse, 1976.

———. "Further Reflections on the Poetics of *Doctor Zhivago:* Structure, Technique, and Symbolism." In *Boris Pasternak and His Times: Selected Papers from the Second International Symposium on Pasternak,* edited by Lazar Fleishman. Berkeley: Berkeley Slavic Specialties, 1989.

———. "Gedichtroman und Romangedicht im russischen Postsymbolismus (Zu einigen tiefgründigen Übereinstimmungen und oberflächlichen Unterschieden zwischen *Doctor Schiwago* und dem *Poem ohne Helden*)." In *Text, Symbol, Weltmodell. Johannes Holthusen zum 60. Geburtstag,* edited by J. R. Doring et al. Munich, 1984.

———. "On the Poetry of Prose: Land- and Cityscape 'Defamiliarized' in *Doctor Zhivago.*" In *Fiction and Drama in Eastern and Southeastern Europe: Evolution and Experiment in the Postwar Period,* edited by Henrik Birnbaum and Thomas Eekman. Columbus: Slavica, 1980.

Blackwell, Stephen H. "Nabokov's *The Gift:* The Image of Reading in Artistic Creation." Ph.D. dissertation. Indiana University, 1995.

———. *Zina's Paradox: The Figured Reader in Nabokov's "The Gift."* New York: Peter Lang, 2000.

Bloom, Harold. *The Anxiety of Influence: A Theory of Poetry.* London: Oxford University Press, 1973.

Boyd, Brian. *Vladimir Nabokov: The Russian Years.* Princeton: Princeton University Press, 1990.

Boym, Svetlana. *Death in Quotation Marks: Cultural Myths of the Modern Poet.* Cambridge: Harvard University Press, 1991.

Bulgakov, Mikhail. *The Master and Margarita.* Translated by Diana Burgin and Katherine Tiernan O'Connor. Ann Arbor: Ardis, 1995.

———. *The Master and Margarita.* Translated by Michael Glenny. New York: Harper and Row, 1967.

———. *Собрание сочинений в пяти томах,* Том пятый. Москва: Художественная литература, 1992.

Burke, Seán. *Authorship: From Plato to the Postmodern: A Reader.* Edinburgh: Edinburgh University Press, 1995.

Carlisle, Olga Andreyev. *Voices in the Snow: Encounters with Russian Writers.* New York: Random House, 1962.

Carrick, Neil. *Daniil Kharms: Theologian of the Absurd.* Birmingham: Department of Russian Language and Literature, University of Birmingham, 1998.

Chudakova, Marietta. "Gogol in the Life and Works of Mikhail Bulgakov." *Soviet Literature* 4 (1984).

————. "*The Master and Margarita:* The Development of a Novel." *Russian Literature Triquarterly* 15 (1976): 177–209.

————. *Жизнеописание Михаила Булгакова.* Москва, 1988.

Clark, Katerina. *The Soviet Novel: History as Ritual.* Chicago: University of Chicago Press, 1985.

Cornwell, Neil. *Pasternak's Novel: Perspectives on "Doctor Zhivago."* Keele, 1986.

Dällenbach, Lucien. *The Mirror in the Text.* Translated by Jeremy Whiteley with Emma Hughes. Chicago: University of Chicago Press, 1989.

Davydov, Sergei. "*The Gift:* Nabokov's Aesthetic Exorcism of Chernyshevsky." *Canadian-American Slavic Studies* 19 (1985): 357–74.

————. *'Teksty-matreski' Vladimira Nabokova.* Munich, 1982.

Descartes, René. *Meditations on First Philosophy in Which the Existence of God and the Distinction of the Soul from the Body Are Demonstrated.* Translated by Donald A. Cress. Indianapolis: Hackett, 1979.

Dewey, John. *John Dewey: The Later Works, 1925–1935.* Vol. 4. Carbondale: Southern Illinois University, 1988.

Dolinin, Alexander. "Nabokov's Time Doubling: From *The Gift* to *Lolita.*" *Nabokov Studies* 2 (1995): 3–40.

————. *О литературе: работы разных лет.* Москва: Советский писатель, 1987.

Эйхенбаум, Борис. *Молодой Толстой.* Петербург, 1922.

Eikhenbaum, Boris, and Yury Tynyanov, eds. *Russian Prose.* Translated by Ray Parrot. Ann Arbor: Ardis, 1985.

Eliot, T. S. *Selected Prose of T. S. Eliot.* Edited by Frank Kermode. New York: Harcourt Brace Jovanovich/Farrar, Straus and Giroux, 1975.

Erlich, Victor. "The Novel in Crisis: Boris Pilnyak and Konstantin Fedin." In *The Russian Novel from Pushkin to Pasternak,* edited by John Garrard. New Haven: Yale University Press, 1983.

————. *Russian Formalism: History–Doctrine.* 3rd ed. New Haven: Yale University Press, 1955.

Ermolaev, Herman. *Soviet Literary Theories, 1917–1934: The Genesis of Socialist Realism.* Berkeley: University of California Press, 1963.

Eysteinsson, Astradur. *The Concept of Modernism.* Ithaca: Cornell University Press, 1990.

Fanger, Donald. *Dostoevsky and Romantic Realism.* Cambridge: Harvard University Press, 1967.

Fedin, Konstantin. *Cities and Years.* Translated by Michael Scammell. Evanston: Northwestern University Press, 1993.

Fleishman, Lazar. *Boris Pasternak: The Poet and His Politics.* Cambridge: Harvard University Press, 1990.

Foster, John Burt. *Nabokov's Art of Memory and European Modernism.* Princeton: Princeton University Press, 1993.

Foucault, Michel. *Language, Counter-Memory Practice: Selected Essays and Interviews.* Edited by Donald Bouchard, translated by Donald Bouchard and Sherry Simon. Ithaca: Cornell University Press, 1977.

———. *The Order of Things: An Archeology of the Human Sciences.* New York: Vintage, 1970.

Frank, Joseph. *The Widening Gyre: Crisis and Mastery in Modern Literature.* New Brunswick: Rutgers University Press, 1963.

Freud, Sigmund. *On Narcissism: An Introduction.* Vol. 14 of *The Standard Edition of the Complete Psychological Works of Sigmund Freud.* Edited by James Strachey. New York: Norton, 1966.

Gadamer, Hans-Georg. *Truth and Method.* 2nd ed., rev. Translated and revised by Joel Weinsheimer and Donald Marshall. New York: Continuum, 1989.

Гаспаров, Борис. «Из наблюдений над мотивной структурой романа М. А. Булгакова *Мастер и Маргарита*,» *Slavica Hierosolymitana* 3 (1978): 198–251.

Ginzburg, Lydia. *On Psychological Prose.* Translated and edited by Judson Rosengrant. Princeton: Princeton University Press, 1991.

Greenleaf, Monika. "Pushkin's Trace in *The Gift.*" *Slavic Review* 53, no. 1 (Spring 1994): 140–58.

Habermas, Jürgen. *The Philosophical Discourse of Modernity: Twelve Lectures.* Translated by Frederick G. Lawrence. Cambridge: MIT Press, 1987.

Hoisington, Sonya. "Fairy-Tale Elements in Bulgakov's *The Master and Margarita.*" *Slavic and East European Journal* 25 (1981): 44–55.

Holquist, Michael. *Dostoevsky and the Novel.* Princeton: Princeton University Press, 1977.

Hughes, Robert P. "Nabokov Reading Pasternak." In *Boris Pasternak and His Times: Selected Papers from the Second International Symposium on Pasternak,* edited by Lazar Fleishman. Berkeley: Berkeley Slavic Specialties, 1989.

Hutcheon, Linda. *Narcissistic Narrative: The Metafictional Paradox.* New York: Methuen, 1980.

———. *A Theory of Parody: The Teachings of Twentieth-Century Art Forms.* New York: Routledge, 1985.

Isenberg, Charles. *Telling Silence: Russian Frame Narratives of Renunciation.* Evanston: Northwestern University Press, 1993.

Jackson, Robert Louis. *Dostoevsky's Underground Man in Russian Literature.* Mouton, 1958.

Jakobson, Roman. *Language in Literature.* Cambridge: Harvard University Press, 1987.

Jameson, Fredric. *The Political Unconscious: Narrative as a Socially Symbolic Act.* Ithaca: Cornell University Press, 1981.

Johnson, D. Barton. "Bely and Nabokov: A Comparative Overview." *Russian Literature* 9 (1981): 379–402.

———. "The Key to Nabokov's *Gift.*" *Canadian-American Slavic Studies* 16, no. 2 (1982): 190–206.

———. *Worlds in Regression: Some Novels of Vladimir Nabokov.* Ann Arbor: Ardis, 1985.

Karlinsky, Simon. "Vladimir Nabokov's Novel *Dar* as a Work of Literary Criticism: A Structural Analysis." *Slavic and East European Journal* 7 (1963): 284–90.

Kermode, Frank. *The Sense of an Ending: Studies in the Theory of Fiction.* New York: Oxford University Press, 1967.

Kohut, Heinz. "Forms and Transformations of Narcissism." In *Essential Papers on Narcissism,* edited by Andrew P. Morrison. New York: New York University Press, 1986.

Kostalevsky, Marina. "The Young Godunov-Cherdyntsev or How to Write a Literary Biography," *Russian Literature* 43 (1998): 283–95.

Kristeva, Julia. *Desire in Language: A Semiotic Approach to Literature and Art.* New York: Columbia University Press, 1980.

Kropf, David Glenn. *Authorship as Alchemy: Subversive Writing in Pushkin, Scott, Hoffmann.* Stanford: Stanford University Press, 1994.

Krugovoj, George. *The Gnostic Novel of Mikhail Bulgakov: Sources and Exegesis.* Lanham: University Press of America, 1991.

Kutik, Ilya. *The Ode and the Odic: Essays on Mandelstam, Pasternak, Tsvetaeva and Mayakovsky.* Stockholm, 1994.

Lacan, Jacques. *Ecrits: A Selection.* Translated by Alan Sheridan. New York: Norton, 1977.

Lévi-Strauss, Claude. *The Savage Mind.* London: Weidenfeld and Nicholson, 1966.

Lodge, David. *The Modes of Modern Writing: Metaphor, Metonymy, and the Typology of Modern Literature.* Ithaca: Cornell University Press, 1977.

Lowe, David. "Bulgakov and Dostoevsky: A Tale of Two Ivans." *Russian Literature Triquarterly* 15 (1978): 253–62.

Lukács, Georg. *The Meaning of Contemporary Realism.* Translated by John Mander and Necke Mander. London: Merlin Press, 1963.

———. *Solzhenitsyn.* London: Merlin Press, 1969.

———. *The Theory of the Novel.* Translated by Anna Bostock. Cambridge: MIT Press, 1990.

Lunn, Eugene. *Marxism and Modernism: An Historical Study of Lukács, Brecht, Benjamin, and Adorno.* Berkeley: University of California Press, 1982.

Malcolm, Donald. Review of *The Gift,* by Vladimir Nabokov, translated by Michael Scammell with the collaboration of the author. *New Yorker* (April 25, 1964): 198, 202–4.

Mandelker, Amy. *Framing Anna Karenina: Tolstoy, the Woman Question, and the Victorian Novel.* Columbus: Ohio State University Press, 1993.

Mandelstam, Osip. *Mandelstam: Critical Prose and Letters.* Edited by Jane Gary Harris, translated by Jane Gary Harris and Constance Link. Ann Arbor: Ardis, 1979.

Mann, Thomas. *Doctor Faustus: The Life of the German Composer Adrian Leverkühn as Told by a Friend.* Translated by H. T. Lowe-Porter. New York: Modern Library, 1948.

Milne, Lesley. "Gogol and Mikhail Bulgakov." In *Nikolay Gogol: Text and Context,* edited by J. Grayson and F. Wigzell. Basingstoke: Macmillan and University of London, 1989.

———. *Mikhail Bulgakov: A Critical Biography.* Cambridge: Cambridge University Press, 1990.

Morson, Gary Saul. *The Boundaries of Genre: Dostoevsky's "Diary of a Writer" and the Traditions of Literary Utopia.* Austin: University of Texas Press, 1981.

———. "Genre and Hero/*Fathers and Sons:* Intergeneric Dialogues, Generic Refugees, and the Hidden Prosaic." In *Literature, Culture, and Society in the Modern Age: In Honor of Joseph Frank.* Stanford Slavic Studies, vol. 4, no. 1. Stanford: Stanford University Press, 1991.

———. *Narrative and Freedom: The Shadows of Time.* New Haven: Yale University Press, 1994.

Morson, Gary Saul, and Caryl Emerson. *Mikhail Bakhtin: The Creation of a Prosaics.* Stanford: Stanford University Press, 1990.

Mossman, Elliot. "Metaphors of History in *War and Peace* and *Doctor Zhivago.*" In *Literature and History: Theoretical Problems and Russian Case Studies,* edited by Gary Saul Morson. Stanford: Stanford University Press, 1986.

———. "Toward a Poetics of the Novel *Doctor Zhivago:* The Fourth Typhus." In *Boris Pasternak and His Times: Selected Papers from the Second International Symposium on Pasternak,* edited by Lazar Fleishman. Berkeley: Berkeley Slavic Specialties, 1989.

Nabokov, Vladimir. *The Gift.* Translated by Michael Scammell with collaboration of the author. New York: Vintage, 1991.

———. *Lectures on Russian Literature.* Edited by Fredson Bowers. New York: Harcourt Brace Jovanovich, 1981.

———. *Собрание сочинений в четырех томах,* том 3. Москва, 1990.

———. *Speak, Memory.* New York: Pyramid, 1966.

———. *Strong Opinions.* New York: McGraw-Hill, 1973.

Natov, Nadine. "Structural and Typological Ambivalence of Bulgakov's Novels Interpreted against the Background of Baxtin's Theory of 'Grotesque Realism' and Carnivalization." In *American Contributions to the Eighth International Congress of Slavists.* Columbus: Slavica, 1978.

———. "The Supernatural in Bulgakov and Gogol'." In *The Supernatural in Slavic and Baltic Literature: Essays in Honor of Victor Terras,* edited by Amy Mandelker and Roberta Reeder. Columbus: Slavica, 1988.

Nietzsche, Friedrich. *The Birth of Tragedy and The Genealogy of Morals.* Translated by Francis Golffing. New York: Doubleday, 1956.

Nivat, Georges. "Deux romans 'speculaires' des les années trente: *Le Don* et *Le Maître et Marguerite." Revue des études slaves* 61 (1989): 269–75.

Paperno, Irina. "How Nabokov's *Gift* is Made." In *Literature, Culture, and Society in the Modern Age: Festschrift in Honor of Joseph Frank.* Stanford Slavic Studies, vol. 4, no. 2. Stanford: Stanford University Press, 1992.

Pasternak, Boris. *Doctor Zhivago.* Translated by Max Hayward. New York: Signet, 1958.

———. *Собрание сочинений в пяти томах,* том 3. Москва, 1990.

Pittman, Riitta H. *The Writer's Divided Self in Bulgakov's "The Master and Margarita."* New York: St. Martin's Press, 1991.

Proffer, Ellendea. *Bulgakov: Life and Works.* Ann Arbor: Ardis, 1984.

Pushkin, Aleksandr. *Eugene Onegin: A Novel in Verse.* Translated and with commentary by Vladimir Nabokov. Princeton: Princeton University Press, 1975.

———. *Сочинения в трех томах,* том 3. Минск, 1987.

Rilke, Rainer Maria. *Selected Poems of Rainer Maria Rilke.* Translated by Robert Bly. New York: Harper and Row, 1981.

Robin, Regine. *Socialist Realism: An Impossible Aesthetic.* Translated by Catherine Porter. Stanford: Stanford University Press, 1992.

Ronen, Irena, and Omry Ronen. "'Diabolically Evocative': An Inquiry into the Meaning of a Metaphor." *Slavica Hierosolymitana* 5–6 (1981): 371–86.

Sahni, Kalpana. *A Mind in Ferment: Mikhail Bulgakov's Prose.* New Delhi, 1984.

Sandler, Stephanie. *Distant Pleasures: Alexander Pushkin and the Writing of Exile.* Stanford: Stanford University Press, 1989.

Segal, D. "Pro Domo Sua: The Case of Boris Pasternak." *Slavica Hierosolymitana* 1 (1977): 199–250.

Sendich, Munir. *Boris Pasternak: A Reference.* New York: Macmillan, 1994.

Shepherd, David. *Beyond Metafiction: Self-Consciousness in Soviet Literature.* Oxford: Oxford Clarendon Press, 1992.

Smirnov, Igor P. *Порождение интертекста: Элементы интертекстуального анализа с примерами из творчества Б. Л. Пастернака.* Vienna: Wiener slawistischer Almanach, 1985.

Spencer, Jerome. "'Soaked in *The Meaning of Love* and *The Kreutzer Sonata':* The Nature of Love in *Doctor Zhivago."* In *"Doctor Zhivago": A Critical Companion,* edited by Edith W. Clowes. Evanston: Northwestern University Press, 1995.

Striedter, Jurij. *Literary Structure, Evolution, and Value: Russian Formalism and Czech Structuralism Reconsidered.* Cambridge: Harvard University Press, 1989.

Struve, Gleb. *Russian Literature under Lenin and Stalin.* Norman: University of Oklahoma Press, 1970.

Tammi, Pekka. *Problems of Nabokov's Poetics: A Narratological Analysis.* Helsinki, 1985.

Taylor, Charles. *Sources of the Self: The Making of Modern Identity.* Cambridge: Harvard University Press, 1989.

Terras, Victor, ed. *Handbook of Russian Literature.* New Haven: Yale University Press, 1985.

Todd, William Mills, III. *Fiction and Society in the Age of Pushkin: Ideology, Institutions, and Narrative.* Cambridge: Harvard University Press, 1986.

Toker, Leona. *Nabokov: The Mystery of Literary Structures.* Ithaca: Cornell University Press, 1989.

Tomashevsky, Boris. "Literature and Biography." In *Readings in Russian Poetics: Formalist and Structuralist Views,* edited by Ladislav Matejka and Krystyna Pomorska. Ann Arbor: Michigan Slavic Publications, 1978.

Tynianov, Yuri. *Архаисты и новаторы.* Ленинград, 1929.

———. "On Literary Evolution." In *Readings in Russian Poetics: Formalist and Structuralist Views,* edited by Ladislav Matejka and Krystyna Pomorska. Ann Arbor: Michigan Slavic Publications, 1978.

———. *Поэтика, история литературы, кино.* Москва: Наука, 1977.

Wachtel, Andrew. *The Battle for Childhood: Creation of a Russian Myth.* Stanford: Stanford University Press, 1990.

———. *An Obsession with History: Russian Writers Confront the Past.* Stanford: Stanford University Press, 1994.

———. "Psychology and Society in the Classic Russian Novel." In *The Cambridge Companion to the Classic Russian Novels,* edited by Malcolm Jones and Robin Miller. Cambridge: Cambridge University Press, forthcoming.

———, ed. *Petrushka: Sources and Contexts.* Evanston: Northwestern University Press, 1998.

Wachtel, Andrew, and Irina Gutkin. Introduction to *What Is Art?,* by Leo Tolstoy. New Haven: Yale University Press, forthcoming.

Waite, Sarah Tiffany. "On the Linear Structure of Nabokov's *Dar:* Three Keys, Six Chapters." *Slavic and East European Journal* 39, no. 1 (1995): 54–72.

Weeks, Laura D., ed. *"The Master and Margarita": A Critical Companion.* Evanston: Northwestern University Press, 1996.

Weir, Justin. "Anna Incommunicada: Language and Consciousness in *Anna Karenina.*" *Tolstoy Studies Journal* 8 (1997).

White, Hayden. *Metahistory: The Historical Imagination in Nineteenth-Century Europe.* Baltimore: Johns Hopkins University Press, 1973.

Wiman, Christian. "Finishes: Notes on Ambition and Survival." *Poetry* 169, no. 3 (1997).

Wollheim, Richard. *Sigmund Freud.* Cambridge: Cambridge University Press, 1971.

Wright, A. Colin. *Mikhail Bulgakov: Life and Interpretations.* Toronto: University of Toronto Press, 1978.

———. "Satan in Moscow: An Approach to Bulgakov's *The Master and Margarita.*" *PMLA* 88, no. 5 (October 1973): 1162–72.

Zholkovsky, Alexander. *Text counter Text: Rereadings in Russian Literary History.* Stanford: Stanford University Press, 1994.

Index

Index